"Spending time in these p[...] in nature. *A Year at Catbird Cottage* reminds us to [...] everything around us and to see beauty and possibility in every corner. This is how Melina Hammer not only approaches cooking food, but also how she approaches growing it, foraging for it, and capturing it through her stunning photography."

—JULIA TURSHEN, BESTSELLING AUTHOR OF *SIMPLY JULIA* AND HOST/PRODUCER OF *KEEP CALM & COOK ON* PODCAST

"With *A Year at Catbird Cottage*, Melina does so much more than welcome us into her kitchen; she invites us out into her garden, seduces us to forage with her the neighboring woods, shows us how to preserve all manner of edibles, and plies us with some of the most enticing recipes I've seen in ages. Her lusciously styled photos and equally evocative prose will leave you torn—do you grab this book and start cooking immediately or do you find a quiet spot to hunker down and get lost in the magical world she's created? Either way is a total win."

—SUZANNE LENZER, AUTHOR OF *GRAZE*

"Melina's photos are evocative and soulful, and everything looks scrumptious. *A Year at Catbird Cottage* is full of nourishing and seasonal meals made with foraged foods or fruit and vegetables you can grow in your garden, and quick meals prepared with everyday staples to share with the ones you love. This is a world I would love to immerse myself in."

—ARAN GOYOAGA, AUTHOR OF *CANNELLE ET VANILLE* AND *CANNELLE ET VANILLE BAKES SIMPLE*

"Any dish at Melina's table is like a cozy embrace. I say this in the best way possible: her cottage reminds me of the comfort I felt at my grandmother's. Melina is a badass, and *A Year at Catbird Cottage* inspires a special nostalgia in a beautiful and delicious way that only she can create."

—GREGORY PORTER, TWO-TIME GRAMMY AWARD– WINNING SINGER AND SONGWRITER, AND EMCEE OF LEGENDARY BED STUY DINNER PARTIES

A YEAR AT
Catbird Cottage

A YEAR AT

Catbird Cottage

RECIPES FOR A NOURISHED LIFE

WRITTEN AND PHOTOGRAPHED BY

MELINA HAMMER

TEN SPEED PRESS
California | New York

CONTENTS

staples

spring

summer

fall

winter

SUSTENANCE, EATING IN BETWEEN THE FEASTS, AKA BONUS TRACKS

INTRODUCTION

This book is a love letter to food, and by extension it is a love letter to Nature, too. I am typing this from my deck nestled on a mossy hillside in the Hudson Valley, a brisk two hours from Manhattan. Years ago I began dreaming of a way to transition my photography and styling career so I could be less beholden to the changing industry. I thought, wouldn't it be wonderful to pull from my husband Jim's and my expertise from years in hospitality and make use of all the family artifacts and one-of-a-kind pieces I'd collected as a stylist. We could create a space that felt like a curated sanctuary, nestled in nature, and give people dining experiences to remember. As we searched for a home, the idea of hosting people was built in, and when we landed on our humble Cape Cod, we saw its potential and began the work of making our home ready, creating Catbird Cottage.

With our two kitties, we took the leap and moved into our cottage a few years ago, and ever since, I have relished witnessing seasons arrive, unfold, then make way for the next. This regular observation of nature's cycles has inevitably deepened my relationship to the foods I eat and the meals I prepare for Catbird Cottage guests.

During my morning garden walks I am met with discoveries of new buds and fruits on our serviceberry and sour cherry trees, thimbleberry shrubs, morning glories, poppies, columbine, monarda, early meadowrue, and innumerable other edible and native plants we installed. I have searched patiently under bush bean leaves to snip their fuzzy, slender fruits. I managed a serious glut of tomatoes two years in a row, canning, roasting, and pickling to preserve the season's jewels. By and large, the garden has rewarded me manyfold through the seasons. I have kept the numerous garden beds more or less tidy. In growing an increasing amount of my food year after year, I have learned to companion plant and succession plant with some confidence. I am definitely not an expert, but three years in, I know some things about what a garden can be.

Perfectly timed, two hummingbirds just whizzed by as if to cheer me on, stopping at our nectar feeder to grace me with their resplendent tiny beings.

How did I get here? I lived in large cities for the majority of my adulthood, and though there was a crucially relevant time and place for that kind of living, I haven't craved it in years. In 2012, when we moved to the Deep South, it dawned on me that I needed a greater connection to nature in my daily life.

After moving back north, we found interim solutions, including daytrips hiking outside of NYC, regular visits to nature preserves, and weekly meanders to forage on a nearby and quaint block that, to our surprise and delight, possessed an abundance of wild foods hidden right in plain sight. Neighbors and passersby scrunched their faces, perplexed at our enthusiasm as we harvested tiny wild black cherries dangling over parked cars or as I snipped purslane from fence openings at lawn edges. We stretched and contorted ourselves (and brought a folding ladder, on occasion) to harvest inky, nectar-sweet mulberries from branches laden with fruit arching over sidewalks, their telltale stains viewed only as a nuisance by the building landlord.

While biding our time and making the most of the city, we set on a path to find a permanent place to resolve my longing for a sturdier connection to the wilds. Years prior, when we moved to Birmingham, Alabama, I grew friendships with family farmers. They lovingly tended all manner of foods. It was cathartic to walk their fields and see the crops growing and observe how they toiled to bring food to market. I learned about elements never found on grocery store shelves, such as okra flowers and cauliflower leaves, about cover crops, and how to milk a goat or a cow by hand. I found ways to forage wild foods easily when I lived in the Deep South, as abundant nature was only minutes away from urban city blocks. These experiences stoked something that, when I returned north years later, made me realize that I needed permanent space in my life. I am now living a life I am in love with. I am lucky enough to walk out my door and be welcomed by a cacophony of beautiful sounds and sights. Nature really is at my fingertips. This brings me enormous peace.

Along with gardening, the move has allowed me to be spontaneous as a forager and explore almost without thinking, because the wilds are everywhere surrounding me. I've learned to seize on my hunches and been rewarded by plump wild berries toppled into many containers. I am party to the anticipation of—and in competition with the innumerable birds and chipmunks—the first ripening black raspberries and am keenly aware of how quickly fragrant chanterelles push from the earth with a few good rainstorms. All this informs the food I prepare throughout the year for guests at the Catbird. Nature has become my partner in crafting menus.

Routine observations around my property and the immediate countryside refine plans as to which ripening ingredients are laced into a dish. Once I've had a chance to explore and test an exciting idea, it becomes a new member of the family of elements in an ever-expanding repertoire. This regular connection is a wellspring for inspiration. I hope this book ignites your curiosity and zeal to explore, too.

HOW TO USE THIS BOOK

I am interested in every one of us falling in love with food so much so that in a daily way, we are met with joyful eating. I also want to reconnect to heirloom ingredients, which have fallen off our modern radar either because they take extra care to cultivate or transport—an automatic strike against many heirloom foods—or because our vernacular has been so seized by what is trendy or by concepts of what will sell in stores (that is, "worth" investing in so as not to have the produce sit forlorn and spoil on the shelves). If you're unfamiliar with any of the ingredients—whether they feel out of reach or too specialized to integrate into your daily life—I want to assure you that the ideas presented here are offered with an eye toward simplicity and immediacy. If ingredients still feel too niche, wherever possible I offer substitutions so that you can succeed.

The foraging and gardening sections are an invitation to greet the natural world around you—to begin to understand foods the landscape graciously offers us and to develop a practice of growing food yourself. Of course, you should always use caution and educate yourself before foraging so that you don't harvest or eat something harmful. You can find more foraging safety guidance on page 25, and further foraging references and resources on page 285. Let these chapters and the resources at the end of the book serve as encouragement and guides to getting your hands dirty, or simply as a way of seeing ingredients in a fresh light.

And, of course, the recipes. You can take any single element in this book to use in your daily repertoire and it would be delicious. The array of staples is made to enjoy simply. The same staples are also meant to be combined within more complex dishes, building greater depth and nuance. These dynamic contrasts in texture and punchy, bright, custardy, chewy, spicy flavors complement each other and make an exquisite affair of eating. I invite you—actually, I urge you—to go the distance to invest in the layers. Make all the staples. Flesh out the more complex recipes. Each of the staples lasts a good long while, and many can be frozen or canned. In between the special, more deliberate meals, you can add a spoonful here and there to everyday basics, giving verve when there would otherwise just be "lunch."

In committing to the more elaborate meals, you will feast on groan-inducing soulful food, perhaps more so than at many a fancy restaurant. You will make wonderful things of thrifty, conscientious food preservation, then revel in the flavors, while *also* bringing a ceremonious occasion to your own table. After the long pandemic isolation, not being able to have friends over for a meal, this piece feels crucially joyful. This is precious community on a plate, growing and harvesting and preserving food with love, and then eating it with those you cherish.

Some of the foods and dishes in this book might feel "fancy." They are some of the most special meals I dreamed up, to celebrate Catbird guests' anniversaries, birthdays, friend getaways, and so much more. They are meals that commemorate living. You can pick from the elements in nearly every dish—without making the whole thing—that are themselves perfectly delicious morsels for any meal, any day. Summery sweet corn–shallot confit with scallops (page 173) is divine on its own. The salsa from Roasted Salmon + Spicy Cucumber-Orange Salsa (page 167) is great with tortilla chips. The aioli—whether the tarragon version made for Asparagus + Artichokes (page 123) or the version in Grand Aioli Summer Feast (page 158)—is sublime no matter what it is served with.

If you seize on the staples and want to tackle the more elaborate dishes but time is your challenge, parcel out the steps over a period of days rather than trying to tackle everything at once. That is almost always how I work. Makes it doable! If you don't have the energy to make a subrecipe, at least add fresh herbs to whatever you're making. Use herbs in abundance, as you would salad greens. Add them to everything, as you will see I do throughout the recipes. Their unique brightness is uplifting, even transformative. If you're doubtful that you'll use a whole bunch of delicate this-or-that, freeze clusters of leaves in an ice cube tray, suspended in pickle brine or olive oil, and then add them to stews, soups, grains, or legumes at a time you can more easily control. That alone is cause for celebration.

Finally—roll with me on this—though they are often considered optional, in my view garnishes are never truly optional. Though they are a flourish contributed at the end of the actual cooking, their specific character adds loft and contrast to every plate of food. Garnishes do not cost much and they deliver big. Garnishes add a special brightness and transform rich dishes such as the Braised Short Ribs + Creamy Beans (page 263) and the Braised Lamb Shanks + Melted Onions (page 214). They add new dimension to the Mussels for Betty (page 127) and even A Rosy Salad for Darker Days (page 251). Depending on the specifics, it's true that garnishes may be harder to come by, or even out of season at times. But in most examples, I try to offer substitutions if you cannot locate a special ingredient so you can succeed no matter the circumstance. Whenever possible, please go the extra distance and add them. Garnishes aren't just an ambiguous wrap thrown on before feasting; they are deliberate and cheery and ephemeral final touches to bring a dish to completion. They bring copacetic to *hot-damn*. Add them and feast first with your eyes on colorful petals and fronds and juicy bits and then be uplifted by amazing food.

A note on "perfection," because, even in nature nothing truly is. My life in food and photography has allowed me to become practiced at making things look beautiful. I did labor over the dishes in this book in the hopes of creating images that look and feel iconic, but by and large they are simple dishes, comprised mostly of choice ingredients, fussed over minimally. Please let any intimidation around the *look* of food fall away. Eating is meant to be sensuous, with your sleeves rolled up, good music playing, and—more than anything—the music of friends or family crowded around, chatting in the kitchen, sipping on something delicious while the final touches are being added to a dish.

Over the years I have amassed a varied collection of implements. It is worth noting here the indispensable tools I use and their special or varied applications. A number of my kitchen tools are inherited from my mother or grandmother, bringing greater meaning and visual character to my kitchen day-to-day.

While this list may present as a rather extensive or particular collection, the aim is that you use what feels most relevant right now, build on your collection, and grow your repertoire as your techniques expand.

Chef's Knife

For nearly all of my prep work, I use an 8-inch pointed tip chef's knife. From slicing, chopping, and mincing to breaking down a chicken or mashing cloves of garlic, it is the most universal tool in my kitchen.

Small and Large Serrated Knives

A good bread knife is crucial. Equally important is a pointed-tip, compact serrated knife to portion flaky pastry, pierce the thin skin of tomatoes, or divide a length of chorizo at a picnic.

Filet Knife

This knife wasn't always part of my collection, but its flexible blade has proven indispensable for finer work, especially breaking down a whole salmon and slicing Wild Salmon Gravlax (page 94). If you have the room and would like greater finesse, it's the right tool for a number of tasks.

Paring Knife

The least used in my knife collection and yet, quite handy for various tasks such as hulling strawberries, sectioning other soft fruits in baking projects, halving custardy boiled eggs in Eat'cha Garden (page 148)—it has a smaller blade surface and therefore produces less friction, leaving less yolk lost to the blade.

Tongs

I use a pair of simple, all-metal 9-inch steel tongs to stir, toss, grip, and turn foods while cooking them in my steel and cast-iron pots and pans. I treat them as an extension of my arm to handle hot foods delicately but firmly. Find a set whose spring tension isn't too strong nor too lax: you don't want to end up fatigued by how much work it is to work with them or preoccupied with worrying if they'll do in an instant what you need for the precision work in front of you. Use a light hand so as not to mar the food as you handle it and any dish will end up cooked to perfection, as well as beautiful to behold.

A Sharp, Fine Pair of Scissors

From snipping herbs in the garden and again while plating, to garden harvests of many kinds (most veg stems including beans, tomatoes, eggplant, even summer squash, lettuces, arugula, and mustard greens), to occasionally cutting pizza or flatbread, I cherish my scissors. There was a two-week period a while back where I'd misplaced them in the garden and it felt like part of me was missing, I use them so regularly.

Stylist Tweezers

I acquired these when I was still a metalsmith (my first career!). As it turns out, these jewelers' tweezers are the absolute perfect tool for daily work on set. What is especially nice about this pair is that the tips aren't too sharp or pointy—which would easily mar tender ingredients such as soft herbs—while still offering needed precision. I use them to turn diminutive tempura-fried milkweed blossoms, the topping to Scallops, Corn Confit, Milkweed (page 173); to nudge trout roe so it captures the light just so; to add windowpane-thin pickled onion rings to Cured King Salmon, Persimmon, Pickles (page 248); and so much more. If these tasks sound like you, tweezers are a must.

Silicone Spatula with a True Squared Blade Edge

On a trip to Japan some years ago, I found a tiny version of this spatula and have since pondered how I survived prior to its discovery. I use two sizes of this tool every single day, multiple times a day, and own four or so in a larger size. Though my original spatula looks all bitten, it remains infinitely useful and I don't dare get rid of it. My mom referred to these broadly as "child cheaters" when I was growing up, because every last bit could be scraped out of the bowl, leaving no frosting for hungry young'uns.

Citrus Juicer

I love a good citrus juicer. My handheld, hinged juicer is ideal for squeezing juice in quantity, when I know I want all the juice from the segment being squeezed, or when I want to squeeze directly onto other ingredients. I also use a porcelain juicer with a handy pour spout when I want to measure a certain quantity of juice, such as when baking.

Dutch Oven

I have a large enameled Dutch oven that I use for braises, such as the Braised Lamb Shanks + Melted Onions (page 214) and Braised Short Ribs + Creamy Beans (page 263), as well as most of my jam-making projects. Its size offers ample surface area for bubbling liquid to evaporate, helping concentrate flavors. I inherited a smaller Dutch oven—also enameled—and a third in cast-iron. The small enameled one is from my husband's grandmother, one of the only physical reminders to conjure her in my own kitchen. She was a proud cook, used it continuously until she was too frail to lift it, and would be so happy I use it. Medium Dutch ovens are indispensable for sourdough bread baking: with the lids on, they trap steam while baking, producing the highly sought-after blistered crust on any good loaf.

Cast-Iron Skillet

I do most of my cooking in a 12-inch cast-iron skillet. Cast-iron is an excellent conductor of heat, works stovetop to oven, and is an all-around workhorse in the kitchen. This is what I use for searing, and, if properly used, it will last a lifetime (or longer)! Use it to cook everything *except* acidic dishes, such as tomato sauce, to prevent the acid from eating into the metal.

Enameled Iron Skillet

This is an inherited piece from my friend Betty, for whom I originally made the mussels on a gorgeous Santa Barbara spring day (page 127). My vintage Le Creuset pan is the go-to for tomato sauce (Pasta Puttanesca, page 217), as well as for dishes incorporating browned butter, which, due to its light surface, makes it obvious when milk solids darken and have separated. This is the pan I use whenever I bake the "Deli Sandwich" Dutch Baby (page 112) and makes a dramatic presentation when brought to Catbird Cottage guests at their morning table.

Mason Jars

As a recipe developer and the daughter of a woman who meticulously keeps a reserve of many things, I maintain an extensive pantry. I have these in every size. The 4-ounce size is excellent for small batch jams, which I like to give as gifts, as well as for condiments such as Pistachio Dukkah (page 64) and Furikake (page 242), and to store the Wild Salmon Rillettes (page 241). The wide-mouth version in any size is great, whether for producing a new ferment or for storing canned tomatoes, grains, or dry beans. I use squat wide-mouth half-pint jars to make the Pâté, Elderberry Gelée, Pickled Ramps (page 119)—they can be sealed and frozen (with adequate headspace) in a cinch. Mason jars are ideal for storing many things, both because it's easy to readily see what's available—a nice jog for the brain on days when inspiration doesn't strike—as well as to ward off any critters who may otherwise lust after your stash for themselves. Living in the countryside, this revealed itself to be a clear issue for us as new homeowners. We quickly made the necessary adjustments, and problems with our dry storage have been a nonissue ever since. In the refrigerator, I use mason jars to keep all manner of jams, pickles, sauces—even iced coffee in summertime.

Canning Funnel

This is a stainless steel wide-mouth funnel that fits perfectly into jars. Excellent for ladling stock, spooning jams, and even transferring dry goods (sugar, beans, and so on) for pantry storage. I also keep a regular funnel handy for transferring batches of cordial or syrups into their longer-term storage jars and bottles.

Mandoline

When I still lived in Brooklyn and we had friends in the restaurant industry, my husband noted the mandoline type his chef preferred and we promptly got one. Inexpensive, portable, and a workhorse, the Benriner mandoline from Japan is simple and has served me for many years. I use it to transform unwieldy vegetables, including cabbage, potatoes, zucchini, beets, and radishes, into lacelike, delicate forms. When you're looking to render uniform slices or want a transformative visual effect—slices so transparent, like a windowpane, or linguine-like "noodles"—this is an excellent investment.

Mortar and Pestle

Since the Stone Age, hunter-gatherers fashioned versions of this tool to grind seeds and grains. This iconic, ancient tool is also a fixture in my kitchen in part because I'm a collector and food stylist—they have beautiful form, and different sizes really do prove useful for different tasks—and in part because they have been used to make sauces and pastes over millennia. I own five of these in varying sizes. The largest is excellent for making Pistachio Dukkah (page 64), traditional pesto, and Punchy Garlic Anchovy Dressing (page 58). The medium and smaller ones are ideal for grinding spices after they have been toasted, the only way to release their delicate natural oils. Select the best mortar and pestle by anticipating how it will most frequently be used in your kitchen.

Dough and Bench Scrapers

The dough scraper is flexible plastic and has a curved edge, and the other is metal with a blunt, straight edge. The curved edge assists in mixing sourdough and conforms perfectly to the shape of a bowl so I can get all the bits organized. The bench scraper's metal, straight edge is ideal for cleanly transferring dough from a work surface and easy counter cleanup and acts as a cool (temperature) set of hands when folding or handling pastry dough.

Rolling Pin

The stylist-collector me has stockpiled pins of varying types over the years. As my technique has clarified, I prefer a single hardwood dowel, sometimes called a shaker pin, or the French tapered style, rather than the traditional pin (rolling dowel with handles). The French and cylinder dowel styles afford more direct connection to the pastry and allow me to make nuanced adjustments as I work. From making Seeded Rye Lavash (page 67) to Sour Cherry Pie dough (page 139), a rolling pin is a beautiful feature in a working kitchen.

Sieves

I have two or three sizes with varying mesh density. I use a large sieve to filter solids from all my stocks, as well as the solids from fermentation projects. I also use it to sift flour when baking to ensure there will be no clumping. I keep a small, fine-mesh strainer on hand for separating seeds and pulp from freshly squeezed citrus (for cocktails, baking projects), for sifting confectioner's sugar onto baked custards, and as a means to be certain that any pomace remains behind when straining cordials, infusions, and vinegars.

Julep Strainer

This is like a mini-colander-sieve mashup originally fashioned to strain—you guessed it—mint juleps. I use mine for removing foods from fry oil, including the buttery potatoes when cooking the tortilla in Spanish Tortilla, Sauce, Pickles, Salad (page 115). If you don't own a spider but have one of these lying around, they work wonders. It is also excellent for skimming foam from the surface while cooking beans, fishing blanched veg from boiling water, and even once in a while straining a cocktail!

9-Inch Springform Pan

There was a moment many years ago where I decided to invest in one of these. I was interested in making straight-sided quiches and cakes, enthralled with the tidy drama they presented, and decided to take the plunge. It felt so specialized and, therefore, a splurge. While I don't use it regularly, when I *do* need it, the springform pan is highly useful and well worth the space it takes up in the cupboard. Most of my cakes are baked in one of these as I'm not much of a layer cake girl. When I want extra impact, a fine short crust draped into one of these makes a gorgeous effect for both pies and quiches.

Fermentation Airlock Lids and Muddler

These are specific, but thankfully they take up little room. I have found peace of mind using the airlock lids, only having to keep track of the water moat and number of days fermenting rather than wondering if the process is going as it should. You can just as easily secure a piece of muslin over the jar opening with a rubber band or kitchen twine. A muddler aids in massaging the ingredients so that they express their liquid— essential in breaking down their membranes and producing the brine they'll need to be submerged in—as well as tamping down the mass in its jar or crock so that it is submerged and can ferment successfully.

Pastry Brush

I paint all of my piecrusts with egg wash or buttermilk for a deeper golden effect, as well as to adhere glittery demerara sugar, bringing crunchy texture to flaky pastry. Additionally, I use a pastry brush for cracker doughs, painting a thin slick of olive oil to coat (to adhere flake salt or other sprinkled toppings). I occasionally use a pastry brush to remove excess flour as I prep the next step in a pastry project. This is a specific tool, but if you bake pies or crackers, you may find it indispensable.

Muslin

This undyed, tightly woven reusable cotton fabric is excellent used as a filter whenever I make labneh (page 177). I also strain many cordials and syrups through a sieve lined with muslin to catch any solid matter as I pour the precious liquid through the funnel into bottles for storage. Muslin makes a great barrier during fermentation projects where I want the atmospheric yeasts to relate to what is being fermented, but not air-borne particles.

Microplane

A Microplane occupies little space, isn't particularly gadgety, and doesn't cost much. Its many small teeth make quick work of dense foods such as ginger and garlic, perfect for the Immunity Elixir (page 81). A wedge of Parmesan gets transformed into lacy shavings in My Mother's Gruyère Soufflé (page 246). A Microplane is indispensable for zesting citrus, as in the Ginger-Pecan Strawberry Streusel Cake (page 141). I use a Microplane when adding nutmeg, too, as in the Sage-Buttermilk-Rye Pot Pies (page 257).

Sheet Pans

Whether you call them cookie sheets or baking sheets, when roasting all manner of veggies, making Spiced Nuts (page 77), Candied Meyer Lemon Ice Cream + Pistachio Tuiles (page 270), Sourdough Crackers (page 75), or you name it, rimmed sheet pans are essential to daily projects.

Parchment Paper

Parchment is a nonstick paper that is also moisture resistant and can be used broadly, including in the oven. It replaces the need for greasing sheet pans and helps minimize cleanup in forming pastry (miso-mugwort shortbread in the Ultimate Nibbles Platter, page 208) and when batch baking Spiced Nuts (page 77). Consider reusing parchment paper (and other disposable products) as I do, to contribute less to landfills.

Food Processor

If there were one machine I had to choose, it would be the food processor. Of course, I like what my small blender does in an instant, and I often use my Ma's 1970s electric mixer, but the food processor offers the greatest versatility in my kitchen. I swear by it and have had the same model for nearly twenty years. I could update for style, but honestly, if it ain't broke, don't fix it.

Small Vessel High Speed Blender

To make the various dressings featured in these pages and especially when I'm on a deadline, using this tool saves time and produces velvety emulsified results to be tossed or spooned onto many things. It gets more use than the larger blender chamber, even though that size is essential for blending batters, pâtés, and a zippy green juice we make for weekday breakfasts.

Cutting Boards

The right board sets the tone for every project. Most often at my workstation sits a large, worn, paneled board I discovered in my grandmother's painting studio when clearing the space out after her passing. She didn't paint on it but rather used it as a cutting surface for mattes, magazine clippings, and other similar tasks. It is large enough to cut a mass of onions for caramelizing, but it has a low profile and feels comfortable to work on day in and out. The many small boards I've collected bring style to the table while offering their utility in transferring wedges of cheese or fruit. Brought along for picnicking, they are ideal for slicing sturdy picnic fare, like saucisson sec or whole cucumbers. Any time I create the Ultimate Nibbles Platter (page 208) to serve guests, I use a handsome board to arrange everything and transport the lot out to the table. Clarify beforehand which boards you don't mind having cut marks on and those that serve as presentation pieces.

A NOTE ON "SUSTAINABILITY"

This book, in part, is a call to waste less, to care about becoming more resourceful, and to change how—and what—we eat. We as a society can't continue the way we are living—in a straight line that will lead us right off a cliff if we keep on in this way, divorced from the repercussions our choices bring. Consider the circle: everything in nature, as well as native peoples' traditions, makes full use of a thing and brings each aspect into value. The Potawatomi people of the western Great Lakes, for hundreds of years, have taught their children about the "Seven Grandfather Teachings" of wisdom, respect, love, honesty, humility, bravery, and truth toward each other and all creations. How do we treat each other? What do we as Americans value? As a society overall, as consumers, as humans? Are we living lives that value economic and gender equality, civil rights, and honor and respect for our planet?

This book is made to show you all kinds of wonderful things to do with food. But there's a sea of underlying systems that get impacted when we make decisions to buy the food we bring home. We want to be aware of the complex web of things and the truth about the choices in front of us. It's also true we each have a finite capacity and our own blind spots. But the climate crisis and human rights transgressions have intensified so greatly, laid bare with the immediacy of social media, serving as cascading alarm calls to us all. I could no longer ignore the layers of issues the world over. I want to choose a different way—a way that is observant and respects living things as much as I possibly can. I'm sure you want that, too.

I don't expect anyone to snap their fingers and address all of these problems at once. They are layered, and it's nearly impossible. I also get that some of these choices come with a financial burden. If you're struggling to put food on the table, this may be especially hard. But to choose a couple, or even a few, directions that speak to you, or to educate yourself more fully and make concerted, regular change really matters. Our great challenge is recognizing disconnection dressed up as greater connection, so that we may build a deeper relationship with nature, and a means to sustain ourselves that empower us all to live more connected, day after day.

With the climate crisis impacting our daily lives, the food we eat automatically incorporates fossil fuels unless we make clear choices to avoid them. Buying foods grown locally literally means fewer fossil fuels are needed for their transport. Consider eating foods that are in season where you live. Yes, it isn't as easy if you live in Boston as if you're in California. But it matters. These choices make a difference. We're already dealing with damaging feedback loops from the concentration of carbon released into our atmosphere. When more havoc comes to our door, it will already have ruined many frontline and coastal communities around the globe, swelling to out-of-control proportions.

Eating with the seasons also means that foods haven't been harvested before they are ripe or need to be pumped with gases like ethylene (this happens all the time with

tomatoes) to make them appear ripe before being tidily arranged on grocery store shelves. Tomatoes eaten in summer aren't transported hundreds or thousands of miles. They are actually ripe. Plus, they actually taste like tomatoes, which is one of life's greatest joys. Eliminating expectations that all foods are available, regardless of the season, honors our planet in more ways than we may imagine. Become a farmers' market zealot. It guarantees you'll eat fresher, riper foods. It's a direct way to vote with your dollar. You support small, family businesses. You support the fabric of your own community.

Growing a garden is one of the simplest and most direct ways to connect to the natural world and give back. Imagine growing and harvesting your own food or learning to forage of-the-moment ingredients. Either of these brings an immediate connection to what it takes to put food on the table and empowers us to choose nutrient-rich foods, because they are right in front of us. Tending a garden builds relationships with others who grow, whether they are our neighbors or farmers at the market. Harvesting a bounty and then preserving it . . . what's this really about? It cuts through the fallacy of year-round availability. Food preservation empowers us to circumvent bad policies and practices by doing it ourselves. The more we learn to preserve food—and save seeds, too—the more independent we are from a chemicalized industry that does not have our health and well-being at its core. And it is more delicious.

PRESERVING, AKA MY PANTRY + FREEZER

I was a child when I learned the value of a well-stocked pantry. My Ma's mama lived through the Depression, and so frugality—and a constant desire to be prepared for harder times—was etched into our own lives.

My parents made a deliberate choice after their college years at Berkeley (which coincided with the times of the continuing Black liberation movement, the free speech movement, and the women's rights movement) to abandon the direction of their previous studies: he, in architecture, and she, in psychology and early child development, and dedicate their lives to the fight for justice. The Vietnam War and the profound antiwar movement that erupted around the world launched their trajectory. They worked in rubber plants in Boston, then ended up moving to Detroit to work in auto plants to help empower workers to organize and fight the myriad inequalities they faced. As a result, I grew up working class. I share this as a means to explain that we went through some hard times, which instilled within me the value of being resourceful. With that as background, I take pride in stocking a mean pantry.

MY PANTRY

My overflowing pantry lives just downstairs from our kitchen, a short jog to all kinds of magic-making waiting to be sparked. The shelves are dedicated to various whole grain flours as well as gluten-free flours for when guests' needs require something delicious but more particular; beans, nuts, and seeds of many varieties; dried things from candied fruits and flowers, to wild mushrooms and pungent fish, to medicinal and culinary herbs. There are sauces, honeys, jams, tinned fish and shellfish, cans of coconut cream, tomato paste. There are indulgent staples such as our beloved coffees and chocolate bars too numerous to seem rational—but we lived through COVID and relied on the real joy small pleasures brought! Plus, they make a great hostess gift for impromptu get-togethers, and I love sorting an array of bars to bring upstairs to our primary cupboards in the kitchen.

The primary cupboards store whole and powdered spices from around the world, delivering special nuances that only those flavors can. I treasure the numerous chile varieties; cardamom pods and star anise; whole seeds such as cumin, coriander, fennel, mustard, and peppercorns; nutmeg; vanilla beans; bay leaves; and myriad aromatics that make foods great.

MY FREEZER

To have harvested the moment's precious bounty, cleared the schedule to process and preserve it, and then, even on the greyest, coldest day, to uncap punchy brightness and floral or herby cheer—that is good eating. This is the task of a successful forager after discoveries in the field or forest. If you grow anything in quantity, you face a similar lucky fate.

Ever since we invested in a second refrigerator and I began curating menus for cottage guests, I have found the raison d'être of my freezers. Many years ago the freezer was sometimes where things went to disappear, never to be seen again. Now, I recognize it as the lifesaver it is. The freezer provides extended storage for all kinds of preserved foods saved in batches for when I am short on time or pine for inspired, other-season fare.

I didn't used to have a FIFO (first in, first out) storage method or a deliberate process, until one day I realized I needed to, to keep track of all the things I was making. My system isn't totally perfect even now, but I have developed a clarity for storage, rotation, and use (the most important!) for sauces, roasted tomatoes and Tomato Confit (page 60), disks of pastry and cracker dough, a half or whole frozen loaf of Sourdough Bread (page 68), heels of old cheese (perfect to fortify a pot of beans, page 263), "snapshot of the season" ice creams (pages 225, 268, and 270), tiny jars of Ramp Salt (page 63), salmon rillettes (page 241), and more.

There is almost always a whole frozen chicken, for when I need to entertain without much notice (a great roast chicken—page 255—is a quintessential comfort). Pot pies made from the leftovers are arguably even more exciting (page 257). A box or two of puff pastry, as well as a container of frozen Brown Butter + Lemon Cecamariti (page 157). There are bags of store-bought frozen peas, summer-harvested frozen berries, and apple or quince peels for future jam-making projects (within their peels is abundant pectin, worth saving for a final glory). And always there is a large bag in the process of being filled with stock-making scraps, along with a container of shrimp shells or a fish frame, for their own stock-making adventures (Bouillabaisse, page 211, Shrimp Umami Stock, page 84). Summer herbs suspended in brine or oil, and various stocks, are frozen in convenient ice-cube portions. Also, straggler leftovers that I simply need to put off deciding what to do with until my frequent Tetris game of managing perishable foods relents.

ON DISCERNING + BEING RESOURCEFUL

I generally advocate you invest in beautiful produce or unusual ingredients. Think of the farmer, maybe even one you know, who gives their wisdom and ongoing labor to grow that beautiful thing. Consider the value in that. If it is a niche ingredient, consider the conditions it must require to grow (such as capers, found only in arid climes and can only be hand-harvested due to their spiny thorns), or what it must undergo to get to you in its final form. Ingredient discoveries birth love affairs with new dishes. I don't use pink peppercorns often, but they send the summer Stone Fruit, Pecan + Pistachio Crisps (page 180) over the top. And they store indefinitely. Trout roe is an indulgence, but its sweet-briny clack brings magic to winter Cured King Salmon, Persimmon, Pickles (page 248). Buy pasture-raised eggs, grass-fed meat and cheese, and sustainably caught wild seafood and fish. These foods will have eaten a more diverse diet, so they'll taste better than their industrially farmed counterparts, and will more likely be treated humanely. Same for vegetables and fruit—try to buy those that are grown with organic or renewable standards. Especially any whose skin you'll eat (berries, lemons and oranges, celery, dark leafy greens such as kale and mustard greens, tomatoes, peppers). They will be more flavorful, nutrient-rich, and free of commonly used, harmful pesticides, herbicides, and GMOs. While it is essential to treat yourself handsomely, it is equally imperative to stretch things to their fullest. It honors all of a thing: the carcass of a roasted bird becomes a soothing broth. Corncobs, stripped of their kernels, and woody asparagus ends flavor summer stock (page 82). Any type of leftover pickle brine (and its aromatic seeds) seasons grains and beans. Cheese heels add depth to creamy beans (page 263). Flat bubbly goes toward braising liquid for Artichokes + Asparagus (page 123). Nearly any food can give, then give again, before bidding its final farewell. Why not make a lifestyle of extracting every bit of flavor?

FORAGING

In 2011, I joined a walk with the acclaimed forager and locavore Leda Meredith. She led us through New York City's Central Park, and my life has not been the same since. I didn't understand you could eat all kinds of things that I previously took for granted, such as pervasive, silvery mugwort leaves. Once my awareness was activated, the landscape came alive in a completely new way. No flower or plant went unnoticed. I was keen to get closer to everything, examine their traits, broaden that day's eating, or make plans for the weeks to come. With the benefit of online resources, there is a vast community to tap into, whether to commiserate on a season's good or bad fortune, for crowd assistance in ID-ing a new food, learning how others may have cooked something to inform how you might, and so on. And in the days before COVID, it was easy to go on nature walks to share or learn together and eat potlucks of various foraged treats; I grew new friends and recipes. This is an invaluable side effect of connecting to wild foods.

When I was a child, I was completely present in the natural world around me, something precious that I lost through the many years living in big cities. Foraging allows me to immediately dip into that same energy, and when I do, it's as if time has stopped. Foraging makes what is right in front of us obvious if we simply stop and notice. Without the attention foraging brings to our surroundings, many things go overlooked. When we forage, we see that the landscape is offering feedback on how quickly a shift in temperature has changed what is ripe or available, how a recent rain has transformed the terrain, or what a very dry season has brought (or what it hasn't). Witnessing these phenomena immediately connects us to plants and the natural world at large.

The first summer we lived upstate, it rained seemingly nonstop for months. It was such a wet summer-through-fall that certain trees in the neighborhood, in the forests, in all kinds of places, just tipped over. They were so saturated that their roots could no longer hold on to the sodden earth. That was one way to mark the profound weather of the season. Another was that there were so many mushrooms proliferating in the forest that when we drove with the windows open, we smelled the earthy rot permeating from the woods. The abundance was in overdrive. Mushrooms of every kind were exploding, and this became an introduction to many mushrooms I'd never personally experienced before.

Central to foraging is the observation of greater and greater subtleties. There are the broad details. As your familiarity with a place deepens, innumerable nuances reveal themselves in plain sight. Whether it is physical change brought by another living thing—deer trampled or ate a colony of berries you had sights on—or by changes in weather that produced a shift in circumstances, such as just-unfurling edible flowers becoming scorched due to sudden or prolonged intense heat. Sometimes these moments signal microclimate fluctuations. Microclimates are variances in local weather conditions, dependent on landscape. If there is a large meadow adjacent to woodlands, the atmospheric condition of one is not going to be the same as the other. The density of trees makes for a cooler, more humid, oxygenated environment, whereas grassy, open fields bear a hotter, drier landscape. Understanding this variance in conditions will help you gauge your hunches more precisely. It's another layer of connection to the things around you, an essential skill as we move toward intensifying climate change as a regular part of life.

To forage well is to be a good steward of our planet and tread more lightly than people just functioning in the relationship of buying food from stores. This connects us to our ancestors, Native peoples, and traditional living that many of us have gotten far away from. Foraging brings us into the web of ecosystems right in front of us, providing something rather splendid in lives that can feel bogged down with obligations or predictability. Nothing about the material world has changed, but because our awareness has increased, things inevitably become more alive, sparking a new relationship with nature around you.

There are some wild foods unique to your region and yours alone—for instance, morel mushrooms do not grow in the Southwest, and prickly pear fruits do not grow in the Northeast. Understanding regional distinctions, that native foods thrive in particular sets of conditions, will aid you in foraging with success. It is of great benefit to assemble a collection of reference guides specific to where you live so you can familiarize yourself with your landscape, as well as properly ID edible plants and affirm your intuition. (I have provided a list of guides on page 285.)

Once you've been bitten by the foraging bug, it is greatly useful to know how to cook or prepare wild foods deliciously. In many cases, it's a pretty straightforward affair. In others, nuance matters. Let the foods in these pages lead you and create confidence, or if you already forage wild foods, may these recipes inspire you to cook in ways you may not already, or layer elements in ways you hadn't thought to. Wherever you've come from, welcome to the exploration of wild and native foods. They are all around us. Slow down, pay attention, use your five senses, and exciting discoveries will unfold.

The more you practice observation, the more you discover and the richer your vocabulary and cooking repertoire become. Think of wild foods as free, highly nutritious food sources. They are foods of-the-moment and absolutely the most local you can find. One crucial service you can do for yourself is to take away the mystery and fear so you can successfully identify foods you love. Mushrooms? Berries? Peppery greens? Build the quest for these into your day-to-day routine. In doing so, you'll connect to their

HEN OF THE WOODS

GARLIC MUSTARD

CHANTERELLES

RAMPS

AUTUMN OLIVES

WILD BERGAMOT

SUNCHOKES

HONEY MUSHROOMS

JUNIPER

PORCINI MUSHROOMS

highly fleeting seasonality and return to wilds you've visited previously with a greater likelihood of right timing—which means a beautiful harvest awaits you.

It cannot be overstated: be sure you have 100 percent confidence. Cross-reference multiple credible sources to positively ID any wild food before consuming. You choose to harvest or consume wild foods at your own risk. That said, most greens will not poison you, and a tiny amount of a thing, chewed—and then spit out if acrid—is a tried-and-true method of testing certain wild foods. When consuming new-to-you wild foods, start with a small quantity and allow a day to pass before consuming again. This timeframe should clarify if you'll have a reaction. This method is especially important for anyone who has other food allergies or sensitivities. I assume no responsibility for any adverse effects from misidentification or incorrect use of featured wild plants.

If you try a wild food and do not like it, know that different plants of the same species may taste different based on microclimate, habitat, or overall weather conditions. It is possible you may prefer it a different way than your chosen initial preparation. It helps to remain open as you broaden your repertoire. And tastes do change.

To experience the most potent flavors and tenderest textures, harvest the part of a plant that is currently growing: a good rule of thumb is leaves in spring; berries, flowers, and fruit in summer; nuts in fall; and roots in winter and early spring. Harvest leaves prior to peak maturity for the most tender results. Fruits and nuts should be at peak ripeness. To harvest roots, the plant growing above ground should be dying back or completely dead, or just beginning to shoot. When harvesting mushrooms, leave some intact so they can release more spores, their reproductive process. Use a knife to cut them from the earth or tree rather than uprooting them to minimize disruption of the mycelium, their underground network of millions of tiny cells essential for future growth. Carry harvested mushrooms in a basket or mesh bag instead of plastic so they can breathe and to allow their spores to disperse as you meander.

Verify the area you're harvesting from has not been sprayed with an herbicide or pesticide. If you don't know, it is best not to take the risk. Only forage on permitted public lands. Check the websites of the National Park Service, Bureau of Land Management, or the specific park you are visiting for guidelines. If you forage on private property, be sure to obtain permission beforehand.

Any plant classified as invasive cannot be overharvested, but do keep the ecosystems and the animals who rely on wild foods in mind, and leave at least half for them. Also consider the ability of the plant to propagate so that you do not overharvest it. Many, but not all, wild foods are considered invasive. Know the difference and treat your harvest accordingly. For instance, it is impossible to overharvest garlic mustard, whereas harvesting ramps should be conducted with great care and restraint, as they multiply very slowly. Their populations have plummeted due to overharvesting and their current popularity.

FORAGING DO'S AND DON'TS

» Do not trample and damage an area in your quest for wild foods. Leave it as pristine as you found it for sustained enjoyment for all.

» Only take one-third to one-half of your discovery and leave the rest for nature.

» Bring a cutter, knife, scissors, hori hori, or other implement to harvest stems, stalks, and shoots cleanly.

» Keep a basket, paper bags or containers, bug spray, a whistle, and a knife or cutter at the ready as part of your impromptu foraging kit.

» When foraging in wild or remote landscapes it is best to forage with a friend, for your safety, should anything unforeseen happen. A whistle is a good friend if you need assistance.

» Always bring or wear waterproof boots. You never know where you may find yourself. This is part of the Seven Ps: prior proper planning prevents piss poor performance. Plus, boots act as a tick deterrent.

» For forest foraging, wear a loose-fitting long sleeve shirt and lightweight pants. They serve as tick and mosquito deterrents, as well as a protective layer against bramble thickets.

» Know what poison ivy and poison oak look like so you safely avoid any contact with them. They can wreak havoc on skin cells for up to a month, a punishment worth avoiding.

» If you inadvertently bring an insect home, show kindness and release it back into nature. However, kill any ticks.

» Always look back from the direction you came. The view is different from this perspective: you may find precious pieces you hadn't originally noticed in doing so, plus it is a way to track your path. Honing your keenness and developing landmarks aids in making successful return visits.

» Beyond personal protection and comfort, be aware of your surroundings. More often than not you'll encounter a few chipmunks or birds, but large berry patches can attract bears. Don't be shy about making a bit of a ruckus when foraging, whether by jangling keys, singing, or blowing a whistle now and then, to let the woodland denizens know you're there, too.

AUTUMN OLIVE (*Elaeagnus umbellata*) is a tree whose berries ripen mid-August through September, and often the last fruits (the sweetest berries of the season) can be seen on trees as late as mid-October in the Hudson Valley, New York. It is native to Asia and is also known as Japanese silverberry, oleaster, or autumnberry.

To Identify: The curvy-edged silvery leaves are leathery, similar to actual olive trees, which may be how they got their name. The shrub was originally brought to the United States in the late 1800s to mitigate against soil erosion. Because the berries are loved by birds, bears, and other wildlife, the spread of autumn olive seeds via their droppings is rampant. Since autumn olive trees fare well in drought and poor soil conditions, they have taken over in some areas, where actual groves of up to 16-foot-tall trees can be found, pushing native varieties out. For the forager, an abundance of berries in one location is excellent news. Their glittery red berries are sweet-tart and slightly tannic and make terrific jams and sauces. But do not plant an autumn olive tree. They are considered invasive by both homeowners as well as by the US government. To ensure you do not start your own autumn olive population after you forage, do not compost the pomace-seed mixture if you make the jam or distribute them elsewhere: to the trash bin they should go.

To Harvest: To harvest autumn olives, hold a berry-laden branch over a large paper shopping bag with handles, looped over one wrist (or a bucket, fashioned similarly), and gently stroke the branches as if you were playing a harp, pulling them from their stems, allowing them to fall into the bag. Berries should be plump and fairly easy to burst when squeezed when you harvest.

To Enjoy: Autumn olives are a powerhouse of nutrients, including lycopene and anti-oxidants. A couple years ago I paired an autumn olive mostarda with lamb chops, and I keep building on the repertoire of ways to enjoy it. Make jam with them (page 99) and add to the Ultimate Nibbles Platter (page 208) with a triple-cream cheese such as Délice de Bourgogne, or a blue cheese such as Saint Agur, Stilton, or a buttermilk blue cheese. Or, make the Autumn Olive Linzer Tart (page 229). Store your harvested berries in the refrigerator until you are ready to use them. Wash them of debris, best done by placing the berries in a large shallow bowl, allowing leaves, twigs, insects, and other matter to float to the top, and then skimming.

GARLIC MUSTARD (*Alliaria petiolata*), also known as wild garlic or Jack by the hedge, is an aggressive-growing, invasive plant in the mustard (Brassicaceae) family, originally brought to the United States as a garden plant. It is a biennial, sprouting vegetation in its first year, then after overwintering the plant produces seeds in spring. Garlic mustard grows at forest edges, in garden beds, in disturbed woodlands, at roadsides, and along walking paths. It is one of the earliest spring plants, growing in squat bunches in March in the Hudson Valley, and reappears in late fall.

To Identify: Garlic mustard's tender foliage is a rich, deep green. Leaves have a wrinkly surface and a rounded, serrated edge. When plants mature, the leaves become more heart-shaped, with leaf tips more similar to knife points. To help identify it, crush a leaf in your hands—if it releases a strong garlicky, mustardy aroma, it is indeed garlic mustard. Once the flower stem (petiole) shoots up from the bunch and flower buds have formed, the top 4 or 5 inches can be readily snapped off and taste similar to broccoli rabe. This is one of my favorite times to harvest garlic mustard. At this stage it is excellent wilted in a cast-iron skillet and added to grains or beans, used as a topping to pizza, or blitzed raw into the versatile Garlic Mustard Pesto (page 62).

To Harvest: You simply cannot overharvest this plant, and in fact you are doing a service to native plants everywhere by harvesting garlic mustard, which suffocates biodiversity. Pull them up by their roots and feast.

To Enjoy: When in full bloom, peppery flower clusters can be harvested and eaten raw on top of all savory foods, from pasta to salads, grains, legumes, fish, and more. All parts of the plant are edible—root (grated as you would horseradish), leaves, tender stems, flowers, and seeds (use as you would mustard seeds or black peppercorns). Garlic mustard has trace amounts of cyanide and should be rinsed or soaked briefly before using to leech it out.

GROUND ELDER (*Aegopodium podagraria*), also known as goutweed, bishops' weed, or snow-on-the-mountain, is a perennial in the carrot family and grows largely in shady areas, such as the understory around trees. It can also be found on stream banks, in pastures, in parks, and in gardens widely, including mine. We have a large front garden that once was a formidable perennial garden. I know this because neighbors who have lived here for decades stop to share, reflecting on it with a sigh and a smile. Alas, I have a lot of ground elder, and due to its vigorous growth via networks of underground rhizomes, it spreads prolifically. It is classified as an invasive and selling it has even been outlawed in some states. Ground elder is highly adaptive and effectively excludes all other plants. Do not worry about overharvesting this plant. You are doing a service to the rest of the ecosystem.

To Identify: To identify ground elder, triangular, hollow stems reach 12 to 36 inches tall, and tiny white flowers spread in dome-like shapes, or umbels, similar looking to Queen Anne's lace. Each of its three leaflets is divided into three leaflets. As part of the family of umbelliferous plants such as parsley, carrots, and fennel, there are also their deadly cousins, like poison hemlock and water hemlock. Don't guess—make sure you can identify ground elder with 100 percent certainty to be safe, not sorry. If you crush ground elder leaves, they should smell like celery.

To Harvest: Snip or pinch stems with scissors or your fingertips.

To Enjoy: Tender ground elder shoots grow in early spring and can be eaten raw (A Rosy Salad for Darker Days, page 251, and Crispy Pork + Fennel Meatballs in Umami

Broth, page 128) and taste herbal, similar to lovage or celery. More mature stems can be cooked to soften their strong herbal quality. I sometimes use mature stems to flavor stocks, extracting their flavor but straining out the fibrous texture.

HONEYSUCKLE (*Lonicera japonica*), also known as Japanese honeysuckle, is a hardy, climbing vine that if given the right conditions will outcompete other greenery and choke out native plants, taking over. Since it is classified as invasive, it is unwise to plant. Honeysuckle can be found in abandoned fields, in open woods, in disturbed areas, along roadsides, and at the edges of lawns. It grows best in full sun and pollinators love the flowers.

Honeysuckle blooms in June in the Hudson Valley, its honeyed floral aroma wafting along our country roads anywhere it grows. Even more than its invasive qualities, honeysuckle is known for its heady fragrance and the tempting nectar inside each flower from which it derives its name.

To Identify: Since there are so many plants (180!) in the honeysuckle family, it is important to know how to distinguish which plants include edible elements and which elements on any plant you should not. The leaves and fruit are generally toxic. For this honeysuckle variety, only the flowers hold interest. The inch-long tubular flowers grow in clusters of two and are bicolor, yellow and white, and grow from strong, fibrous, twining, trailing stems. Pointed-tip ovate leaves grow in pairs opposite from one another.

To Harvest: Collect flowers in a paper bag. If you must use plastic, do not seal the container, as they'll sweat and risk becoming slimy through the condensation.

To Enjoy: Use within a day to make syrup, jelly, or fermented Honeysuckle Cordial (page 104), as their floral brightness fades the longer they sit.

MUGWORT (*Artemisia vulgaris*), also called wormwood, is a perennial herb and grows in forests, on field edges, along roadsides, in backyards, and along waterways.

To Identify: Mugwort leaves are dark green, feathery with many sharp points, and resemble chrysanthemum leaves. They are pinnately arranged, and their undersides look soft and silvery due to a surface of fine hairs.

To Harvest: It grows quickly so the best time to harvest mugwort is in early summer, pinching off the top tender growth and outermost leaves, into fall, when the flowers may be harvested.

To Enjoy: Mugwort leaves smell spicy and bright and taste similar to sage. They are excellent in savory baked goods such as Sourdough Crackers (page 75) and miso-mugwort shortbread (page 210). The stems are deep burgundy colored. Mature plants can reach up to 5 feet tall. Mugwort has long been used as a healing herb in many traditional cultures through the ages. It is best used in moderate quantity, whether in medicinal uses or as a culinary flavoring.

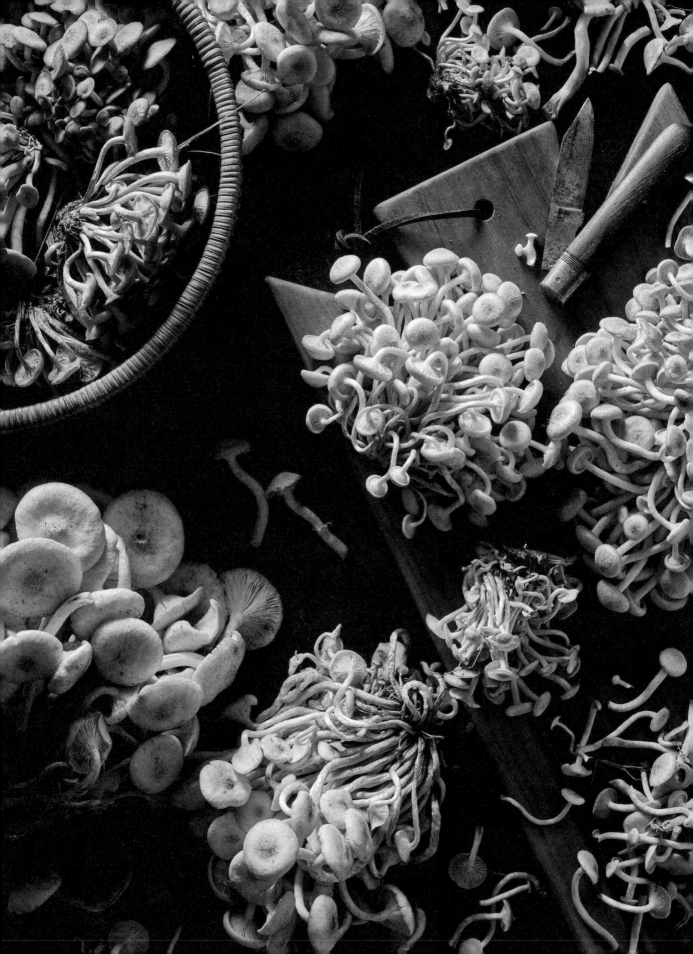

RINGLESS HONEY MUSHROOMS · FIELD GARLIC + HOARY BITTERCRESS

NATIVE PLANTS

BLACK RASPBERRY (*Rubus occidentalis*), also known as black caps, black cap raspberry, or bear's eye blackberry, is a plant native to North America. In the wild, black raspberries grow sparsely but in clusters, thanks to runners that extend from their canes. They can be found in disturbed areas, open woods, and meadows and along trails, steams, and roads. If you forage black raspberries, best to have patience as your yield will grow only by visiting more shrubs. They grow on my property, and over the few years we have lived here, I have taken to training and pruning, or heading, them to stimulate more prolific fruiting. Even still, black raspberries ripen over an extended period, rather than all at once. So, it's a little here, a little there type of harvest and therefore difficult to amass a quantity unless you have many plants.

To Identify: To identify black raspberries, notice their chalky red, thorny canes or stems. Black raspberry leaves are green on top and nearly white on their undersides. Their fruits are cup- or cap-shaped, exhibit a more tightly clustered flesh, have numerous fine white hairs, and are purple-black when ripe. (They appear similar in hue to cultivated raspberries when unripe.)

To Harvest: In upstate New York, black raspberries ripen mid-June into July, and every bird (and even squirrels and chipmunks) has its eyes on the ripening jewels, so you better beat them to it. Since the berries grow from upright stems, they are easy to pluck when ripe. Be mindful of thorns as you move from cane to cane—wearing long sleeves during harvest is helpful to avoid being scratched.

To Enjoy: The slightly tart-sweet berries are a delicious addition to Bourbon Mascarpone Tartlets (page 185), and can be made into jam, syrup, ice cream, shrubs, or eaten simply fresh off the shrub.

BLUEBERRIES (*Vaccinium angustifolium* and *V. corymbosum*) are native shrubs with both highbush and lowbush species. Lowbush blueberries (such as *V. angustifolium*) grow up to 18 inches tall. Highbush blueberries (such as *V. corymbosum*) grow up to 7 feet tall, and unlike other berry shrubs, they do not have thorns. Blueberries growing in the wild are tiny compared to cultivated blueberries and have twice the antioxidants of cultivated blueberries, due to a greater concentration in the flavonoid anthocyanin.

To Identify: Fruits have a five-pointed crown on the underside of the berry; leaves are green and broad with a defined point and turn a scarlet red in the fall. The flowers are small, bell-shaped, and pink or white. They typically ripen mid-July through mid-August here in the Hudson Valley.

To Harvest: If you harvest wild blueberries, do so with a friend. Bears also like blueberries, but instinctively do not want to be near humans. In company you're likely to make conversation or noise, alerting any bears that may happen upon you by surprise.

Ripe wild blueberries should detach easily from their stems with a gentle roll of your fingers. If you have to pull the fruit off with any force, it's likely not yet perfectly ripe. Fruit on a single bush ripens over a period of several weeks, depending on the exposure it receives, so it is feasible to visit shrubs at the beginning of ripening season, as well as toward the end and expect to find delicious berries.

To Enjoy: These tiny berries pack a flavorful punch, but be sure to sample from different shrubs, as well as different areas on a plant—not all have robust flavor and it's best finding that out before you harvest a container-full.

COMMON MILKWEED (*Asclepias syriaca*), also known as butterfly flower, is a tall perennial herb, endemic to North America, and grows in open fields and meadows, along roadsides, and in gardens. Its leaves are the sole food source for monarch butterfly caterpillars. Any area with abundant sun and sandy soil is likely to grow milkweed. I am doing my best to develop a milkweed colony on our hillside, in a sunny spot just in front of the edge of our woods.

To Identify: Common milkweed has thick pointed oval leaves that grow in opposite pairs along the lone stalk. Plants grow up to 4 feet tall, and their tiny flowers look like loose pompom clusters when they bloom in early summer, in shades from purple to pink to white. Pods, which follow the flowers, are teardrop shaped and green and bumpy and grow 4 to 5 inches long. They contain seeds attached to gossamer tufts that travel easily, becoming airborne for disbursement. All parts of the plant exude milky latex if cut. Milkweed provides many edible parts over the course of its growth cycle.

To Harvest: To harvest leaf shoots, do so when they are still compact (6 to 10 inches tall). Flower bud clusters appear in late spring and resemble a tight head of broccoli. All edible parts should be harvested stems pointing down, to prevent the sticky latex from bleeding all over.

To Enjoy: The flower bud clusters are delicious fried (page 173), tasting similar to green beans or asparagus, and the pods are often compared to okra. Blanch shoots, pods, and buds for a few minutes, then shock in an ice bath to retain their bright green hue before further preparation or consumption.

ELDERBERRY (*Sambucus canadensis*) is a perennial shrub and member of the Adoxaceae family, native to North and Central America. Its flowers show in midsummer (June and July), then the plant forms purple-black berries in late summer here in the Hudson Valley. Elderberry shrubs prefer sunny locations and grow along roadsides, in woodland clearings, and along stream banks. I planted a pair of shrubs our second summer at the cottage after we undertook a large landscape project to clear invasive plants. Though they experienced a vulnerable period where some forest denizen thought to munch the farther away of the two, they both have since grown vigorously. They need very little care and have been a joy to see coming into bloom up on our hillside.

To Identify: Shrubs can grow up to 12 feet tall. Their greyish-brown limbs have warty bumps, and the older bark is brownish-grey with shallow fissures, with thin, platelike scales. Elongated, pointy tip dark green sawtooth leaves grow in opposite pairs, from five to nine leaves per stem. Numerous tiny five-petaled creamy white flowers sit flat on umbrella-shaped clusters. Berries grow from the flowers into flat, sometimes droopy clusters, up to 10 inches across. Berries are first green in color, then ripen to purple-black. Berries are round and ⅛ inch in diameter.

To Harvest: Harvest freshly opened flowers early in the day to retain the greatest concentration of nectar. Snip flower umbels from their stalks and shake or dislodge the many florets, as any stem matter is toxic. Harvest berry clusters when fruits are shiny and purple-black, plucking individual berries from their stems.

To Enjoy: Although the flowers and berries are edible, all other parts of this shrub are poisonous, containing toxic calcium oxalate crystals. Only consume berries when they are fully ripe and only when cooked. Flowers can be eaten raw, made into syrups or other infusions, and fried into fritters. If you harvest flowers, leave at least half on the shrub so they may mature into berries. Berries can be cooked into a syrup or jam or made into cordial.

JUNIPER (*Juniperus species*) is an evergreen that can grow either as a shrub or as tall as a tree. It prefers sun but is not particular about good soil conditions.

To Identify: The berries—actually fleshy cones—form in tight green clusters on female trees, and when ripe they turn a powdery blue. And a little goes a very long way. This pricey spice is available in abundance growing throughout the New York region, ripening in September. Juniper berries are invigorating, tasting somewhat piney or resinous, and slightly citrusy-sweet.

To Harvest: Harvest juniper berries from late fall into winter. Wear gloves as you harvest the berries because the plant is prickly and can give a stinging, albeit temporary, rash. It's said that juniper berries become sweeter by late winter, so experiment: taste berries from different trees, at different points through the cold weather months, and see.

To Enjoy: I use juniper berries in many wild cured salmon recipes (such as on page 94) in my fermented Juniper + Cumin Meyer Lemon Kraut (page 90), and in a host of other preparations during cold weather months, including an aromatic rub for game meats. Store harvested berries sealed in a jar at room temperature where you keep other spices.

PAWPAW (*Asimina triloba*), also known as custard apple or wild banana, this fruit is a native deciduous tree in eastern and southern North America. It is part of the same family as cherimoya, soursop, guanabana, and ylang-ylang. It is an understory tree, growing up to 30 feet tall in fertile, well-drained soils, and is the largest edible indigenous fruit in the United States. Fruits ripen in the Hudson Valley in October.

To Identify: The large, 10- to 12-inch-long simple leaves are clustered at the ends of branches. Six-petaled maroon flowers show in early spring. Ovular, kidney-shaped fruits range 2 to 6 inches long and start as green, then change to yellowish-green skins when ripe. Creamy yellow flesh contains several glossy brown or black seeds.

To Harvest: Pawpaws are ready to eat when they emit a tropical aroma and the skins give slightly, becoming yellowish or blemished with brown spots. If you have perfect timing, cut the ripe fruits at their stem with a sharp blade. Or harvest recently fallen fruits—this is the more likely option of the two, as the tendency of the tree is to let the fruits go, the weaker branches bending with their pregnant weight.

To Enjoy: Pawpaws taste like a cross between pineapple, mango, and banana and can be eaten raw, simply scooped from their shells; made into ice cream, sorbet, or crème brûlée (page 232); added to baked goods; or puréed for making cocktails. Puréed pulp can be frozen for later use.

SPRUCE TIPS (*Picea abies*) are the new growth at the ends of evergreen spruce tree branches.

To Identify: When the spruce tips grow in the middle of spring, late May to June in the Hudson Valley, they are initially encased in brown, papery sheaths, which then peel away to reveal soft, frondy, light green clusters of needles. Before the new needle clusters stiffen, they are prime for harvest.

To Harvest: Any harvested tips will stop the year's growth on that part of the tree, so choose carefully to work with its natural form. Given this, it is more advisable to harvest from mature, grander trees rather than young ones that need time to grow undisturbed. Never harvest more than 20 percent of the tips from any given tree. To harvest, gently twist-pull or pinch off the tips with your fingers.

To Enjoy: Spruce tips from different trees will taste different from one another. Our towering Norway spruce produces floral, slightly citrusy tasting tips, and it is these I use to perfume honey, sugar, and salt, and to make syrup (Rye + Spruce Tip Last Word, page 103).

RAMPS (*Allium tricoccum*), also known as wild leeks, are one of the earliest plants to break through newly thawed spring ground. The aromatic plants show shoots before the hardwood forests they grow in have leafed out, which provides necessary sunshine to the forest floor for these plants to mature.

To Identify: Ramps grow in clumps. They have broad ovate leaves, similar in appearance to lily of the valley, and exude a pungent, sweet oniony aroma. Leaves emerge from a sometimes pink sheath membrane, sprouting from white stalks.

To Harvest: It is crucially important that foragers harvesting ramps only harvest the leaves, not the bulbs, and *definitely not* the roots. Ramps are notoriously slow to regenerate—they take seven to ten years to multiply—and due to their popularity on restaurant menus everywhere, they have succumbed to overharvesting. Their populations are in peril. The only circumstance where harvesting bulbs can be done safely is when ramps grow in enormous abundance, on land you have more than a fleeting connection to. I am extremely fortunate that a true forest of ramps grows in a woodland just a few minutes' drive away, and I only harvest the entirety of a plant when it has been damaged by other foragers' exploits or by tractor tracks from recent forest clearing projects (sad, but can't be controlled, as it is on someone else's property). To harvest, only take fatter, more mature bulbs, cutting well above the root. Trim leaves at the stem, up to a few from each clump if you are harvesting from an abundant patch. If it is a small patch, harvest only a few leaves so that the group may continue to regenerate and provide a greater bounty down the road.

To Enjoy: The intensely aromatic leaves preserve well in Ramp Salt (page 63). The bulbs make an excellent, pungent pickle (page 85) and can be paired with richly flavored pâtés (page 119) and cured fish (page 248).

SUNCHOKES (*Helianthus tuberosus*), also known as Jerusalem artichokes, are a hardy perennial sunflower endemic to central United States. They are neither from Jerusalem, nor are they artichokes. Sunchokes propagate via their tubers. Their vigorous growing nature risks outcompeting other plant life, and they also produce phytotoxins that prevent competitive species from germinating. It is precisely these traits that make these prolific tubers a reliable food source, once you land on an established colony.

To Identify: Sunchokes grow up to 12 feet tall, with sandpaper-textured woody stems and alternating ovate leaves. Each plant bears multiple yellow 2- to 4-inch flowers between August and October. The tubers are reddish or whitish knobby shapes, resembling stubby-looking ginger with white flesh.

To Harvest: Harvest tubers in late fall, as the flowers are dying or have died back. For the best tasting sunchokes, wait until one or two frosts have passed; they will concentrate fructose, rendering them sweeter.

To Enjoy: The inulin present in Jerusalem artichokes makes them excellent for gut flora, but too much produces gassiness. They are infamously sometimes referred to as "fartachokes." Fermenting Jerusalem artichokes makes them easier to digest without issue. Sunchokes can be eaten raw, and when eaten this way, they are similar to jicama or water chestnuts. Roasted, boiled, or fried, their flavor is slightly sweet and subtly nutty. The sunchokes featured in this book were harvested by my neighbor Ruthie, who has been waging a small battle in her garden beds for some years.

WILD BERGAMOT (*Monarda fistulosa*) is also called bee balm. This native perennial is a favorite among pollinators and grows in fields, in sunny clearings, in open woodlands, along roadsides, and in gardens.

To Identify: Mature plants grow up to 4 feet tall. Leaves grow in opposite pairs on a square, hairy stem and are tapered and pointy with wide serrated edges. Tubular flowers arrange in a circle and bloom early to midsummer. Whenever I see them, I am reminded of spiky 1980s rock hairdos or cartoon spaceships.

To Harvest: Cut the flower heads off their tall stems when in full bloom, in early morning to preserve their abundant fragrance.

To Enjoy: Part of the mint family, wild bergamot smells like oregano and tastes similarly spicy. It makes an excellent addition to salads (Oaxaca-Meets-the-Mediterranean, Tomatoes, Corn, page 162), desserts (Black Raspberry–Bourbon Mascarpone Tartlets, page 185), and grilled meats. Pluck petals from flower heads for a colorful pepperiness, or snip the topmost toothed leaves and use fresh or dried as you would oregano.

Mushrooms

CHANTERELLE MUSHROOM (*Cantharellus lateritius* or *C. cibarius*) is an orange, meaty mushroom. They are a summer mushroom, their bright golden forms push from the forest floor after abundant rainfall. Chanterelles grow in loose clusters in established deciduous forests, most commonly growing out of the forest floor near maple, beech, poplar, and oak trees.

To Identify: Chanterelles have "false gills": forked ridges that appear as gills and run down the solid stem. They appear somewhat trumpet- or vase-like in shape. They grow as individual mushrooms, sometimes in pairs, but do not share a stem. Spore print is pale pinkish yellow. This mushroom has lighter interior flesh and a fruity aroma, often compared to apricots.

To Harvest: Use a knife or other blade to slice the stem where it meets the earth. Collect chanterelles in a basket so they may spread their spores as you wander.

To Enjoy: As with nearly all wild mushrooms, chanterelles should be cooked before being consumed. Simple preparations, using oil or butter in a cast-iron skillet to cook them, make chanterelles taste their best, such as for Buttery Scrambled Eggs + Chanterelles (page 152).

GOLDEN OYSTER MUSHROOM (*Pleurotus citrinopileatus*) **AND COMMON OYSTER MUSHROOM** (*P. ostreatus*). Golden oyster mushrooms are a warm weather oyster mushroom, requiring consistently warm temperatures to fruit. Common oysters are a winter-to-spring mushroom. Both are saprotrophic in nature, decomposers of dying tree matter.

To Identify: Golden oysters are trumpet-shaped polypores. Their bright, saffron yellow caps are situated on longer stems than their grey cousins and are very fragile when mature. They have white gills and grow in clusters, similar to the common oyster mushroom. The common oyster mushroom has pale to dark brown flesh. It has white decurrent gills attached to a short, nearly nonexistent stem and produces a white to

ELDERBERRIES · BLUEBERRIES

lilac-grey spore print. The oyster mushroom cap is convex when young, flattening to broad and fan-shaped and growing to span 8 to 10 inches across when mature. Its flesh is firm and white. This polypore fungus is easily recognizable by the way in which it grows: shelflike, in clusters, on deciduous tree trunks.

To Harvest: Oyster mushroom clusters can be heavy but also delicate: use a knife or other blade to slice them close to but not at the inception point at the tree bark, leaving the more fibrous stem material behind. Transfer to a large-handled paper bag or a basket so they may spread their spores as you meander further.

To Enjoy: Golden oysters impart an earthy, nutty flavor when cooked. Some people describe common oyster aroma akin to oysters or scallops. It is a specific but mild aroma, ultimately. These are both mild-tasting mushrooms with a meaty texture. Each is excellent in the Wild Mushroom Escabeche (page 93)—which gets added to the Vegan Umami Udon (page 172).

HEN OF THE WOODS (*Grifola frondosa*), also known as maitake, is a polypore that most frequently grows at the base of established oak trees.

To Identify: Hen of the woods can be recognized by its pale-grey to dark-brown wavy caps, organized into clusters of ruffles, fanning out from a single base. This fungus does not have gills, but instead pores that are in the shape of rounded tubes. It produces a white spore print. Like various other fungi, it is parasitic to living oaks and other hardwoods, causing a white rot. This mushroom is one of the prizes of fall: once temperatures dip to the 40s and the earth is damp from recent rain, the conditions are right to go hunting for this savory autumn treat.

To Harvest: Cradle the mushroom cluster in one hand and slice it at its base with the other, using a knife or other sharp blade. Transport in a large-handled paper bag or basket, so that it may spread its spores as you continue on.

To Enjoy: Hen of the woods is excellent seared hard in a skillet, enough so that certain areas are rendered crispy, as in the Roast Chicken, Hen of the Woods, Leeks, Pan Sauce (page 255). If I've scored a large haul, any drier parts make an excellent Mushroom Stock (page 80). It is deeply nourishing and adds flavor to anything you add it to—grains, beans, soup, stews, you name it.

HONEY MUSHROOMS (*Armillaria mellea*) grow one of the largest underground mycelium networks of any living organisms. Honey mushrooms grow in clusters from a single base on decaying hardwood stumps, the base of tree trunks, or on the forest floor. They often grow from oak trees in a parasitic relationship (saprophytic) that ultimately kills their hosts.

To Identify: To properly identify honey mushrooms, confirm their somewhat spotted yellow or reddish brown-to-tan cap surface and a convex cap when young, and that the mushroom produces a white spore print. The stipe (stem) may or may not have a ring: it is a called a ringless honey mushroom if there is no ring, otherwise it is called a honey mushroom.

To Harvest: Look for younger mushroom clusters, which are a firmer texture and easier to clean. Their caps will be small and unopened, therefore not revealing the gills. Gently hold the mushroom cluster in one hand and slice it at its base using a knife or other sharp blade, keeping the clump intact. Transport honey mushrooms in a large-handled paper bag or basket, so that they may spread spores as you walk.

To Enjoy: Brush any debris away, then trim stems so only a very short length is consumed, as the stems tend to be fibrous. Parboil honey mushrooms for 5 minutes, then strain in a colander before using in a final preparation. This is said to reduce the likelihood of any bitter flavor or potential gastric upset. Use honey mushrooms in the Wild Mushroom Escabeche (page 93), stews, or other sautéed mushroom dishes.

PORCINI (*Boletus edulis*), also referred to as the king of mushrooms, penny bun mushroom, and cep, porcini has a richer, more deeply mushroomy flavor than other mushrooms.

To Identify: In the northeastern United States, it grows in the soil underneath pine, spruce, and hemlock conifers, but also sometimes underneath large oaks. They can be found in the Northeast between September and November.

To Harvest: Harvest younger button or "bouchon"-size mushrooms whenever possible, as tiny worms will often have burrowed into larger specimens. Porcini have white to greenish-yellow spongelike pores rather than gills. To tell if you have a prime specimen, slice it in half vertically. If it is white through and through, it is prime. Larger porcini may have tubes (pores) turning yellowish green, still edible, but may impart a less than ideal texture once cooked.

To Enjoy: These boletes have a very short shelf life. Use them within two or three days or lose them to incubating pests.

GARDEN "WEEDS"

DANDELION (*Taraxacum officinale*) has a long history as a medicinal and health food and is one of the most nutrient-dense plants. It is a perennial and grows everywhere, from roadsides, pavement cracks, and pastures, to garden beds and meadows.

To Identify: Dandelions grow from a sturdy taproot in a rosette pattern and sprout jagged or sharply irregularly toothed, dark green leaves. Their sunny yellow flowers grow from a single stalk and are ubiquitous, thwarting perfect lawns and fueling childhood fancy everywhere.

To Harvest: Never harvest dandelion from chemically treated areas, roadsides where walking dogs pass by, or areas of frequent car traffic.

To Enjoy: You can eat all parts of the plant: root, leaves, and flowers. Dandelion greens are packed with vitamins and antioxidants. Younger leaves can be eaten raw in salads, snipped at the base of the crown, whereas more mature leaves—once temperatures are consistently warmer causing the plants to flower—are more bitter and tough and therefore better harvested as single leaves for wilting (Vegan Umami Udon, page 172). If you have a garden, harvest your dandelion at will—it grows vigorously and is labeled a survivor for a reason!

FIELD GARLIC (*Allium vineale*) is similar to cultivated garlic in that it is a bulb forming plant, but unlike cultivated garlic, it is a perennial. Field garlic grows everywhere. Find it in parks, meadows, forests, pastures, disturbed areas, and even urban lots.

To Identify: Field garlic grows 12 to 16 inches tall in patchy bunches and becomes more fibrous as it matures, with subtle ridges along the length of each of its stems. Look for garlicky-smelling, tender, hollow leaves that resemble chives in early spring or late fall. Any plant that smells like garlic or onions is edible and will not lead you astray. Once mature, an edible pinkish flower bulblet grows from the tip of field garlic's central stem, and opens to a burgundy flower sphere made of juicy garlicky florets. Field garlic's main method of reproduction is via the underground bulbs that sprout adjacent to the parent plant.

> "What is a weed? A plant whose virtues have not yet been discovered."
>
> —*Ralph Waldo Emerson*

To Harvest: The bulbs are tricky to uproot and so the task is best done after rainfall with a forked weeding tool or trowel. Harvest tender field garlic shoots late fall to early spring. Harvest the underground bulbs April to June when plants are mature. Leaves from mature plants are more fibrous and indicate larger, plumper cloves underground. Gently thwack the bunch you uproot against a stone or tree trunk to release clumping soil. Then rinse in an outdoor water source to free up any remaining earth from the bulbs or, alternatively, fill a bowl with cold water and swish the bulbs in it, then toss the water outdoors. Repeat as needed until they are clean. There is absolutely *no risk* of overharvesting field garlic, so have at it. In fact, in some regions it is considered invasive.

To Enjoy: Use field garlic stems as you would chives (Field Garlic Oil, page 58), the bulbs as you would garlic, and bulblets for vinegar or pickling projects (Moroccan Pickled Carrots, page 86).

HOARY BITTERCRESS (*Cardamine hirsuta*), also known as hairy bittercress and pepperweed, is a winter annual, germinating in fall, surviving winter, then flowering and going to seed in spring. This diminutive green in the mustard family grows in multiples in yards, along clearings and roadsides, and in disturbed areas. It is a prolific, spicy, slightly tangy-tasting herb and grows broadly across the United States.

To Identify: Bittercress has smooth lobed leaves that grow in a rosette formation around the stem, often layered in four to eight leaflets, arranged alternately and diminishing in size. During flowering, the stem extends 8 to 10 inches tall, and at its tip there is a cluster of tiny white flowers, also edible. Leaves all originate from a single point.

To Harvest: Gather leaf rosettes into a cluster to reveal its base. Use scissors to snip the rosette from the root. Rinse any dirt or debris by plunging rosettes into a bowl of cold water and allowing debris to sink to the bottom. Shake rosettes and pat them dry.

To Enjoy: It can be eaten raw or cooked and makes an excellent bright, slightly spicy garnish to rich stews (page 263), a topping for smoked fish (page 241), or as a salad green.

LAMBSQUARTERS (*Chenopodium album*), a cousin of quinoa, is also known as white goosefoot or wild spinach and is an opportunistic, fast-growing annual that thrives in disturbed areas, including fields and gardens. Its leaves and seeds are edible.

To Identify: Lambsquarters grow 3 to 4 feet tall, on grooved stems, often tinged with red. Lambsquarters leaves are triangular or coarsely toothed, diamond-shaped, sort of like the webbed foot of a goose. Their undersides appear silvery, due to a naturally occurring (and harmless) slightly white-grey powdery crystalline wax, which, when the leaves are run under water, causes the water to bead up.

To Harvest: Notice where you're harvesting lambsquarters from: if the area is polluted or chemically farmed, skip it, as the plants concentrate potentially toxic nitrates from the soil. Harvest by pinching the tender tips, or the top 3 to 4 inches on each stem.

To Enjoy: Strip leaves from the fibrous stem and use in salads (pages 156 and 162).

PURSLANE (*Portulaca oleracea*) is a delicious weed. Also known as pigweed or little hogweed, it grows just as easily in pavement cracks as it does in flowerbeds. This plant is not picky: it thrives in warm conditions and tolerates drought. Purslane is a low-growing succulent, its stem, though substantial, is juicy and crunchy as are its leaves, and it can be eaten raw or cooked. Many years ago, I found one of the lushest colonies of purslane on a meager berm in a neighborhood in Bushwick, Brooklyn. The leaves were broad and cheery, the numerous stems fat and sturdy. I exclaimed out loud as I discovered it and decided to harvest some, even though I knew it might have been susceptible to passing dogs. A good wash made any issues go the way of the drain, and they were quite a prize for a random excursion.

To Identify: To identify purslane, look for multiple smooth blush-red stems, originating from a single taproot. The leaves are small, spoon-shaped, flat, fleshy, and green. They are broadest at their rounded tips. Each part of the plant is juicy and tastes lemony sour.

To Harvest: Snap the top 5 or so inches off of mature plants, leaving the rest to regenerate for future harvests.

To Enjoy: Purslane is one of the most nutrient-dense foods you can find. It is rich in antioxidants, contains the highest omega-3 fatty acids—next to salmon—and is packed with a whole slew of vitamins and minerals. I mostly eat purslane raw, added to salads (Oaxaca-Meets-the-Mediterranean, Tomatoes, Corn, page 162), in ceviches, and as garnishes to sautéed and grilled foods (Scallops, Corn Confit, Milkweed, page 173).

WOOD SORREL (*Oxalis* spp.), also known as sourgrass, is a diminutive green often mistaken for clover. Wood sorrel is a common perennial, flanking park paths and hiking trails, and grows easily in garden beds, disturbed areas, and meadows.

To Identify: Wood sorrel is most commonly green but can also be purple or burgundy. It commonly grows 8 to 9 inches tall. Each leaf is comprised of three heart-shaped leaflets. Leaflets are creased along each midvein, like a folded paper heart. They fold up at night along that crease and reopen during the day. Seedpods are approximately ¾ inch tall and grow upright from their stems, resemble tiny okra, and pack an extra lemony punch.

To Harvest: Wood sorrel leaves, flowers, and seedpods are edible. To harvest, pluck leaves, flowers, and pods from the fibrous stems in morning time. Eat the flowers the same day before they close and the leaves or pods within a few days as the delicate leaves will wilt once picked.

To Enjoy: Many cultivated vegetables, including spinach, kale, and broccoli, contain oxalic acid, as does wood sorrel. Oxalic acid can be toxic when consumed in large quantities because it inhibits the absorption of calcium. But don't let this scare you from eating wood sorrel, as there isn't any issue when these foods are eaten as part of a varied diet. People who suffer from gout, rheumatism, and kidney stones, however, should avoid oxalic acid. Wood sorrel imparts a tart lemony flavor and is excellent paired with charcuterie, eggs, and smoked or seared fish, added to salads, and as a topping for beans or grains

IN THE GARDEN

I have always wanted a garden. When I was growing up, my mother tended one and taught me a foundation, including various flowers that grow through the seasons: peonies, petunias, daylilies, snapdragons, hostas, and more. Now at my own home, I am working to tend the land with care. We have made a great effort to remove invasive brambles and shrubs and installed hundreds of pollinator-attracting native plants. We have assessed the land many times over to clarify where the water flows so we can dig trenches and swales and plant appropriate species to thrive at particular points in the landscape.

I have weighed what critter may or may not munch on what I diligently install. Knowing I wanted to grow many vegetables, we constructed the raised-bed vegetable garden and then built a cedar-post fence to enclose it. I was so green, but equally driven. After the first season I made further investments in the landscape, including dozens of new plants, some rescued from where-plants-go-to-die at nurseries, and others, choice, precious specimens. I sourced more planters to accent the fence posts and sowed numerous fuchsia morning glory seeds and black-eyed Susan vines for them, so they'd climb the fence netting and create their own dedicated moment of beauty.

My process didn't start as a rational plan. I had a vision of elements I wanted to experience each day, ideas of a meandering flow and a feeling in mind, but they weren't tethered in pragmatic know-how, initially. Through the numerous rounds of research that followed, I was able to anchor logistics into the growing of things, lacing ways to build success into my vision, and make a beautiful, layered garden for both our enjoyment as well as health of the soil, and overall biodiversity.

It's become a point of pride to amend the soil with our compost, and twice or so through the growing season, make compost tea to give everything a boost in flourishing with worm castings from a vermicompost setup we maintain in our basement. We started vermicomposting when we still lived in a city apartment. I couldn't reconcile tossing all the food scraps produced from my commissioned work, and this provided a better, regenerative solution. As spring inches closer and temperatures are warm enough, I stir the compost, feeling its heat radiate from the squat barrel. I plot out the full list of early season efforts: limb pruning, all manner of spring cleanup, fertilizing and mulching, and the highly anticipated seed starting. In February and March I sow the first of many seeds, cultivating numerous, often new-to-me heirloom tomatoes, celery, onions, peppers, early flowers, and eggplants. Cut-and-come-again salad greens are directly sown into beds, along with radishes and other root veg, head lettuces, and then later, once warmer days are certain, I push bush and pole bean seeds into the earth, dusted in inoculant to encourage nitrogen fixing for subsequent crops. Those beans sprout soon enough with days of consistent warm temps, just like from the pages of a fairy tale.

There are unusual herbs I've made a point to grow at the cottage gardens, such as pipicha (see more about it on page 162) and shiso. Though originally a volunteer, shiso reminds me of my mother's garden and is extremely versatile, and it grows in abundance. I love dill and cilantro and their umbelliferous flower heads and always want to grow more. Young coriander seeds, as well as their wispy flowers, are often incorporated into my dishes.

I like growing a variety of alliums since they are universally useful: chives, garlic chives, garlic (used through its growth cycle as green garlic, garlic scapes, and lastly, as mature bulbs), bulb onions, and shallots. Growing nasturtium is one of my greatest joys. To see such a full, cheery plant whose leaves and flowers are edible, and one so important, serving as a trap crop for pests, keeping other precious plants safe. I love purslane and one season had to fiercely protect it behind chicken wire, sealed on all sides, as the rabbits and woodchucks liked it as much as I do. I grow unusual peppers so I can accent dishes throughout summer with their juicy, colorful verve. Summer squash is another versatile crop and feeds my penchant for squash pickles and shaved raw salads. Celery is a cathartic, albeit long-season crop to grow. It is immeasurably greener, livelier, and more packed with flavor than grocery celery, putting it to utter shame, and through its season I harvest individual stalks as needed. I installed five rhubarb plants our second year here and cannot wait for them to mature enough to harvest for pies and sauce. A currant shrub planted a year ago was obediently prolific with fruits, but they were all lost to a hungry forest dweller before even ripening. I inherited a gooseberry plant from Marie Viljoen, expert garden designer, writer, and fellow forager, whose plant adoption party introduced intriguing new varietals that I giddily carted home, stuffing our small car full. They now thrive on my grounds: the gooseberry started producing last year and is now loaded with delicate orbs along all its branches, prompting fantasies about what to make—if the catbirds don't beat me to the harvest.

Incremental learning permeates my life. Along the way, there are moments where the imperceptible dots connect, and a beautiful "aha!" is born, making all the steps I'd tread at last make sense. It's been the curse and gift of being self-taught in nearly everything. For example, caramelizing ingredients in a hot pan. What "don't crowd the pan" actually means after years of not exactly getting it. Lots of quiet listening to things, observing, feeling the rhythm of a thing, then feeling empowered to act with spontaneity—this is what has guided me over time. The garden is becoming that for me now.

I adopted square foot gardening as a means to bolster finite growing space and boost overall harvests on the recommendation of a family friend. After practicing it for a season, I'm sold. The raised beds are lush and overflowing. With the square-foot gardening grid, the cells for growing lay forth a clear map. Instead of planting in a row, derived from how farmers traditionally grow crops (at a much larger scale), the idea is to use a square-foot space to determine how much of a thing can be planted for optimal conditions and the resulting harvest. This is especially suited for raised beds. In square foot gardening, I can grow sixteen radishes in a square foot, or one eggplant, or nine bulb onions, and so on. This has been particularly helpful for me, especially since it clarifies what space is actually available for succession planting as the season evolves. If you're not familiar, succession planting is growing one crop after another has ripened and been harvested, maintaining a momentum to maximize the space you have to grow things, keeping a continuous harvest until the growing season ends. In years prior I couldn't figure out where new veg would fit in as summer tapered into fall, having used the apparent space to capacity. Square foot gardening made a clear map.

Hand-in-hand with square foot gardening, I expanded my knowledge to adopt companion planting. It's basically the idea that certain plants grown next to each other help each other maximize yields, deter predatory pests, or multiply nutrients in the soil. It's a philosophy of polyculture rather than monoculture. For example, tomatoes and basil—a classic combination—grow well together. Alliums such as garlic or onions do not grow well with peas and beans. Eggplant and marigolds grow well together and planting them together enables me to bypass chemical pesticides, since marigolds kill harmful soil-dwelling nematodes and serve to attract beneficial insects, such as ladybugs, lacewings, parasitic mini-wasps, and other predatory insects that eat aphids and other pests. This practice has served me well as I map the raised beds in early spring.

Lastly, I practice crop rotation. To change where you grow a thing means the pests that pulverize your plants do not continue to have an available food source, which means they die off. This practice gives crops a fighting chance. If you do not rotate crops every two years (or thereabouts), there is a greater likelihood of the bugs wreaking havoc. After growing more than fifty tomato plants across the raised beds and most of my containers for two seasons in a row, I was faced with the hard decision of overhauling how and what I grew the following season. Which meant downsizing the number of tomatoes I could produce. The importance of rotating crops cannot be overstated.

My garden routine is simple. I spend time observing, I research based on my observations, and I modify. And repeat. Get down low with your plants. Like, really low, where the shoots grow from the soil. There, I can see the layers of growth and the textures, one plant to the next, and decide whether to trim away dead matter or pull a stray weed, or witness beautiful new growth. Or collect a pest whose time has come. I examine the gardens from every vantage point so I'm less likely to miss important changes. I make a daily practice of trimming dead matter, to maintain good airflow among the many plantings and prevent fungal disease from manifesting. Everything also looks prettier when kept tidy. If I'm going to harvest, I try to do so early in the day before the heat sets in. I bring my scissors and a basket and pluck or snip, without cutting away too much of any single plant. If I'm harvesting flowers for bouquets for guests, I bring a vessel filled with water to immediately transfer cut stems. I also try to water first thing in the day, to give all the very best foot forward. A cup of coffee is a good companion, since these chores tend to take a little while.

I installed three terra-cotta reservoirs in the raised beds as a supplemental means to mitigate against drought, so hungry plant roots could absorb water through the ceramic membranes as needed, in addition to receiving water from the hose. This season, we've laid a plan for drip irrigation for the same beds, to free us from at least one area of watering. In the other garden beds, I've researched and established plants that naturally thrive in the conditions they're planted. Last season, I transplanted a host of plants, as their needs weren't being met by current conditions to really flourish. One of those included a trio of peonies that hasn't bloomed since we've lived here, planted by a previous dweller years ago. This season will reveal if I made smart choices, hopefully to discover each thriving. There is great satisfaction in seeing the results of good choices or efforts I've made come to fruition.

Walking among the garden beds each day is a good teacher. It is a quiet time and a time of discovery and wonder. This regular connection to plants reveals changes that occur, sometimes literally overnight. One day a plant is fledgling. The next day plump buds have emerged, ready for *just the right moment* to debut their glory. Or, evidence of munching and limbs gone missing or stems riddled with aphids. Connecting to the garden ecosystem routinely means I'm able to nip a problem in the bud, no pun intended. The internet has been an excellent second teacher. I consult a number of resources to solve many mysteries. Why do my tomato plants have those spots? Why are promising young cucumbers dying after flowering? And more. When time permits at the farmers' market, I consult the farmers for their take on a particular problem. We often end up commiserating, its own kind of affirmation.

Because I want to tend a garden without administering harmful chemicals, I have amassed a collection of organic sprays and powders to effectively fight the plant survival battle. Neem oil and diatomaceous earth are the ones I use most. To help my plants thrive and produce abundantly, I diligently fertilize with organic compounds, such as bone meal, blood meal, vermicompost, regular compost, compost tea, liquefied seaweed, and more. It is a lot to keep track of, but creating a routine helps. This work is important to help establish a healthy ecosystem, especially since I came in and changed a lot of things. The perennial beds needed to settled in and establish themselves. The garden is a long journey, and everyone needs to be in the right seat at the show.

DRYING SCARLET RUNNER BEAN PODS · GARLIC HARVEST

staples

I relish stacking the staples, building unexpected complexity even if I'm only preparing a sustenance dish such as the Brown Rice, Pickled Spices, Potatoes (page 275) or Stewed Scarlet Runner Beans (page 276). It's a saving grace to be able to pull any bottled gems-from-a-season at a moment's notice. Layering elements also produces a rich sensory experience so that no matter the meal, it is robust.

Savory umami charges the salivary impulses, helping us taste all foods even more. Tomato Confit (page 60) and Garlic Mustard Pesto (page 62) can (and should) be generously added to everything. Sourdough Crackers (page 75) and Seeded Rye Lavash (page 67) bring a pleasing flaky crunch to dishes through the seasons. The stocks enhance anything they are added to. They make equally satisfying nourishment sipped straight from the pot. Wild Blueberry Compote (page 100) and the Autumn Olive Jam (page 99) share a silky lushness. Each is versatile within cheese board pairings, as well as Pillowy French Toast (page 151) and Autumn Olive Linzer Tart (page 229). Fermented and briny foods meaningfully deepen flavor with their punch. Tarragon-Shallot Summer Squash Pickles (page 98) and Moroccan Pickled Carrots (page 86) add unexpected, delicious flavors to grilled foods, salads, grains, and more. The Wild Salmon Gravlax (page 94) is wonderful piled onto salad or toast. It is also great swapped in to the "Deli Sandwich" Dutch Baby (page 112). Though they vary in the means to arrive at their umami, Juniper + Cumin Meyer Lemon Kraut (page 90), Fermented Green Garlic (page 89), and the Wild Mushroom Escabeche (page 93) deliver redolent, zippy flavor and should be added to everything.

PUNCHY GARLIC ANCHOVY DRESSING

MAKES ABOUT ½ CUP

A version of this dressing regularly occupies space in my fridge. The rich savoriness makes an excellent foil to all manner of salad and vegetables, plus, a spoon added here and there adds punch to pasta or grains. Use it also as a flavor layer in making sauce for fish, lamb, and ragus.

3 garlic cloves

4 or 5 anchovy fillets

1 tablespoon Dijon mustard

¼ teaspoon freshly ground black pepper

2 teaspoons white wine vinegar

¼ cup extra-virgin olive oil

Mash the garlic and anchovies in a mortar and pestle to make a thick paste. Add the mustard, black pepper, and vinegar and whisk to combine. At a bare drizzle, whisk in the olive oil to emulsify. If you are unsure about the consistency or if the dressing is in fact emulsifying, drizzle the oil more slowly, or stop altogether and look at the whisked mixture—if there is a film of oil on top, it needs further whisking. The end result will be velvety and uniform. Taste the dressing and adjust the seasoning as needed. The dressing keeps for up to 3 weeks, sealed in the refrigerator.

FIELD GARLIC OIL

MAKES ¾ CUP

Use this slightly sweet garlicky oil to top Brown Rice, Pickled Spices, Potatoes (page 275) or to season other grains and bean dishes. It makes a delicious salad dressing base, can be baked into bread, or can top fish or meat dishes. If you cannot find field garlic, chives work just as well.

1 cup tender field garlic stems or chives, cut into 1-inch lengths

½ cup sunflower oil

½ teaspoon kosher salt

Use a small high-speed blender to liquify the garlic stems, sunflower oil, and salt until smooth, bright green, and largely uniform. There will be a small amount of field garlic solids which you may strain through a fine-mesh sieve, or use them as you spoon the oil onto dishes.

Transfer to a jar and seal. The bright oil keeps for a couple weeks, stored in the refrigerator, but will lose some of its vivid green hue after a few days.

HARISSA

MAKES 1 CUP

My friend Bryant Terry, who wrote the foreword to my first cookbook, is a force in understanding the African Diaspora and is renowned for killer vegan food. He inspired me to make my first scratch-made harissa. I hadn't grasped how simple it was nor how unique and flavorful making my own would be. Ever since, I've riffed on different versions depending upon what chiles populate my fridge or garden, and experimented with how different sweeteners affect the overall results. I quite like date syrup for its thicker texture and also because it is only mildly sweet.

Warm the olive oil over medium-low heat in a small saucepan. Add the red pepper flakes, cumin, coriander, both paprikas, and cayenne and stir, blooming the spices in the oil until very fragrant, 3 to 4 minutes.

Add the minced chile pepper, garlic, and preserved lemon and cook 2 to 3 minutes, stirring occasionally, until fragrant. Lower the heat slightly if the mixture bubbles too vigorously—aim for a mild simmer.

Add both tomatoes and the paste, along with the lemon juice, date syrup, and salt. Stir to combine and cook for another 5 minutes to meld the flavors, stirring to prevent scorching. Taste and adjust the seasoning as needed. Remove from the heat and allow the mixture to cool. Transfer the harissa to a lidded jar and seal once cooled to room temperature. Harissa will keep, sealed in the refrigerator, for up to 2 weeks. It can be frozen in ice cube trays or in jars for up to 4 months.

¼ cup extra-virgin olive oil

1 tablespoon red pepper flakes

2 teaspoons cumin seeds, toasted in a dry skillet and ground in a mortar and pestle

2 teaspoons coriander seeds, toasted in a dry skillet and ground in a mortar and pestle

2 teaspoons Hungarian paprika

1 teaspoon smoked paprika

½ teaspoon cayenne

1 fresh chile pepper, minced—jalapeño, serrano, chile de arbol, and chipotle all work (about 1 teaspoon)

3 garlic cloves, finely grated on a Microplane

Flesh from a quarter of a Preserved Meyer Lemon (page 97), minced

¼ cup canned tomatoes, minced

1 tablespoon roasted tomatoes, chopped (page 128; optional)

2 tablespoons tomato paste

Juice from half a lemon

1 teaspoon date syrup

¼ teaspoon flake salt

TOMATO CONFIT

MAKES I QUART

When it is high tomato season, this is an easy way to capture their rich flavor for use well past summer days. Sometimes I add shallots. Other times it's just a pot of the rosy gems and a handful of herbs. Use the confit wherever you want bold tomato flavor, such as in the Spicy Tomato Clams + Thick Sourdough Toast (page 252) and Two Toasts (page 203). Save leftover confit oil for Pasta Puttanesca (page 217) and Piquant French Lentils (page 272).

2 cups small, cherry, or Roma-style tomatoes such as Blue Beech paste varietal

3 to 5 shallots, cut in half lengthwise (optional)

7 to 9 sprigs fresh thyme

Kosher salt

½ teaspoon black peppercorns

1½ to 2 cups extra-virgin olive oil, enough to submerge the tomato mixture

Flake salt for serving

If you are using paste tomatoes, slice them into ½-inch coins. If using smaller tomatoes, leave them whole: they will collapse once confited.

In a small saucepan, layer the tomatoes with the shallots and thyme sprigs. Add a generous pinch of salt and the peppercorns and pour enough olive oil to cover. Over medium heat, bring the mixture to a bare simmer, then lower the heat to maintain it—there should be a bubble or two every few seconds, showing you that there's activity without bubbling vigorously.

After 20 minutes, check for doneness. Use the back of a spoon and gently press against a tomato: it should readily give. If that isn't so, continue on a bare simmer for another 5 to 10 minutes or until all the tomatoes are soft.

Remove the pan from the heat and allow it to cool to room temp. Transfer the tomato confit into a squat jar and pour in the olive oil to submerge. When serving the confit, discard the herb stems and peppercorns.

Once cooled, the confit keeps in its oil, sealed in the refrigerator for up to 1 month, or frozen up to 6 months.

GARLIC MUSTARD PESTO

MAKES 1½ CUPS

In early spring I am overjoyed to discover tender garlic mustard, one of the first green things to sprout from the still-dormant upstate New York landscape. This joy is twofold, since garlic mustard is also an aggressively invasive plant: I diligently do my part to hamper its spread by harvesting it by the armful. Firstly, for this unctuous sauce; secondly, a couple weeks later I harvest the tender shoots and flower buds, eaten similar to broccoli rabe. Use emerging tiny garlic mustard shoots as you would microgreens. Once in bloom, its wispy white flowers give punch to salads, pizza, pasta, fish, and more. Even garlic mustard roots are edible, akin to horseradish. Pull the whole thing and don't look back. Biodiversity thanks you, and delicious eating awaits.

4 cups packed tender garlic mustard stems and leaves, stems coarsely chopped

1 cup extra-virgin olive oil, plus more as needed

⅓ cup sunflower seeds, toasted until golden

3 tablespoons nutritional yeast

1 teaspoon kosher salt

Blend all the ingredients thoroughly in a food processor, pausing to scrape down the sides of the vessel and reincorporate. Taste and adjust the seasoning as needed. I prefer a thicker paste consistency but sometimes thin the sauce further with water, depending on its end use.

Transfer the pesto to jars and pour a thin film of oil to top. Wait at least an hour or up to 1 day for the flavors to mellow before using. Use to top Spanish Tortilla, Sauce, Pickles, Salad (page 115) and the sustenance dishes (page 272–276), or swapped for the Oaxaca-Meets-the-Mediterranean sauce in Oaxaca-Meets-the-Mediterranean, Tomatoes, Corn (page 162) and Two Toasts (page 203). Garlic mustard pesto keeps sealed in the refrigerator for up to 2 weeks, or frozen for up to 8 months.

VARIATIONS: I have made variations using pecans or walnuts in place of the sunflower seeds, and sunflower oil—or a mix of half olive oil, half avocado oil—in place of the 1 cup olive oil.

RAMP SALT

Salt is the vehicle to make a time capsule of intensely aromatic ramp leaves. Making ramp salt is straightforward and a great way to preserve their fleeting season, using equal weight ramps and kosher salt, with whatever quantity of ramp leaves you have. Use ramp salt on Eggs, Beans, Garden Greens (page 111) or anytime you seek a hit of salty oniony funk. The mixture will stay bright green if you store any surplus jars in the freezer. Whichever jar is in active use, store it in the refrigerator for the same results.

Coarsely chop the ramps, then transfer them to the bowl of a food processor. Pulse to pulverize the ramps. Add the salt and pulse until incorporated. Once the mixture is uniform, transfer it to a parchment-lined sheet pan. Spread and flatten it until the bright green paste is quite thin, about ⅛ inch thick.

Dehydrate ramp salt in a very low oven, 150°F, for 4 to 5 hours or until the salt crumbles easily when folded. Break the sheet into sections halfway through dehydrating, arranging edges that faced center to the perimeter to accelerate the drying process.

Transfer fully dried ramp salt into small jars and seal. Store all but the one you'll use in the freezer. Store the active-use ramp salt jar in the refrigerator to retain greatest potency and extend its green hue.

6 ounces ramp leaves
(about 4 cups, loosely packed)

6 ounces kosher salt
(roughly 1 cup)

PISTACHIO DUKKAH

MAKES 1 CUP

I was late to the dukkah appreciation party. Now that it's in my wheelhouse, I always have a jar nearby to add a hearty sprinkle to any dish that might benefit. This aromatic condiment hails from Egypt, and its name refers to the process for making it: *dukkah*, or *duqqa*, means "to crush" or "to pound" in Arabic. It makes a lovely crunchy topping for Spring Fling Salad in Green (page 124). It can be used interchangeably as you would the Spiced Nuts (page 77) or crispy bread crumbs, sprinkled onto beans, eggs, and the sustenance dishes (see page 272). Traditionally, it is also eaten as a snack on its own. I have done just that on many an occasion.

⅔ cup lightly salted pistachios, toasted on a sheet pan until golden and fragrant

2 teaspoons cumin seeds

2 teaspoons coriander seeds

1 tablespoon sesame seeds

1 tablespoon black sesame seeds

1 teaspoon flake salt

Gently crush the pistachios in a large mortar and pestle (see Note) until you've produced a mix of coarse pistachio crumbs and small bits of pistachio, scooting finer meal out of the way so you can pummel the larger bits effectively. A ratio of two-thirds meal to one-third larger chunks is ideal. Transfer the pistachio mixture to a small mixing bowl and set aside.

In a small, dry cast-iron skillet set over medium heat, toast the cumin seeds once the pan is warm. Agitate the pan occasionally to prevent the spice from burning. Once the cumin becomes fragrant, it is ready, about 3 minutes. Transfer to a small mortar or the one you used for the pistachios. Coarsely grind the cumin and empty it into the bowl with pistachios. Add the coriander seeds to the pan. Toast until fragrant, agitating the pan as you did with the cumin, 2 to 3 minutes. Transfer the seeds to the mortar and coarsely grind them, then add to the bowl with the pistachios.

Lower the heat to medium-low to toast the plain sesame seeds, stirring regularly once they begin to turn golden, moving the skillet away from the heat as needed so you can retain control of the process—this takes no more than 3 minutes. Transfer to the pistachio bowl as soon as they become golden and fragrant. Repeat toasting, now with the black sesame seeds. Since the pan is hot and the seeds are black, use the prior timing as your gauge and agitate the pan or stir often to prevent them from burning. As soon as they become fragrant, they are ready. Transfer to the mixing bowl and set aside.

Add the flake salt to the mixture and stir to combine. Taste and adjust the seasoning as needed. The dukkah keeps for up to 1 month at room temperature, sealed in a jar.

NOTE: If you do not have a mortar and pestle, you may crush the pistachios by laying them in a single layer on a cutting board, placing a cast-iron or heavy skillet over them, and leaning on the pan. Shift your weight to one side and then the other until the nuts are crushed to the appropriate consistency. You can also use a coffee or spice grinder to grind the spices—just wash it afterward.

SEEDED RYE LAVASH

MAKES EIGHT 11 BY 4-INCH CRISPY FLATBREADS

These lavash can be whipped up in a single day. As long as you keep in mind rolling them quite thinly—think sheet-of-paper thin—you'll succeed in achieving a crisp, wafer-like result. If you prefer different seeds, this recipe adapts well to any crunchy sprinkle: you can use sesame seeds, cracked pepper, or just flake salt. Adjust the quantity of salt you add based on what you'll pair with the crackers, to ensure the perfect salty balance.

In a measuring cup with a pour spout, combine the honey, yeast, and warm water and stir until uniform. Set aside for 5 minutes or until the yeast activates and foams.

In a medium bowl, add together the flours and kosher salt and stir to combine. Make a well in the center and add the avocado oil and the yeast mixture. Stir until a rough dough forms, then transfer to a clean work surface, and knead for 4 to 6 minutes, until the dough is smooth and supple.

Place the dough into a lightly oiled bowl and cover with a damp tea towel or plastic wrap. Set in the proofing drawer of your oven (or in the oven with the light on) for 30 minutes or until slightly risen.

Preheat the oven to 400°F. Set the dough on a lightly floured work surface and divide it into eight segments. One at a time, roll the dough out, both lengthwise as well as widthwise. After the first round of rolling it out, compact the edges using your fingers to minimize any splitting. Roll the dough quite thinly into a shape roughly 11 inches by 4 inches. The lavash should be nearly paper thin. Brush the dough edge-to-edge with a slick of olive oil and carefully place it on a parchment-lined sheet pan.

Repeat with remaining segments. You will need two or three sheet pans to accommodate the flatbreads in a single layer without any overlap. Generously sprinkle them with the fennel seeds and then scatter the flake salt. Press lightly with the flat of your hand to better adhere the sprinkles to the dough.

Bake two pans at a time, rotating the pans between the upper and lower racks after 12 minutes. I also rotate individual flatbreads on their respective pans for even baking during this step.

After 14 minutes, the flatbreads should be crisp and golden brown, with slightly bubbled air pockets. When the lavash are ready, transfer them to a wire rack to cool fully. Store at room temperature in a sealed container. Lavash keep for up to 10 days.

1 teaspoon honey or date syrup

1 teaspoon active yeast

½ cup lukewarm water

1 cup all-purpose flour, plus more for dusting

1 cup rye flour

1 teaspoon kosher salt

¼ cup avocado oil

Olive oil for brushing

Fennel seeds for sprinkling

Flake salt for sprinkling

SOURDOUGH BREAD

MAKES 2 LOAVES

Baking sourdough bread is a precision-filled process. As I learned it using the metric system, I am sharing it this way in hopes it will bring you success, too. Except when I feed my starter, I use ounces as a quick step to get me closer to the more complex process, aka baking bread. If you do not already maintain a starter, you may make one or purchase a fresh starter (see Note) as I had to, on assignment for the *New York Times* many years ago.

Sourdough baking spans two days. I use my starter weekly—if your use isn't as frequent, do two rounds of feeding to jump-start its activity. I usually bake between 8 and 9 am, which means the day before, I bring my starter out from the fridge around 11 am, feed it, then let it proof Once the starter pushes its way up to—and sometimes beyond—the lid, aka peak activity, it is ready to be added to the autolyse at 3 or 4 pm.

FEEDING THE STARTER

At least 1 cup starter (see Note, page 74)

4 ounces flour (I use exclusively Farmer Ground Flour brand High Extraction Half-White bread flour)

4 ounces filtered lukewarm water

AUTOLYSE

650 grams all-purpose flour, plus more for dusting

100 grams unbleached bread flour

100 grams half-white bread flour

60 grams spelt flour

550 grams filtered water, heated to lukewarm

20 grams kosher salt

50 grams filtered water

½ cup toasted walnuts, coarsely chopped

2 tablespoons chopped fresh rosemary or sage leaves

Feed the starter: Take your starter out of the refrigerator and discard all but 2 ounces or 1 cup, whichever is less, saving the discard to make Sourdough Crackers (page 75). Add the flour and filtered lukewarm water to the remaining starter. Mix thoroughly until uniform, place the lid loosely on the jar, set it on a small plate or tray to catch the starter should it overflow, and place in the oven with the light on or at the proofing setting. Check the starter periodically to monitor its growth. It will take about 2 hours to reach peak activity, but ideally at around the 45-minute to 1-hour mark it will have grown by about half its original volume and this is when you want to start the autolyse.

Make the autolyse: In a large bowl, combine the flours and the 550 grams of water with a spatula initially, then work the remaining dry flour bits that cling at the bottom of the bowl with your hands until uniform. Use a dough scraper to aid in incorporating the dry mixture and scrape any sticky dough off your hands, reincorporating it into the autolyse. Once it is uniform, cover the autolyse with a damp tea towel or wrap it in a large plastic bag and place the bowl inside the oven next to the starter. The autolyse needs to hydrate for an hour before adding the starter, so timing the autolyse to coincide with the remaining time needed for the starter is key. Ultimately, you want the autolyse to be hydrated just as the starter has reached peak activity.

About 1 hour later, once the starter has reached peak activity, nearly overflowing the jar, with bubbles at the surface (see photo, page 70, top left), add 190 grams of the starter to the autolyse, followed by the salt and 50 grams water. (The remainder of the starter can go back in the refrigerator to be fed and used again another day.) The more you practice, the better your timing will be.

CONTINUED →

Vigorously squeeze the autolyse for a minute to absorb some of the starter. Transfer the mixture to a work surface—the mixture will be wet, soupy, and messy (see photo opposite, top right). Do a round of slap and fold (see Slap and Fold Process under "Fermentation, Preservation, and Baking," page 286): slap one end of the dough onto your work surface (see photo opposite, bottom left) and toss the other end over, onto itself (see photo opposite, bottom right). Rotate dough 90 degrees and repeat about four more times, beginning to bring the dough together. If, however, you see the dough tearing—more so than coming together as you work—pause for 15 to 30 seconds to allow the dough to rest, then resume slap and fold. As you repeat this process, the dough should form a cohesive, somewhat tacky but smooth ball. Place the dough back into the bowl, cover with the tea towel or plastic bag, and return to the oven to proof for 25 minutes. This is the beginning of bulk fermentation.

Bring it out from the oven, remove the covering, and add the nuts and herbs. Perform a round of stretch and fold: lightly moisten your hands and scoop up the dough at the far side of the bowl, pulling that end up until you're met with resistance (see photo, page 73, top left). Fold it forward onto itself in the bowl. Give the bowl a quarter turn and repeat—think of hands on a clock, 3, 6, 9, 12, as you turn the bowl to make the remaining three stretches (or four, depending on your dough). Remoisten your hands as needed to ensure the dough does not stick. With each stretch and fold, the dough will give more resistance. Do not pull so hard that the dough tears. Instead, work with the weight of the dough, using gravity to help it stretch as you work. Observe its elasticity—once it's hard to stretch without tearing, stop. This observation should serve as a guide to how many stretches you perform. Cover the bowl with the tea towel or plastic bag and return it to proof in the oven.

Repeat five more rounds of stretch and fold at 30-minute intervals. Each time, remove the bowl from the oven, perform four to five stretches as described above, and return the bowl to the oven. This process helps trap air in the dough and builds its elasticity and structure.

Thirty minutes after the final round of stretch and fold, it is time to pre-shape. Flour a work surface. Use a plastic dough scraper to transfer the dough from the bowl in one large mass onto the floured work surface. Use a metal bench scraper to divide the dough into two even portions: to minimize sticking when dividing, dip the bench scraper first into flour and tap it lightly to remove any excess.

To form a boule (a round loaf), stretch the dough, pulling it from two opposite sides, left and right. Fold one side over the other as if swaddling a baby then tuck the dough in onto itself as you roll the dough forward into a ball (see photo, page 73, top right). Turn the boule over so the smooth side faces up. With floured hands cupped around the boule, pull it toward you to tighten its form, using a

CONTINUED →

slight downward dragging motion against the work surface to increase friction. Repeat this tightening two or three times, rotating it slightly as you pull, until the boule feels tidy.

Lightly flour a sheet pan and, in a swift motion, scoop the boule up with a bench scraper and place onto the pan off to one side, leaving space for your second boule. Repeat the shaping process with the second portion of dough, then place it alongside the first on the pan. Cover the sheet pan with a damp tea towel or a large plastic bag and place it in the oven for a final 20-minute rest.

Sieve a light dusting of flour into two 8-inch cloth-lined bannetons. If you do not have bannetons, the natural cane baskets used for sourdough bread baking, use two mixing bowls nearly the same size as the boules, lined with undyed linen fabric or napkins. You may also use sesame seeds or oats in place of the sifted flour.

Repeat the shaping process the way you did the first time for each boule. At the end—this is final shaping—place each boule seam-side-up into the bannetons. This will allow them to continue to expand as they proof overnight in the refrigerator.

Cover each with a damp tea towel or plastic bag and place in the refrigerator for the final rise and fermentation. I usually allow loaves to proof for about 10 hours, though depending on the atmospheric conditions and the flours you use, it could take 6 to 14 hours. Press your finger into the dough. If the impression doesn't bounce back, the dough needs more time to proof. The timing is a wide range, because there are so many variables that contribute to how long dough needs to proof. In a way, it's understanding how they all relate that makes successfully baking bread so magical. The more you bake, the clearer the timing will be for what you adopt to achieve the best results.

The following day, prior to bringing the first loaf from the fridge, preheat a cast-iron Dutch oven with the lid on, at 525°F. After it has reached temperature, give it 20 more minutes to heat before baking.

Bring the first boule out just before you're ready to bake. Tear a length of parchment slightly larger than the size of the boule and set it on a similar-size cutting board. Place the cutting board on top of the banneton (parchment layer between boule and board) and in a smooth motion, clasping the bowl and board together, invert the banneton onto the board and set on the work surface. Carefully lift the banneton away to reveal the boule.

Hold a fresh razor or lame at an angle parallel to your work surface and, in a swift motion, score a ½- to 1-inch-deep cut lengthwise along the side of the dough (see photo opposite, bottom left). This cut creates direction for the dough to expand as it bakes, aka, the highly prized "oven spring." You may add additional

CONTINUED →

shallower decorative score marks. Try to have the design clear in your mind once the dough is on the board, so that this step takes only a few seconds before transferring it to bake.

Set the board with the scored boule near the oven. Acting quickly, with heavy-duty potholders, bring the Dutch oven out of the oven. Remove the lid and set it aside nearby. Grasp either end of the parchment and gently lower the boule into the Dutch oven. Quickly and smoothly replace the hot lid, return it to the oven, and bake for 25 minutes. The steam produced inside this closed environment is essential in forming the desired blistered crust. After 25 minutes, bring the Dutch oven out, remove the lid, and return to bake for 10 more minutes or until the bread is deeply golden. When returning the Dutch oven to bake for this round, place the lid beside it or on another rack in the oven, to keep it hot for the next loaf.

Remove the bread from the Dutch oven and allow it to cool fully on a wire rack before slicing, as the crumb structure is still forming. While it cools, place the lid back securely on the Dutch oven for the second loaf and allow 10 minutes to pass as the heat builds again inside the Dutch oven. Follow the same process to bake the second loaf.

You can (and should) retoast bread once sliced! Store unused bread in a paper bag at room temperature for up to 1 week. You may freeze cooled whole loaves (or for quicker thawing, slice a loaf in half) by wrapping them in a layer of parchment, followed by aluminum foil and sealing in a resealable bag to prevent freezer burn, for up to 3 months. Thaw half loaves in a paper bag to retain their ideal texture on the counter for 1 hour or until fully thawed, and whole loaves for 2 hours.

NOTE: You can purchase a fresh starter at www.kingarthurbaking.com. Store starter in a wide-mouth pint-size mason jar. Feed it 4 ounces of lukewarm filtered water and 4 ounces half-white bread flour. Stir the flour and water into the starter until fully incorporated and uniform. Loosely place the lid on and leave the jar to sit at room temperature (or inside the oven with the light on), ideally 70°F ambient temperature. Check the starter to see its activity after 1 hour. If your starter is new, it may take significantly longer (up to a day) to ripen and become active. When the starter reaches peak activity—lots of bubbles throughout and on its surface—it can be used toward making sourdough bread or other baked goods. Store starter in the refrigerator unless you plan to bake daily. Whenever feeding the starter, first remove 1 cup: this is the discard, and is excellent for making crackers and other baked goods. The feeding routine is to add 4 ounces lukewarm filtered water and 4 ounces half-white bread flour, stir to incorporate, and leave at room temperature to ripen, then use for baking and return to the refrigerator. If the starter is unused for a longer period, it may require multiple feedings to reawaken it.

SOURDOUGH CRACKERS

MAKES 2 SHEET PANS OF THIN CRACKERS

Ever since I have maintained my starter, I have been making these crackers. Every batch is a delight to eat. They produce a flaky snap, and the tang of the sourdough evokes a subtle, sharp cheesiness (in the best way possible), due to the fermentation. If you maintain a starter, this is an excellent way to use the discard rather than to toss it. *Everyone* oohs about how delicious they are—whether Catbird guests, family and friends, or lucky clients for whom I've baked a batch (see photo, page 121).

This recipe is adapted from the cracker recipe from King Arthur Baking Company. I often swap in different flours for more flavor and nutritional value, as well as various fresh herbs and aromatics to create limitless combinations of crispy, flaky good times ahead. I have used all-purpose flour, as well as rye and spelt. They are all quite good. Really, it's up to you to discover what you like best. Be sure to drop me a line and report back!

In a small bowl, use a dough scraper or spatula to mix the sourdough discard, the flours, butter, rosemary, and salt together until uniform. The dough should be smooth, not tacky. Divide into two, shape into rectangular blocks, and wrap each with plastic wrap. Chill for at least 40 minutes for the dough to meld.

Bring dough from the fridge 15 minutes before rolling it out. Lightly flour a piece of parchment the size of a rimmed sheet pan, unwrap the dough (reserving the plastic) and place it onto the parchment, then lightly flour the dough. Lay the plastic wrap over the dough and roll out $\frac{1}{16}$ to $\frac{1}{8}$ inch thick, pausing at intervals to unpeel it from the dough and re-flour it or the parchment as needed.

If dough becomes smeary, chill it for 10 minutes, sandwiched between the plastic wrap and parchment on the sheet pan. Repeat all steps with the second batch of dough.

Preheat oven to 400°F. Use a pastry brush to paint the dough with a light slick of olive oil all the way to its edges. Use a pastry cutter and cut the dough into crackers—sometimes I make larger oblong strips, and on other occasions I make a grid of smaller, more typical cracker shapes. You will need to rotate whatever shapes you cut partway through baking for even browning, so keep this in mind.

Sprinkle the crackers with flake salt. If you refrigerated the crackers before baking, transfer the lot on its parchment to a pan that is not cold, then bake for 6 to 8 minutes, or until they begin to turn golden. Remove the sheet pans from the oven to rotate the crackers on each pan: less-golden shapes move to the perimeter, and vice versa.

1 cup sourdough discard (see page 68)

½ cup all-purpose flour

½ cup rye flour

4 tablespoons salted butter, room temperature

2 tablespoons finely chopped fresh rosemary

1 teaspoon kosher salt

Extra-virgin olive oil for brushing

Flake salt for sprinkling

CONTINUED →

SOURDOUGH CRACKERS CONTINUED

Check at 2- to 3-minute intervals, continuing to rotate or swapping lesser-baked crackers with those that are more golden. Crackers will likely be done by the 12-minute mark—monitor your oven to see where the hottest zone is so you can ensure the crackers bake evenly.

Transfer any deeply golden crackers to a wire rack as the remainder finish baking and allow all to cool fully. Crackers will keep 1 to 2 weeks wrapped in a layer of parchment, stored in a sealed container at room temperature.

NOTE: If you prefer to prep two batches and only bake one, the cracker dough can be frozen for up to 3 months, wrapped in plastic wrap and then sealed in a resealable bag.

VARIATIONS: Some of my favorite seasoning variations over the years include

Fresh field garlic and sesame seeds

Chives, cracked pepper, and sea salt

Mugwort, sage, or fennel seeds and Himalayan salt

Flake salt and pink peppercorns

Rosemary, za'atar, or Aleppo chile flakes and flake salt

"Everything" bagel sprinkle

Fresh herbs should be mixed into the dough. Crunchy elements get sprinkled on top, just before placing the crackers in the oven to bake.

SPICED NUTS

In 2002 we settled into new lives in New York City. Lauren was the chef at a restaurant I found work at, a place that was under the radar and possessed some of that New York City magic, enough so that foodies like Alec Baldwin dined there on occasion. She influenced me in many ways with her food, rooted in Roman and Sicilian cultures. Years later when I'd begun my career as a photographer, she shared a staple she loves. It's something I return to again and again, riffing on the spices, which seeds or nuts to include, or what to pair with the crunchy treat. This mixture is an excellent topping for ice cream (Persimmon-Date Ice Cream, page 225), root vegetables (Two Toasts, page 203), and Quinoa + Quince Porridge (page 197), or eaten straight from the pan.

Preheat the oven to 375°F. On a parchment-lined sheet pan, toast each kind of nut in separate batches until fragrant: 3 to 5 minutes for the sunflower seeds and pistachios, 4 to 5 minutes for the pecans, 5 to 7 minutes each for the almonds and walnuts. When one batch of nuts is done, transfer it to a medium bowl, followed by the next batch, and so on, until all are finished and together in the bowl.

Once the nuts are room temperature, after 7 to 10 minutes, add the brown sugar, rosemary, nutmeg, salt, cayenne, and black pepper and stir to combine fully. With an electric mixer, beat the egg white until soft peaks hold. Transfer the beaten egg white to the nut mixture and use a silicone spatula to fold it in until uniformly covering the nuts.

Transfer the mixture to a parchment-lined sheet pan, spreading it out into a rough single layer, then roast for 8 minutes. Use the parchment edges to fold the outermost clusters toward the center and use the silicone spatula to scoot the centermost nuts toward the periphery. Roast for another 3 to 5 minutes, until deeply golden and fragrant. The mixture will be a collection of burnished chunky clusters when it's ready.

Cool the spiced nuts fully on the sheet pan. Gather the parchment ends to pour them into a quart-size mason jar. Sealed, they will keep up to 1 month at room temperature.

TOASTED SEEDS VARIATION: Increase the sunflower seeds to 1 cup, and use 1 cup pepitas and ½ cup sesame seeds in place of the pistachios, pecans, almonds, and walnuts. Toast the seeds, each on their own tray, until fragrant. Pumpkin seeds will begin to make popping sounds when they are ready, about 5 minutes. Sesame seeds only take 2 to 3 minutes, so keep a close eye on them. Follow the instructions above to coat the seeds in spices and then toast the spiced seeds for 8 to 10 minutes or until deeply golden, turning halfway through, as above.

½ cup lightly salted sunflower seeds

½ cup lightly salted pistachios

½ cup pecans

½ cup unsalted almonds

1 cup walnuts

2 packed tablespoons brown sugar

1 tablespoon finely chopped fresh rosemary

½ teaspoon freshly grated nutmeg

½ teaspoon flake salt

¼ teaspoon cayenne

¼ teaspoon freshly ground black pepper

1 egg white (save the yolk for aioli, page 158)

IN PRAISE OF STOCKS

There is something unique and elemental about stock. Combine water with some odds and ends, give them a long soak at a bare simmer, and you have produced magic. For years, the concept of stock eluded me. I didn't understand that it was basically making a savory tea. At least, that's how I ended up thinking about it so it made sense. Stocks are infusions. They absorb the aromatics they are given. Simple, right? The more you make stock, the more fulfilling your results will be. I say that because you can make soulful, robustly flavored stock from almost anything, and, connecting to stock-making on the regular helps to refine your proportions. What mood are you in? How will you use it? Would you enjoy sipping it all on its own?

I treat stocks as elixirs to supercharge other dishes, as much as I like to wring out every last bit of flavor in the foods used to make them. I hate waste. I love flavor. So I make stock. Stocks also serve as time capsules for the seasons. As you'll see in the recipes to follow, there is a group of ingredients that form the basis for many stocks. With each season, I use additional ingredients to capture their essence: asparagus in spring, corn in summer, mushrooms in fall, and bones or garlic plus ginger in winter. Especially beneficial is that stocks are immune boosters: we all could use a boost when the brittle, cold days drag on. You may add seasonal wild ingredients such as ground elder or turkey tail, hen of the woods, and Dryad's saddle mushrooms, among others to fortify the nutritive density even further.

Begin a stock routine. Keep a large resealable bag in your freezer and add the remnants or odd bits from other cooking projects: mushroom stems or dried mushrooms; leek roots and tips, outer onion layers (but not the papery skin—they impart a bitterness that is not enjoyable); carrot peels; celery ends; parsley stems; chicken bones; shrimp shells; fish frames; ginger and turmeric knobs. Add a handful of spices and voilà, stock. When the bag contains enough elements to mostly fill your stockpot or slow cooker, it is time to make stock.

I choose the stock I make based on what I have the most of and what will reduce the volume of the scraps bag fastest. The only work is straining solids at the end, expressing the last savory liquid, then planning how you'd like to use it.

CHICKEN STOCK

MAKES 2 QUARTS PLUS 1 PINT

Stock imbues richer flavor to all foods. Chicken stock is one of the most universal of stocks, delicious added to so many dishes. Make this stock for Roast Chicken, Hen of the Woods, Leeks, Pan Sauce (page 255) or when making soups or risotto.

Place all ingredients in a slow cooker and top with the water. Turn the dial on low setting. Place lid on and cook overnight, or 8 hours.

The next day, taste and adjust the seasoning as needed. Use tongs to transfer solids into a colander placed over a bowl. Ladle the stock through a sieve placed over a canning funnel, set on a quart-size mason jar. When one jar is full, move to filling the next, until there is no more stock to strain.

When the solids are cool enough to handle, squeeze the remaining liquid from them and discard for compost (meat solids should be discarded). Add the remaining liquid to the jars and cool to room temperature before sealing and refrigerating.

Stock can be poured into ice cube trays for smaller portions, or into 1 cup plastic containers for easy stacking in the freezer. Stock may be stored frozen up to 6 months, or in the refrigerator for up to 5 days.

Bones from a leftover roast chicken

Roots and tips from 6 to 8 onions, plus any outer layers (but not the skin)

Peels and ends from half a bunch of carrots

4 to 6 parsley stems

Ends from half a bunch of celery

Half a lemon, juice squeezed into the pot and then lemon added

1 tablespoon kosher salt

1 bay leaf

1 dried chile pepper

½ teaspoon coriander seeds

½ teaspoon peppercorns

PLUS ANY OR ALL OF THESE, FOR EXTRA NUANCE:

10 mushroom stems (from chestnut, crimini, or oyster mushrooms)

Ends from 2 leeks, both the white root and dark green parts

Woody ends from 1 bunch asparagus

5 to 7 spruce tips (page 35)

10 cups water

MUSHROOM STOCK

MAKES 2 QUARTS PLUS 1 PINT

Each season I hunt wild mushrooms. Often I'm met with needing to discard the tough stems or drier parts. This made me want to find ways to extract their delectable mushroomy flavor, even if I couldn't eat them directly. You may use a mix of any flavorful mushroom to produce this earthy elixir. Use it in Eggs, Beans, Garden Greens (page 111) or Braised Short Ribs + Creamy Beans (page 263).

Stems from ½ pound mushrooms, any mix of chestnut, crimini, hen of the woods, shiitake, or oyster mushrooms

Root ends and tips from 6 onions, plus any outer layers (but not the skin)

Peels and ends from 1 bunch carrots

4 to 6 parsley stems

Ends from half a bunch of celery

Woody ends from 1 bunch asparagus

1 dried chile pepper

1 bay leaf

1 tablespoon kosher salt

½ teaspoon coriander seeds

½ teaspoon peppercorns

10 cups water

Place all the ingredients in a slow cooker (see Note) with the dial on low setting. Place the lid on and cook for 2 hours. Remove the lid, taste, and adjust the seasoning as needed.

Use tongs to transfers solids to a colander placed over a bowl. Ladle stock through a sieve placed over a canning funnel, set on a quart-size mason jar. When one jar is full, move to filling the next, until there is no more stock to strain.

When the solids are cool enough to handle, squeeze any liquids from them and discard for compost. Add the remaining liquid to the jars and cool to room temperature before sealing and refrigerating.

Stock can be poured into ice cube trays for quick use or smaller portions, or into 1 cup plastic containers for easy stacking in the freezer. Stock may be stored frozen up to 6 months, or in the refrigerator for up to 7 days.

NOTE: For even richer flavor, make this recipe on the stovetop, in a stockpot. Sear the mushroom fragments in a drizzle of oil until well caramelized, followed by the other veg. Add the aromatics and water and bring the mixture to a boil. Cover with a lid, lower to a bare simmer, and follow the remaining process as laid out.

IMMUNITY ELIXIR

This is a tonic adaptable to any season. Sometimes I drink a warm bowlful without adding anything to it to start the day, especially in winter when I can use an extra immune boost. In spring and summer, I dice chunky wedges of avocado, snip handfuls of herbs from the garden, and add them to a cup, barely warm, with a squeeze of lemon. In fall, the flavors pair wonderfully with roasted pumpkin or squash and brown rice. It can be layered into more complex meals as a foundation flavor, too. It will impart a different character depending on the type of stock you begin with; the mushroom stock might be my favorite, producing a deeply soothing—and vegan—result.

In a saucepan over medium-low heat, warm the olive oil, then grate the garlic directly into the pot. Stir to prevent the garlic from sticking. Sauté until the garlic becomes fragrant, about 3 minutes. Grate in the ginger and turmeric and stir, sautéing for 3 to 5 minutes more, until fragrant. Add the stock and stir to combine all. Heat until steaming, then ladle into bowls. Squeeze a wedge of lemon on top and enjoy.

1 tablespoon extra-virgin olive oil

2 garlic cloves, finely grated on a Microplane

1 tablespoon peeled and finely grated fresh ginger, using a Microplane

1 teaspoon, peeled and finely grated fresh turmeric, using a Microplane

3 cups homemade stock (corn/mushroom/chicken all work, pages 79, 80, and 82)

Lemon wedges for garnish

CORN STOCK

MAKES 2 QUARTS PLUS 1 PINT

Every year I make batches of corn stock, freezing most for colder days. This snapshot-of-summer adds a gently sweet richness to the poaching liquid in the Grand Aioli Summer Feast (page 158), Halibut + Poached Vegetables with Aioli Slather (page 222), and Maple-Gochujang Ribs, Pickle Platter, Cornbread (page 168).

5 corncobs

Woody ends from 1 bunch asparagus

10 to 13 parsley stems

1 onion

1 stalk celery

1 dried chile pepper or ¼ teaspoon red pepper flakes

1 bay leaf

2 teaspoons kosher salt

½ to 1 teaspoon coriander seeds

½ teaspoon black peppercorns

10 cups water

Place all ingredients in a slow cooker (see Note). Turn the dial on low setting. Place the lid on and cook for 2 hours. Remove the lid, taste, and adjust the seasoning as needed.

Use tongs to transfers the solids to a colander placed over a bowl. Ladle the stock through a sieve placed over a canning funnel, set on a quart-size mason jar. When one jar is full, move to filling the next, until there is no more stock to strain.

When the solids are cool enough to handle, squeeze the remaining liquid from them and discard for compost. Add the remaining liquid to the jars and cool to room temperature before sealing and refrigerating.

The stock can be poured into ice cube trays for quick use or smaller portions, or into 1 cup plastic containers for easy stacking in the freezer. The stock may be stored frozen up to 6 months, or in the refrigerator for up to 7 days.

This stock is excellent to enhance the flavor of anything that requires liquid, from rice to barley or quinoa, beans, stews, ragù, risotto, soups, and more.

NOTE: If you do not have a slow cooker, place the ingredients into a stockpot, bring it to a boil, cover with its lid, then lower to a bare simmer. Follow the remaining process as laid out.

SHRIMP UMAMI STOCK

MAKES 2 QUARTS

Of the sea, with grounding and brightening aromatics, this delicate, flavorful stock deepens many dishes. Use this recipe in Crispy Pork + Fennel Meatballs in Umami Broth (page 128). There is an additional seafood-fortified stock in making the bouillabaisse on page 211.

Shells from 1½ pounds shrimp

1 bunch cilantro stems

2 star anise

1 piece kombu (approximately 5 inches by 4 inches)

1 bay leaf

2 tablespoons thinly sliced ginger (3-inch piece)

1 tablespoon kosher salt

8 cups water

In a large saucepan, place all the ingredients and bring to a boil. Place the lid on and lower the heat to low. Simmer the mixture for 30 minutes.

Use tongs to transfer the solids into a sieve or colander set over a bowl. Filter any small particles with another sieve as you transfer the stock to jars. Once cool enough to handle, squeeze any juices from the solids, wrapping the sharp shrimp shells inside the seaweed so as not to cut yourself. Transfer the expressed juices to the jars.

Cool the stock to room temperature, jars set on wire racks, then freeze for up to 3 months, or store in the refrigerator for up to 1 week.

QUICK PICKLED RED ONIONS

MAKES A HALF-PINT

These pretty, pink slices boost dishes throughout the seasons at the Catbird and could not be simpler to make. To top Spanish Tortilla, Sauce, Pickles, Salad (page 115), the "Deli Sandwich" Dutch Baby (page 112), or the Lamb Skewers with Alliums Three Ways (page 177), they are beautiful and deliver a bright pickly punch. Use any leftover brine to season bean or grain dishes or to rev up soups or stews.

Halve the onion top-to-root and peel, then trim the ends. Slice thinly on a mandoline and pack the slices into a jar. Fill the jar with white vinegar, submerging the slices. Press the slices down as needed. Marinate for at least 15 minutes before using. They keep for 1 month, sealed in the refrigerator.

1 small red onion

White vinegar

PICKLED RAMPS

MAKES A HALF-PINT

This recipe suspends precious ramp bulbs in an aromatic, spicy brine, extending their life by months. Only harvest or buy ramp bulbs if you can confirm they have been sustainably harvested (see "Foraging," page 21).

Cut off the ramp leaves to use for making Ramp Salt (page 63) and reserve the bulbs and stems. Place the mustard seeds, coriander seeds, and black peppercorns in a half-pint jar. Pack the bulbs in and slide the bay leaf in between the bulbs, followed by the chile pepper.

Add the vinegar—it should come only halfway up the side of the jar. Dissolve the sugar and salt in ¼ cup of the filtered water in a small saucepan set over high heat, whisking to help expedite the process, then pour the mixture into the jar. Add the remaining ¾ cup filtered water to the saucepan, swirl to collect any salt-sugar residue, then add it to top off the jar.

Press down the bulbs to submerge all, seal, and refrigerate. Pickled bulbs need 3 to 5 days to meld and will keep, refrigerated, for up to 1 year.

1 bunch ramps (about 30)

½ teaspoon mustard seeds

½ teaspoon coriander seeds

½ teaspoon black peppercorns

1 bay leaf

1 dried chile pepper

1 cup white vinegar

1 tablespoon cane sugar

1 teaspoon kosher salt

1 cup filtered water

MOROCCAN PICKLED CARROTS

MAKES 1 PINT

Forager and expert food preserver Leda Meredith shared this delicious recipe with me, and to this day it is one of my favorites. The combination of spices hits every note. I sometimes use garlic cloves as per Leda's original recipe, and other times I use segments of green garlic from the kitchen garden or, as here, field garlic flower buds. The flower buds and brine are excellent cooked into legumes or grains, as in the Brown Rice, Pickled Spices, Potatoes (page 275), once all the carrots have been munched. Even if your carrots are organic, you must peel them for the aromatics to fully absorb. Save the peels to enliven stock. These pickled carrots pair delectably with the Maple-Gochujang Ribs, Pickle Platter, Cornbread (page 168) and are part of the regular rotation in the Ultimate Nibbles Platter (page 208).

1 bunch carrots

1 teaspoon mustard seeds

½ teaspoon whole cumin seeds

Pinch black peppercorns

Peel from 1 lemon, white pith shaved off

2 dried chile peppers

3 field garlic buds

1 bay leaf

⅓ cup filtered water

1 teaspoon cane sugar

½ teaspoon kosher salt

½ cup white vinegar

Peel and cut the carrots in half lengthwise (save peels for stock, page 80), then trim the spears to fit height of the jar, leaving some portion of the carrot greens as space allows.

Place half of the mustard seeds, cumin seeds, and peppercorns into the jar. Set the jar on its side and pack the carrots in as tightly as they'll fit, tucking in the lemon peel, chiles, garlic buds, and bay leaf as you go.

Heat the water, sugar, and salt in a small saucepan until they dissolve, whisking to help expedite the process. Set aside to cool slightly.

Turn the jar upright and top with the remaining mustard seeds, cumin seeds, and peppercorns. Pour the salt-sugar liquid into the jar, followed by the vinegar. Push the carrots down to completely submerge them. Seal jar and invert a couple times to incorporate. Refrigerate for at least 2 weeks to allow flavors to meld. Carrot pickles keep refrigerated up to 3 months.

FERMENTED GREEN GARLIC

Through garlic's life cycle, there are numerous ways to use this essential plant. I reserve most of my harvest to mature fully into bulbs, but I select a number of thinner stalks each season to harvest as green garlic, when the green leaves are still tender, before scapes send up their shoots. Use this condiment to bring garlicky funk to any dish. Since it carries a wallop of flavor, a little goes a long way.

Slice the green garlic stems in half lengthwise, then slice thinly on a diagonal. Tare (zero out the weight) a medium bowl on a scale, add the green garlic to the bowl and weigh it, then calculate 2 to 3 percent of the green garlic weight to determine the quantity of kosher salt. Weigh the salt and then add it to the green garlic. Toss to coat, then vigorously massage the green garlic until it begins to break down and express its juices.

6 to 8 tender green garlic stems, ends trimmed

Kosher salt

1 to 1½ teaspoons red pepper flakes, depending on your penchant for spice

When the mixture is bright green and juices are apparent, about 3 minutes, transfer any remaining garlic from your hands back to the bowl and add the red pepper flakes. Use a silicone spatula or spoon to fold in the pepper flakes.

Pack the mixture into two half-pint jars. Use a muddler to compress the mixture. Place a clean river stone, glass canning weight, or fermentation weight to submerge the mixture under the juices. If there isn't enough liquid to submerge, add 1 to 2 tablespoons water for additional brine.

Once the mixture is submerged, cover each jar with a piece of muslin secured with a rubber band or kitchen twine, and place them out of direct light in a cool place, such as a cupboard or closet. After 2 days, the mixture should be aromatic and slightly funky. Taste and either seal and refrigerate at this point, or ferment one additional day, then seal and refrigerate. This condiment is used throughout the recipes, including the Piquant French Lentils (page 272), Vegan Umami Udon (page 172), and more. Fermented green garlic keeps refrigerated for 1 year.

JUNIPER + CUMIN MEYER LEMON KRAUT

MAKES 1 QUART

More and more of us are aware of the numerous benefits of fermented foods. The savory lovers among us can doubly rejoice: this take on kraut is zingy and quite aromatic, thanks to Meyer lemons, toasted cumin seeds, and foraged juniper berries. While the initial mass looks like a lot (and it is, at its beginning), once you've massaged the salt into the veggies, the mixture breaks down quite a bit. I've provided metrics in this recipe so that you can scale it up or down. Weigh your main ingredients (cabbage, carrots, lemon), then add 3 percent salt by volume to your mixture. Keep in mind this isn't a main course but rather a punchy component laced into other dishes, such as the Stewed Scarlet Runner Beans (page 276) and Piquant French Lentils (page 272), or to go with the Eggs, Beans, Garden Greens (page 111). Experiment, adding a couple spoonfuls alongside rich foods such as meats or stews or mild dishes such as beans and grains. You'll discover new favorites along the way, opening up a whole new facet of layered and nourishing eating.

17 cups (800 g) green cabbage, sliced thinly

4 carrots (175 g) peeled, sliced into thin coins, about 2 cups

1½-inch piece (20 g) fresh turmeric, peeled and shaved with a vegetable peeler

1.1 ounces (32 g) sea salt

Half a small Meyer lemon (100 g), seeds and ends removed, thinly sliced into half-moons

1 small jalapeño (15 g), thinly sliced on a mandoline

½ teaspoon cumin seeds

½ teaspoon juniper berries

In a large mixing bowl, combine the cabbage, carrots, and turmeric. Sprinkle the salt to cover and allow the mixture to sit as you toast the cumin seeds. Toast the cumin seeds in a dry skillet over medium heat until fragrant, 3 to 5 minutes. Transfer them to a dish to cool for 3 minutes, or until at room temperature.

Vigorously squeeze the salt into the veggies, breaking down the membranes so that the mixture collapses and creates its own brine. This brine is what will ultimately submerge the veggies as they ferment. Once you've produced ample liquid, add the lemon slices and squeeze them briefly into the mixture until combined throughout.

Sprinkle the cumin seeds and juniper berries over the cabbage mixture and add the jalapeño slices. Do not massage the jalapeño slices in with bare hands, otherwise you'll be in for a burning sensation for hours to follow. Rather, fold them into the mixture with a large stainless spoon until all are incorporated.

Pack a quart jar with the kraut. Use a muddler or smaller jar to compress the mixture, so that the brine submerges it. Use an airlock lid to keep the contents submerged or a ceramic or glass fermentation disk or a clean river stone. If using an airlock system, fill the water moat and maintain over the fermentation period. If using a disk or stone, cover the jar with muslin and secure it with a rubber band or kitchen twine.

During fermentation, store the kraut in a moderate temperature, 60°F or so, away from light.

Taste after 6 or 7 days. If it is pleasant, seal with a lid and store in the refrigerator. Fermentation will continue in the refrigerator, but at a slowed rate. If you prefer more tanginess, allow the kraut to ferment a few days more, then seal and store it in the refrigerator. The kraut will keep refrigerated up to 2 months.

WILD MUSHROOM ESCABECHE

MAKES 2 PINTS

Preserving the season holds true for mushrooms just as much as for any other seasonal prize. I like to bottle fresh mushrooms so I can enjoy their lushness any time of year. Between this recipe and a conserva I sometimes make, I've found a consistent means to retain their meatiness.

This condiment is an excellent topping to nearly any savory food. I add it to batches of grains or beans, such as the Piquant French Lentils (page 272), to top scrambled eggs in place of the butter-cooked mushrooms in Buttery Scrambled Eggs + Chanterelles (page 152), mixed into the Vegan Umami Udon (page 172), and more. The mixture must marinate for 1 week before using and stores well once prepared. It isn't a good candidate for water bath processing due to its high oil content.

Combine the salt and sugar with the orange and lemon juices and both vinegars in a large bowl and whisk until they have dissolved. Add the garlic and stir to incorporate.

Slice all mushrooms and cook by type in batches in a large cast-iron skillet over medium to medium-high heat, adding a tablespoon of extra-virgin olive oil and sautéing until lightly browned on both sides. Transfer each cooked batch to the bowl, following with the next round until they are all cooked.

Add the onion slices, parsley, ⅓ cup oil, and red pepper flakes and stir to thoroughly combine. Taste a little of the marinade and adjust the seasoning as needed.

Spoon the escabeche into pint or half-pint jars, pressing the mixture down to submerge under the liquid. If the escabeche is not fully submerged, top with additional olive oil. If there is any leftover marinade, you can use it as cooking liquid for beans or grains or toward making salad dressing.

Store for at least 1 week, sealed in the refrigerator to allow the flavors to meld. Stored with enough of its marinade to cover, the escabeche will keep sealed in the refrigerator for up to 4 months.

1½ teaspoons kosher salt

½ teaspoon cane sugar

⅓ cup orange juice

1 tablespoon lemon juice

1 tablespoon sherry vinegar

¼ teaspoon red wine vinegar

1 clove garlic, finely grated on a Microplane

1½ pounds mixed mushrooms—any mixture of shiitakes, chestnut, oyster, honey, maitake, and chanterelles work well

Extra-virgin olive oil for sautéing the mushrooms, plus ⅓ cup for marinade and more as needed

1 small red onion or medium shallot, finely sliced on a mandoline

⅓ cup chopped parsley

1 teaspoon red pepper flakes

WILD SALMON GRAVLAX

MAKES EIGHT 4-OUNCE SERVINGS

Cured fish is a staple on both the Nordic and Jewish German sides of my family. Lox and bagels is a tradition carried down from my Oma and Opa, my father's father and his wife, as well as Noni and Fred, his mother and her husband. Though my mom is Swedish and Welsh, I attribute my ardent love for cured or smoked fish broadly to my Scandinavian heritage.

My parents, brother, and I punctuate every special occasion with a platter of lox and bagels with all the fixings. Know that you are loved if you are part of this meal. If I can plan for the two days it requires, I make my own lox, usually a version of gravlax, with wild salmon from Drifters Fish in Alaska. This preparation appears in Cured King Salmon, Persimmon, Pickles (page 248) and Wild Salmon Rillettes + Seeded Rye Lavash (page 241) and would be completely at home on the Buttery Scrambled Eggs (page 152) minus the chanterelles, or swapped in for the "Deli Sandwich" Dutch Baby (page 112).

1 cup kosher salt

½ cup cane sugar

2 teaspoons black peppercorns, toasted and ground in a mortar and pestle

2 pounds wild, skin-on coho or king salmon fillet, pin bones removed

2 teaspoons coriander seeds, toasted and coarsely ground in a mortar and pestle

1 tablespoon juniper berries, toasted and mashed in a mortar and pestle

2 small lemons

1 orange

A third of a bunch fresh dill, coarsely chopped

Lay a considerable length of plastic wrap onto a work surface, with a similar piece laid perpendicular on top of it. Combine the salt, sugar, and black pepper in a bowl and stir to combine. Sprinkle an even layer of the mixture in a shape resembling the fish onto the plastic wrap. Position the fish on top of it, skin side down.

Sprinkle the coriander onto the fish, followed by the juniper. Finely zest one lemon and the orange to coat the fish, then arrange the dill over the entire surface. Zest the remaining lemon on top of the dill, then sprinkle enough of the salt-sugar mixture to completely coat the salmon, as well as all sides. You may be left with extra of the salt-sugar mixture. Save, seal, and store it at room temp indefinitely for the next cure recipe.

Pull the plastic wrap from one side tightly over the fish, followed by the opposite, as if you are swaddling a baby. Repeat with the top and bottom sections and secure tightly.

Place the fish flesh side up on a rimmed sheet pan into the refrigerator, evenly weighed down by heavy objects such as cans or a pan or two. Allow the salmon to cure for 48 hours, checking every 12 hours or so to drain any accumulated liquid.

After the second day, rinse the aromatics from the salmon and discard the plastic wrap. Slice away a small corner of the fish and taste. Rinse it further if it is still too salty. Pat the cured fish dry and store sealed in a container in the refrigerator for up to 5 days, or frozen, wrapped tightly in layers of plastic wrap and sealed in a resealable bag, for up to 3 months.

To serve, slice very thinly on a shallow diagonal with a thin, sharp knife. Test the thickness by holding a slice up to the light—you should be able to see through it.

PRESERVED MEYER LEMONS

MAKES 1 QUART

To prepare these salty, lemony pickles, a hermetic bail-hinged jar with rubber gasket is excellent. If you use a mason jar, choose a plastic lid so the interior surface is not corroded over time by the salt, or place a square of parchment as you affix the lid to act as a barrier. Be sure that the jar is sterilized before using.

Scrub 7 lemons under cool running water and set aside in a colander. Place enough kosher salt at the base of a quart jar to evenly coat it. Slice each lemon twice from its tip to within ½ inch of its base, almost cutting them into quarters but leaving them intact at one end, as if they were flower petals opening up.

Place a lemon cut sides up at the bottom of the jar. Spoon kosher salt to coat all cut surfaces, then bring the quarters back together to reshape the fruit. Press it down slightly, then sprinkle more salt to coat the lemon. Add the peppercorns and bay leaves, and repeat with all remaining lemons until you have filled the jar.

Press down onto the stack of lemons so that they release more of their juices, packing them in as tightly as possible and creating a brine to submerge them. If there isn't enough liquid, add juice from one or two additional lemons and once again press down on the fruits. Add enough kosher salt to form a layer on top.

Seal and store the jar at room temperature away from sunlight for 30 days. Invert the jar a few times to aid in dissolving the brine and coating the fruits, every day or two. After this period, the skins will have turned slightly translucent.

When 30 days have passed, store the sealed jar in the refrigerator. Use the brine or minced flesh to season grains, beans, soups, and stews, and the sliced or diced skins to flavor Seared Scallops + Veggie Gravel (page 133), Roasted Whole Cauliflower with Harissa + Yogurt (page 207), Chicken Thighs, Quince, Cipollini, Preserved Lemon (page 221), potatoes, salads, pastas, and more. You may choose to rinse the skins before using, depending on the desired saltiness. Discard any seeds as you find them. Refrigerated, preserved lemons keep indefinitely.

7 lemons (Meyer lemons if you can find them) plus 1 or 2 additional lemons, for juice, as needed

Kosher salt, such as Diamond Crystal brand

1 teaspoon peppercorns

2 bay leaves

VARIATIONS: Other spice combinations besides black pepper and bay leaf make for unique, delicious flavors as well.

1 teaspoon coriander seed, 1 teaspoon cumin seed, bay leaf, and dried chile pepper

1 teaspoon pink peppercorns and bay leaf

Cardamom pod and vanilla bean

Dried chile pepper, cinnamon stick, and bay leaf

1 teaspoon fennel seed, cinnamon stick, and 1 teaspoon coriander seed

TARRAGON-SHALLOT SUMMER SQUASH PICKLES

MAKES 1 QUART

Crunchy and mild summer squash beckons to be pickled. These refrigerator pickles retain their crunch and receive new verve from alliums and herbs. Pair them with succulent Maple-Gochujang Ribs, Pickle Platter, Cornbread (page 168).

1 medium to large yellow summer squash, sliced no more than ⅛ inch thick using a mandoline

1 or 2 small shallots, sliced a similar thickness as the squash

2 or 3 stems fresh tarragon

½ teaspoon coriander seeds

1 cup white vinegar

1 tablespoon cane sugar

1 teaspoon kosher salt

1 cup filtered water

Layer the squash slices, shallots, and tarragon in a quart jar and top with the coriander seeds. Add the vinegar—it should come only halfway up the side of the jar. Dissolve the sugar and salt in ¼ cup of the measured water in a small saucepan set over high heat, whisking to help expedite the process, then pour the mixture into the jar. Add the remaining water to the saucepan, swirl to collect any salt-sugar residue, then add it to top off the jar.

The liquid should fully submerge the squash mixture. Press down gently if needed. Seal the jar and invert it a couple times to blend the contents fully. Chill in the refrigerator for at least 1 day before serving. Squash pickles keep refrigerated for up to 3 months.

AUTUMN OLIVE JAM

MAKES A LITTLE MORE THAN 8 HALF-PINTS

This autumn olive jam is thick and luscious. Its pleasing tartness is similar to that of cranberry or lingonberry, and it is full of antioxidants. I use a method that requires you to dramatically reduce the volume of liquid—essentially boiling off most of the water added. This helps prevent the jam from separating into a watery layer and a pulpy layer. I use apple or quince peels—keep quince peels left over from Rosé + Spice Poached Quince (page 101) frozen in a bag for occasions such as this, as their high pectin content helps the jam set. I used ½ cup sugar for every 1 cup of juice and pulp. Because autumn olive is an invasive plant (see page 27), it is an ecological problem here in the United States. If you do not have it growing in your area, please do not plant it. Instead, purchase frozen autumn olive berries harvested from the wild, available online. This jam is spread into a glossy layer when making the Autumn Olive Linzer Tart (page 229), spooned to pair with rich cheeses in the Ultimate Nibbles Platter (page 208), and makes an excellent PB&J.

Place the frozen peels in a muslin pouch and secure with kitchen twine. In a large nonreactive pot, cook the berries, apple or quince peels, and water over medium heat for about 15 minutes, gently mashing the berries with a potato masher and stirring at intervals. Remove the muslin bundle. When it is cool enough to handle, express any remaining liquid from it back into the pot and discard the bundle.

Put the hot mixture through a food mill to separate the pulp from the seeds, working in batches as the food mill reaches capacity. Though it is said that once autumn olives undergo a good boil, the seeds can no longer germinate, I don't like to risk putting them in my compost and instead drop the mash off for my neighbor's chickens or discard it as trash.

Clean the pot and return it to the stove. Add the pulpy liquid with the sugar, lemon juice, and salt. Bring it to a boil and simmer, stirring frequently, 35 to 45 minutes, until the setting point is reached (see Note). You'll need to stir fairly constantly toward the end to prevent scorching. Pay special attention to the pot after the 30 minute mark, and begin testing to see if the jam sheets off a large, shallow spoon, otherwise known as the "gel test."

Pour into sterilized half-pint jars, leaving ½-inch headspace. Cover with sterilized lids, screw on the rings, and process in a boiling water bath for 15 minutes.

Scant ¼ cup frozen apple or quince peels (from 2 or 3 fruits)

14 cups ripe autumn olive berries

4 cups water

3 to 3½ cups cane sugar

2 tablespoons fresh lemon juice

½ teaspoon kosher salt

NOTE: For the gel test, dip a large stainless steel spoon sideways into the jam. When two drops of the liquid meet and form into one as they slide down the edge, the setting point has been reached.

WILD BLUEBERRY COMPOTE

MAKES 3 OR 4 HALF-PINTS

This compote is a simple method to preserve berries through the seasons, highlighting their peak-ripe glory with not much else in the way of ingredients. That said, you may add herbs to offer further interest to this inky topping. Delicious options include a sprig of fresh rosemary, lavender, or anise hyssop, a bay leaf, or a few sprigs of thyme, tied in a bundle with kitchen twine for easy removal. The recipe scales up easily for larger batches and can be hot-water processed for 15 minutes for longer term storage.

4 cups wild blueberries

½ cup cane sugar

Juice from half a lemon

Pinch kosher salt

Bring all the ingredients to a boil in a medium saucepan over medium heat, stirring occasionally. Once the mixture is bubbling, mash some of the berries using the tines of a fork or a potato masher and turn the heat down so that the mixture simmers. The berries will express more juices as they cook, but this gives them a head start. Reduce the heat to low as needed to avoid scorching the compote. Simmer, reducing the liquid by a third, 8 to 10 minutes or until somewhat thickened. Taste and adjust the seasoning as needed.

Spoon the compote into three or four half-pint jars and allow to cool to room temperature. Seal and refrigerate or use a hot-water process for 15 minutes.

ROSÉ + SPICE POACHED QUINCE

Quinces are intensely floral-smelling, knobby orchard fruits that require cooking before eating. Native to the Caucasus region in western Asia, Greece, Armenia, and Iran, they are used in these cuisines in both sweet and savory dishes. In recent times this aromatic fruit has been labeled a specialty item here in the United States and is more widely available as prepackaged membrillo, aka quince paste. This is an unfortunate shift in perception since the fruits are quite versatile, imparting a special floral quality that cannot be replaced by apples or pears. When choosing quince, look for large, firm, unblemished, and fragrant fruit that is more golden yellow than green, a sign of ripeness. Some at farmers' markets may even still have their downy fuzz, a protective coating quince produce as they ripen.

Quinces make their appearance at markets in late September, ending in November or early December. The poached quince can be eaten with their liquid, spooned to top yogurt or ice cream, or reduced to make other delectable recipes, such as the Quince Tarte Tatin (page 226), Chicken Thighs, Quince, Cipollini, Preserved Lemon (page 221), and the Quinoa + Quince Porridge (page 197).

Place the wine, water, and sugar in a medium saucepan over medium heat. Dissolve the sugar completely, stirring occasionally, then add the quince wedges, lemon peel, cinnamon stick, and cardamom pods.

Bring the mixture to a boil. Lower the heat to simmer, cover the liquid surface with a parchment cartouche—a paper lid that fits flush to the surface—and cook at a gentle simmer for 30 minutes.

Gently lift the cartouche and check the quince, piercing the quarters with a thin sharp knife. If the knife readily pierces, they are done and should be transferred to a bowl using a slotted spoon. If any are still hard, return the cartouche flush with the surface and poach until they are soft enough to pierce with little resistance.

Once the quinces have been poached, cool to room temperature. Discard the cinnamon stick and cardamom pods, but keep the lemon peel to incorporate in the Quinoa + Quince Porridge or Quince Tarte Tatin. Store the quince in their liquid in a sealed container in the refrigerator for up to 2 weeks.

2½ cups rosé wine

¾ cup water

½ cup cane sugar

5 quinces, peeled, cored, any hard tissue along inner spine cut out, and cut into quarters (see Note)

6 strips lemon peel

1 cinnamon stick

7 cardamom pods, bruised with the butt end of a knife

NOTE: If you cannot find quince but would like to make this—and any of the secondary recipes—you can substitute tart, firm apples such as Pink Lady, Braeburn, or Evercrisp. Poach the apple quarters for half as long as you would the quince, otherwise following the recipe as stated.

CANDIED MEYER LEMONS + SYRUP

MAKES 1 PINT CANDIED LEMONS AND 1 CUP (8 OUNCES) SYRUP

Like sunny windowpanes, these citrus wheels sparkle, bringing cheer to colder days. Make the Candied Meyer Lemon Ice Cream + Pistachio Tuiles (page 270) with the fruit, and swap citrusy syrup for the spruce tips in mixing a Meyer lemon version of the Last Word cocktail (opposite) to keep the chill at bay or add to other baking projects.

1 cup cane sugar

1 cup water

3 to 5 Meyer lemons, ends discarded, thinly sliced, seeds removed

Combine the sugar and water in a medium shallow pan over medium heat and stir occasionally to dissolve the sugar. Arrange the lemons in the pan, submerging them below the surface. Simmer the slices for 35 to 45 minutes, or until the lemons become translucent. Use tongs to remove the candied slices and place them onto a wire rack set over a sheet pan to catch any drips. Reserve the syrup in a bottle in the refrigerator for up to one month.

Allow the slices to dry for a day so they become less tacky. This can be done up to 1 week in advance of making the Candied Meyer Lemon Ice Cream + Pistachio Tuiles. Candied slices keep up to 2 months, stored in a sealed container at room temperature.

RYE + SPRUCE TIP LAST WORD

This is my favorite cocktail. It sips too easily, refreshing the palate, making you desire more of it. This version of the Last Word, a Prohibition-era cocktail invented in the 1920s at the Detroit Athletic Club, incorporates rye whiskey, a spirit we always have on hand at the cottage. True to the cocktail's origins, it incorporates green Chartreuse, a botanically derived liqueur made by Carthusian monks since the 1600s in France, and is how the similarly named color got its name. I make spruce tip syrup when my enormous Norway spruce sprouts its new growth in spring and use it to sweeten the cocktail before shaking. Beware, this pretty drink is boozy and will creep up on you. It is also excellent with mezcal or tequila swapped in as the base spirit. Santé!

Combine all the ingredients in a cocktail shaker. Fill with ice, seal, and shake vigorously for 15 seconds. Strain into coupe glasses. Prost!

4 ounces Old Overholt rye whiskey

2 ounces green Chartreuse

2 ounces Dry Curaçao

1 ounce fresh lemon juice

1 ounce spruce tip syrup (recipe follows; see Note)

1 dash habanero bitters

NOTE: You may substitute syrup from the Candied Meyer Lemons (opposite) for the spruce tip syrup, or simply use maple syrup.

SPRUCE TIP SYRUP MAKES 8 OUNCES

You may omit the water, opting to simply layer sugar and tips in a jar set in a sunny spot for a month or two, allowing days in the sunshine to dissolve the sugar into syrup—it is a slower method that Alan Bergo, the forager chef, recommends to extract the richest flavor. If you'd like syrup sooner, use the quick method below to extract the citrusy, coniferous sweetness from tender spruce tips. The syrup keeps in the refrigerator for up to a year.

Dissolve the sugar into the water in a medium saucepan set over medium heat, stirring to completely dissolve. Bring the simple syrup to a boil, then remove from the heat. Once the liquid is steaming but no longer boiling, add the spruce tips. Stir until they are well combined. Allow the mixture to cool to room temperature. Transfer the mixture to a jar and store in the refrigerator to continue steeping overnight. I sometimes strain the syrup after a day or two, and other times, I allow the spruce tips to continue infusing for months. Taste as you go to decide your preference. Make sure the spruce tips stay submerged in the syrup. Strain them through muslin laid onto a fine-mesh sieve when you plan to use the syrup, squeezing any excess syrup from them before discarding.

1 cup cane sugar

1 cup water

1 cup spruce tips (page 35)

HONEYSUCKLE CORDIAL

MAKES 7 CUPS

This simple fermented cordial extracts honeysuckle's perfume in a luscious, lightly effervescent alcoholic drink. I credit Marie Viljoen with the basis of this recipe, which is adaptable to many edible flowers. Refer to page 29 for honeysuckle identification and harvesting, and bottle the season into this elixir.

2½ cups cane sugar

6 cups filtered water

4 cups honeysuckle flowers

In a large saucepan, dissolve the sugar in the water over medium heat, stirring to expedite the process. Remove the pan from the heat once the sugar is fully dissolved and allow the liquid to cool to room temperature. Transfer it to a large, wide-mouth jar and add the flowers. Stir to combine.

Place muslin to cover the jar opening and secure with a rubber band or kitchen twine. Place out of direct light and every other day or so, stir the mixture, pushing the flowers down into the liquid, then reseal with the muslin. When the surface is bubbly, airborne yeasts have begun to feed on the sugars, fermenting the mixture. Depending on how warm the weather is, this may take only 3 days or up to 10. Stir again once fermentation is well underway, submerging the flowers.

Steep them one more day, then strain the mixture through muslin laid over a large fine-mesh sieve, squeezing the solids to extract all their liquid. Transfer the cordial to swing-top bail-hinge bottles and refrigerate. The cordial will keep for up to a year refrigerated but is at its best within 6 to 8 months. Be careful when releasing the bail to serve: carbonation will have built up pressure inside the vessel and will exit with an impressive *foomph*.

spring

Spring is the season I anticipate most. When the brown and grey late winter days drag on, I catch myself staring longingly out the window, impatient for productive time once again spent outdoors.

Before moving to the countryside, I certainly enjoyed spring. But since I didn't have a front row seat, the magnificent shifts of this season, both small and enormous, more or less blended into one. Spring is the season when everything is having sex or giving birth! Living amidst those layers of creation is stunning. Watching—and listening to—all the birds gathering materials for nests, choosing their mates; beholding the very first, most tender, and still-transparent leaves unfolding from maple trees; seeing tight, sculptural buds transforming into floriferous poofs of color everywhere. When I go foraging or tend the garden, I get to witness in real time everything erupting back to life. The verdant transformation of the landscape at large is afoot, and there is nothing more riveting.

In spring, I break ground, too—not just in the garden. I have all my seeds ordered and laid out by late winter—rather in a jumble, with eyes bigger than time or wherewithal allow at first. Then I begin the task of deciding what goes where and why. Seeds sown at a station in the basement become promising shoots, and I grow into my confidence about the coming season and all the new menus I'll create with a snip here and there, harvesting pods, flowers, and fruit.

Spring cleanup is initially daunting, so many beds to yank and rake layers of dead matter from the season past. But doing so reveals the very exciting first pointed crowns of new shoots. The perennials emerge deep burgundy red and alien. The red, as it turns out, is photo protection against the sun's rays, a concentration of anthocyanins. Like nature's sunscreen. It is a miracle to see everyone emerge as if planned somehow, a grand choreography nature has long rehearsed.

MAY 26

The squash and cucumbers are showing new purpose in their stems and darker leaves. The garlic is nearly 3 feet tall. The red frill mustard greens resemble feather finery: fanned, upright, showy. Only today did I witness the first creased heart-shaped scarlet runner seedling emerge. It is my first time growing them and I cannot wait to see their necks wind up around the 8-foot maypole I fashioned out of twine and metal. Oh, and the hummingbirds are back. Iridescent coral pink throats flashing as they hover at the newly reinstalled nectar feeder, just a few feet from where we take breakfast, lunch, and sometimes cocktail hour.

JUNE 3

Early this growing season I decided to allow one cell of radishes to go to seed so I could save seeds for next year. The process of seed heads forming, then maturing, and drying out has been quite lengthy as it turns out. All the veggies in adjoining cells have caught up with them and are now clamoring for the prime real estate it occupies. With this unforeseen timeline I took advantage—a kind of stroke of insight—to incorporate some of these immature seedpods into spring Catbird menus. Green, juicy, crunchy like a snap pea, but sweet-sharp like a radish. And resembling funny spaceships. This discovery has made waiting (and waiting) worth much more than the original intention.

EGGS, BEANS, GARDEN GREENS

When spring's bounty begins to flourish, I seize on the first opportunity to snip tender greens during early morning garden walks. Every shoot is dew-covered, perky, ready for the day. These discoveries inspire the meals I end up making, both the immediate and curated creations. Sweet-peppery mustard greens are added by the fistful to brighten creamy beans and custardy eggs, both mainstays here at the cottage. A generous shower of ramp salt finishes all in fine form— obviously salty, but also slightly sweet, sharp, tenderly green-savory, uniquely itself. Since the dish is so simple, it's crucial to use the freshest, highest quality ingredients.

Prepare the beans: Soak the beans in cold water to cover by 2 to 3 inches for 8 hours or overnight.

The next day, drain the beans in a colander and transfer to a medium saucepan. Add the stock, olive oil, thyme sprigs, and red pepper flakes. Bring the mixture to a boil, then cover and lower to a simmer. Cook the beans 45 to 55 minutes, until tender. Add the kosher salt, stir to incorporate, taste, and adjust the seasoning as needed. Remove the pan from the heat and replace the lid.

In a small saucepan, bring enough water to cover the eggs to a rolling boil (do not add the eggs yet). Gently lower refrigerator-cold eggs into the water and return to a rolling boil for 30 seconds. Lower the heat to a simmer and cook for 6 minutes. Remove the eggs using a slotted spoon and plunge them into an ice bath. Set aside as you do the remaining prep, peeling their shells once the eggs are cool enough to handle. With their shells left on, the eggs can be cooked up to 3 days in advance.

Slice the toasts in half and arrange them on plates. Ladle the beans and some of their liquor onto the toasts. Slice the eggs in half and nestle them into the beans. Sprinkle with Ramp Salt and freshly ground black pepper. Place a cluster of greens next to the piled toasts, to gather leaves for each mouthful.

BEANS

1 cup dried cannellini beans plus cold water to cover

About 2 cups stock or water, enough to cover the beans when cooking

3 tablespoons extra-virgin olive oil

3 sprigs fresh thyme

½ teaspoon red pepper flakes

½ teaspoon kosher salt

4 eggs

4 slices Sourdough Bread (page 68), toasted until golden

Ramp Salt (page 63)

Freshly ground black pepper

1 bunch tender mustard greens or arugula, ends trimmed if needed

"DELI SANDWICH" DUTCH BABY

MAKES 2 SERVINGS

This impressive dish requires a scorching hot oven and pan to give the batter loft. Crispy edges and a fluffy interior are a dynamic canvas for zippy elements such as cornichons, cured meat, salty cheese, and bright greens. Feel free to swap elements to suit your own tastes or what is available. Later spring versions are chock-full of tender green veg, and when I make this for guests in summer, it's usually loaded with a colorful tomato salad and sometimes creamy burrata. Don't open the oven to check on its progress—uninterrupted heat is the key to producing those swollen, puffed edges.

DUTCH BABY

½ teaspoon kosher salt

½ teaspoon freshly ground black pepper

¼ teaspoon freshly grated nutmeg

3 eggs, at room temperature

¾ cup whole milk, at room temperature

½ cup all-purpose flour

3 tablespoons salted butter, cubed

TOPPINGS

2 slices blue cheese, such as Saint Agur triple-cream blue

3 to 5 cornichons, thinly sliced lengthwise

4 slices prosciutto, salami, or mortadella

Quick Pickled Red Onions (page 85) for garnish

2 cups microgreens, shoots, soft herbs, or a combination

Freshly ground black pepper

Preheat the oven with a heavy enameled 9-inch pan inside it to 425°F.

Make the Dutch baby: Combine the salt, pepper, and nutmeg in a small bowl. Crack the eggs into a high-speed blender and blend on medium-high for 45 seconds, until the mixture is very frothy. With the cap removed, stream in the milk on the same speed until well incorporated.

Stop the machine and add the flour and spice mixture. Run the blender for only a few seconds to incorporate the dry ingredients, then stop.

Carefully remove the hot pan from the oven and add the cubed butter. It should sizzle immediately on contact. Gently and quickly replace it in the oven to finish melting. Scrape down the sides of the blender, then bring the pan back out of the oven, swirl the melted butter along the sides to coat, then carefully but swiftly pour the egg mixture into pan. Quickly return the pan to the oven and bake 20 to 25 minutes, until deeply golden and puffed. Do not open the oven at any point except to remove the pan when the Dutch baby is done, as the hot air required to give it loft will dissipate, hampering its rise.

Add the toppings: Have all toppings at the ready, as the Dutch baby will begin to deflate as soon as it is taken out of the oven. Shingle the cheese onto the Dutch baby. Next to the cheese, add a cluster of cornichons, followed by prosciutto ribbons draped in a pile. Nestle in a bunch of pickled onions and lastly, a tangle of greens. Bring the Dutch baby to the table, set on a trivet, finish with a few grinds of black pepper, and eat at once.

SPANISH TORTILLA, SAUCE, PICKLES, SALAD

MAKES 8 TO 10 SERVINGS

If you're flush with fresh eggs, a great way to use them is in this traditional Spanish dish, one of the most widely available foods throughout Spain. I diverge from tradition and first caramelize the onions, which enriches the flavors. I'm also not stringent about the potatoes: If some become golden while cooking, I do not mind. I find the resulting depth of flavor quite pleasing, and the overall "pancake" tender. The tortilla makes a good brunch centerpiece. It is equally perfect for a picnic, much like its origin as a Spanish tapa. Bracing pickled red onions are an ideal counterpoint to the buttery tortilla. The green sauce—Garlic Mustard Pesto—makes use of spring's favorite invasive wild green and can be spooned liberally onto this (and anything). The onions and pesto can be made days ahead and keep just as long. While the tortilla will keep for a few days, don't be surprised if it's gobbled up.

In a medium bowl with a pour spout, crack the eggs, add the salt, and beat vigorously until uniform and frothy.

In a large nonstick skillet, heat the oil over medium heat. Oil-poach the potato slices in two or three batches so all potatoes can lie flush to the pan surface, lowering the heat to medium-low if the slices cook too quickly. Turn them using a silicone spatula and a julep strainer or slotted spoon, cooking 5 to 7 minutes on one side, then 3 to 5 minutes on the second, until the slices are translucent, golden, and tender when pierced with a thin, sharp knife. It is okay if some slices brown slightly.

Use the slotted spoon to drain as much excess oil as possible from the potatoes and transfer them to the egg mixture. Add the caramelized onions.

Remove the pan from the heat and pour off all but 1 tablespoon of the hot oil. Return the pan to the heat, set over medium-low. Pour in the egg-potato-onion mixture. Use a silicone spatula to stir the eggs at the center of the pan, then in different areas around the pan until the eggs begin to set, arranging the potatoes and onions as you go around, creating a more-or-less uniform surface so that once cooked, each wedge cut will have ample potatoes and onions.

Tip the pan to one side to slide any lesser-cooked egg mixture toward that edge, then tilt pan to opposite side to move any remaining egg mixture toward the other edge. Continue cooking the tortilla over medium-low heat, jiggling the pan after a couple minutes to see how much wobble remains in the center.

8 eggs

1 teaspoon kosher salt

1 cup extra-virgin olive oil

5 to 7 medium Yukon gold potatoes, peeled and sliced ⅛ inch thick

1 cup caramelized onions (recipe follows)

ingredients continued →

CONTINUED →

RADISH SALAD

7 to 10 radishes, including
a mix of French breakfast,
watermelon, pink beauty,
purple, and green luobo
varieties for a range in hues
and flavors

1 jalapeño, seeds removed
if you prefer less spicy

2 colorful bell peppers, sliced
into thin rings

⅔ cup chopped fresh parsley

2 tablespoons fish sauce

4 teaspoons sherry vinegar

2 tablespoons extra-virgin
olive oil

Freshly ground black pepper

Quick Pickled Red Onions for
garnish (page 85)

Garlic Mustard Pesto for
garnish (page 62)

When the mixture only slightly wobbles when agitated the pan, remove from
heat. Position a plate slightly larger than the pan on top of it. Hold the pan
handle with one hand and the plate with the other. Carefully and swiftly, in one
motion, invert the pan. The tortilla should release in one piece onto the plate.

Set the pan down and tip the plate to slide the tortilla (bottom side up) back into
pan to cook for 1 more minute, just long enough to set the innermost mass. Once
you have slid it into the pan, tuck the edges down. After the tortilla has cooked
for 1 minute, tip the pan to slide the tortilla back onto the plate. Allow to set for
5 minutes.

Make the salad: Using the main plate on a mandoline, thinly slice the radishes
and jalapeño into delicate disks. In a medium bowl, toss them with the bell
pepper slices, chopped parsley, fish sauce, vinegar, oil, and black pepper. Taste
and adjust the seasoning as needed.

Bring the tortilla to the table. Serve alongside the zippy radish salad, the Garlic
Mustard Pesto, and the Quick Pickled Red Onions for guests to mix and match
as they slice the tortilla into wedges. The tortilla can also be eaten at room
temperature. Any leftovers can be stored in a sealed container in the refrigerator
for up to 3 days.

CARAMELIZED ONIONS MAKES ABOUT 2 CUPS

Sweet-oniony, this jammy condiment deepens the flavors of anything to which
you add it. It's nice to make a large batch and scoop a tablespoon here and there
for an array of dishes, such as for Stewed Scarlet Runner Beans (page 276) and
the Wild Mushroom–Potato–Onion Tart (page 194).

Olive oil, for sautéing

4 medium onions, cut in half,
thinly sliced

Kosher salt

Get a large cast iron skillet hot over medium-high heat and add a generous drizzle
of oil. Add the onions, toss thoroughly to coat in oil, and season with salt. Sauté
until onions begin to soften, 7 to 10 minutes. Stir at intervals, lowering the heat to
medium if they begin to brown. Lower heat to medium-low and continue to sauté,
adding another drizzle of oil if the pan looks dry.

Stir occasionally as they soften further and begin to caramelize, spreading them
out in an even layer as they cook. Stir the mixture to turn the slices, then spread
them out in an even layer again. Repeat like so throughout the process until
onions are deeply golden, translucent, and collapsed, 30 to 40 minutes. They will
have cooked down dramatically once they are ready. Set aside. These can be
made up to 3 days in advance and stored in a sealed container in the refrigerator.

SPRING SKILLET: DUCK EGGS + CRISPY BROWN RICE

MAKES 2 SERVINGS

As someone who both hates waste and likes to experiment in the kitchen, this dish was born when my pan sat with a sheen of fat, left over from cooking the Lamb Skewers with Alliums Three Ways. I didn't want to just toss it. The flavor-packed fat is perfect to revive leftover rice, giving it new personality and purpose. Savory, chewy, crispy grains make a great foil to creamy duck egg yolks and their own crispy fried edges. The soft-crunchy temperament of wilted romaine ushers in a welcome brightness. Add hot sauce or a scatter of herbs, and it serves as good eating for any time of day.

Leftover pan fat from Lamb Skewers with Alliums Three Ways (page 177)

1 small onion, cut in half, thinly sliced lengthwise

3 garlic cloves, chopped

Kosher salt

2 cups day-old brown rice

1 head romaine lettuce, stem trimmed and sliced in half lengthwise

2 duck eggs

Extra-virgin olive oil

Freshly ground black pepper

Flake salt for garnish

1 handful soft herbs such as parsley, basil, or dill

Heat a large cast-iron skillet over medium-high heat to melt the leftover fat and get the pan hot. Add the onions and sauté for 3 minutes undisturbed. Sauté 2 more minutes, stirring the onions occasionally until translucent and browning in parts, lowering heat to medium as needed to avoid burning them. Add the garlic, season with salt, and sauté for 1 minute or until fragrant, stirring once or twice.

Scoot the onion mixture to a pile at the coolest zone of the pan. Add the rice and spread it in a single layer over the base of the pan. Season with salt to taste and cook 7 to 9 minutes. During this time, flip the rice with a firm spatula every 2 to 3 minutes, then smooth it out and press it flush to pan. Repeat this process, cooking the rice undisturbed, then flipping and smoothing it out to develop a crust, rendering the grains crunchy as the rice sizzles.

Once the rice is browned and crispy, scoot the rice mixture to the onion pile and combine. Add the lettuce halves face down on the pan surface and season with salt. Cook undisturbed for 2 to 3 minutes, until they begin to collapse and become translucent, then turn the pieces and any stray extra leaf sections over. While the lettuce cooks, crack the eggs into two small dishes.

Move the lettuce to the periphery and add a small drizzle of olive oil to pan if it looks dry. Gently tip in the eggs. Pan-fry the eggs until crispy at their edges and the whites are cooked through, 4 to 5 minutes. Rotate the eggs as needed for even frying.

While the eggs cook, turn the lettuce halves so that all surfaces become visibly wilted and burnished in parts.

Bring the skillet to the table, set on a trivet. Divide the rice mixture, lettuce, and eggs evenly between two plates. Add a few generous grinds of pepper and season the eggs with flake salt. Pluck the herb leaves from their stems, tear the leaves, and scatter over all.

PÂTÉ, ELDERBERRY GELÉE, PICKLED RAMPS

I've always loved the velvety indulgence of pâté. I attribute this, at least in part, to my European roots. I am the first generation born in the United States on my father's side. Many family rituals pull from who we were before fleeing Europe during the Holocaust. Traditional foods are a matter of course in Europe, along with a frugal interest in transforming less desirable or leftover bits into delicious fare. For example, my father used to delight in a snack of cold consommé—essentially beef gelatin—with a spoonful of sour cream.

This recipe is adapted from my friend chef Joshua's chicken liver pâté, a recipe he most recently served guests at the Chicago Museum of Art, which won him a Bib Gourmand. Before either of us left Birmingham, he, his partner Jon, and I went foraging in their neighborhood one hot spring evening. We gleefully plucked wild berries from their hedge and heady honeysuckle, too. Pulling from this memory, I thought it'd be fitting to pair a wild ingredient with the pâté. Elderberry syrup gets rendered into a gelée to seal in the mousse-like spread. It's like velvet and jewels. The pâté is equally excellent with toast or crackers. If you know me, I say all rich foods are better with pickles. Cornichons or other pickles would be just as good if you don't have pickled ramps. If you cannot forage elderberries, you can purchase elderberry syrup, sold as a health tonic, from many green grocers.

Make the apricot purée: In a small saucepan set over medium heat, combine the chopped apricots, ¼ cup each of the brandy and water, and bring to a boil. Lower the heat slightly and reduce the liquid by three-quarters, 3 to 4 minutes. Apricots should be quite soft and the liquor will have largely cooked off. Set aside to cool slightly. Use a small blender to purée the mixture until uniform, adding 1 tablespoon water to loosen the mixture and 1 teaspoon brandy. If the purée is not completely uniform at this point, add the remaining teaspoon brandy and purée once more. Taste and add a final tablespoon of water as needed to thin.

Make the pâté: Place the butter in the top of a small double boiler and warm over medium heat until just a third of it has melted. Quickly remove the top pan from the double boiler to prevent the butter from melting further. Stir until uniform, blending the melted butter with the solid and smoothing any lumps with a silicone spatula. If any lumps persist, replace the pan on the double boiler very briefly, until the butter starts to melt again and repeat: remove the pan from the double boiler and smear the lumps along the pan sides to incorporate until the mixture is uniform. This is tempering the butter. The results should appear an opaque, light yellow and resemble the texture of melted chocolate. Set aside.

CONTINUED →

APRICOT PURÉE

⅓ cup chopped unsulphured dried apricots

¼ cup brandy plus
1 to 2 teaspoons

¼ cup water plus
1 to 2 tablespoons

PÂTÉ

12 tablespoons salted butter, coarsely chopped, at room temperature

12 ounces chicken livers

1¾ teaspoons fine sea salt

1 teaspoon ground white pepper

2 egg yolks

1 tablespoon plus 2 teaspoons sherry vinegar

8 ounces heavy cream

ingredients continued →

ELDERBERRY GELÉE

1 teaspoon powdered gelatin

2 tablespoons dry white wine or flat prosecco

1 tablespoon water

½ cup plus 1 tablespoon elderberry syrup

Sourdough Crackers (page 75) for serving

Pickled Ramps (page 85) for serving

Remove any stringy connective tissue from the livers and discard. Combine the livers, salt, pepper, egg yolks, apricot purée, and sherry vinegar in a high-speed blender. Blend until uniform. Stream in the heavy cream, blending on low until uniform. Repeat with the tempered butter, until the pâté is very creamy and completely uniform.

Place an empty roasting pan on a rack set in lower third of the oven, with the other rack placed in the middle. Preheat the oven to 225°F.

Set a large kettle and a medium kettle of water to boil. Divide the pâté evenly into eight heatproof wide-mouth half-pint jars, leaving at least ½-inch headspace in each. Wrap each tightly with two layers of heavy-duty plastic wrap. Place the jars into a baking dish. Carefully pour the larger kettle of hot water into the roasting pan inside the oven and pour the medium kettle of hot water to fill the baking dish halfway. Transfer the pâtés in the baking dish to the oven and bake for 1¼ hours, or until the pâtés barely wobble when agitated.

Transfer the pâtés from the baking dish to a cooling rack until only mildly warm, then chill on a level surface in the refrigerator overnight. The pâtés will keep for up to 1 week, sealed in their plastic wrap, in the refrigerator. They can be wrapped tightly (or lids screwed on) and frozen for up to 3 months, without the gelée (make the gelée and top once they have thawed in the refrigerator).

Make the gelée: Combine the gelatin with the white wine in a small bowl. Add the water and stir well. Bloom the gelatin for 5 minutes.

Meanwhile, heat the elderberry syrup until steaming. Pour it onto the gelatin and stir until the gelatin is completely dissolved, about 1 minute. Allow the syrup to cool until tepid. Bring the pâtés out and unwrap them. Pour a thin layer of the gelée to coat, dividing it evenly among them. Rewrap and chill the pâtés for 1 hour or up to overnight.

Serve the pâté slathered onto Sourdough Crackers, alongside Pickled Ramp bulbs.

ASPARAGUS + ARTICHOKES

This dish is a celebration of juiciness. Artichokes can be fiddly to work with, but their nutty, meaty hearts make the labor well worth it. A slow braise renders them tender, and the remaining cooking liquid may be used for all kinds of things later (such as cooking beans or grains in the sustenance dishes, page 272). Asparagus is quickly steamed to bring out its bright greenness, and homemade aioli receives an infusion of fragrant tarragon, perfect for dragging the veg through. If you don't like tarragon, you can substitute other soft herbs, such as dill or chervil. When I immediately want a dish to read as "extra special," sparkling roe is an easy addition. Here, its salty clack is a good foil to the soft textures.

Make the artichokes: Add the water, wine, olive oil, red pepper flakes, salt, and lemon peel to a medium Dutch oven or other braising pot wide enough so artichokes can be arranged more or less in a single layer, 8 to 9 inches wide.

Starting with one artichoke, peel and trim its stem and rub the area thoroughly with the cut side of a lemon to prevent it from oxidizing. Peel away most leaves until the softer inner leaves are revealed. Cut the top 2 to 2½ inches off (depending on how tall the artichokes are), rubbing all exposed surfaces with the lemon as you go. Cut the artichoke in half lengthwise and scoop out the hairy choke, being sure to rub again with the lemon. Place the cut sides down in the pot. Repeat the process with the remaining artichokes.

When all artichokes are arranged, bring to a simmer and cover, cooking for 10 minutes undisturbed. Remove the pan lid and turn each half over, nestling them in the cooking liquid. Replace the lid and cook for 10 to 15 minutes more, until tender when pierced at the thickest point with a sharp knife. Remove the lid and allow the artichokes to cool to room temperature. This step can be done up to 3 days in advance with the artichokes stored in their braising liquid and sealed in a container in the refrigerator. If you prepare them in advance, set them out 1 hour before preparing the rest of the dish, so they can come to room temperature.

Prepare the aioli: Fold the chopped tarragon into the aioli, taste, and adjust the tarragon as needed. Replace the lid and return to the refrigerator until it is time to plate.

Arrange the asparagus spears in a steamer basket, placed inside a saucepan with 1 inch of water. Place the lid on and steam over high heat until the asparagus turns bright green and the stems become just tender, about 5 minutes. Shock the asparagus in an ice bath until they are cool to the touch. Pat dry and set aside.

Drag a couple dollops of aioli across serving plates and nestle a pair of artichoke halves, a lemon peel from the braising liquid, and a cluster of asparagus on top. Dot with trout roe and season with freshly ground black pepper.

ARTICHOKES

¾ cup water

½ cup dry white wine

¼ cup extra-virgin olive oil

½ teaspoon red pepper flakes

½ teaspoon kosher salt

Strips of lemon peel from half a lemon

4 medium artichokes

1 or 2 lemons, cut in half to rub on artichokes to prevent oxidizing

TARRAGON AIOLI

2 tablespoons fresh tarragon leaves, finely chopped, plus more as needed

1 cup aioli (page 158)

1 bunch plump asparagus, woody ends snapped off (save for stock, pages 79, 80, and 82)

Trout roe for garnish

Freshly ground black pepper

SPRING FLING SALAD IN GREEN

MAKES 2 TO 4 SERVINGS

When presented with an opportunity to make a thing I favor something that jostles you to attention, such as this vernal theme: punchy dressing enrobes tender spring greens. Butter and gem lettuces, juicy snap peas, abundant herbs. Every forkful is crunchy, juicy bliss.

ROASTED GARLIC

4 bulbs garlic

5 sprigs fresh thyme

1 sprig rosemary

1 dried chile pepper

1 cup extra-virgin olive oil

Pinch kosher salt

DRESSING

5 cloves roasted garlic

6 tablespoons extra-virgin olive oil, plus more as needed

2 tablespoons freshly squeezed lemon juice

1 tablespoon Dijon mustard

2 teaspoons white wine vinegar

1 teaspoon lemon zest

¼ teaspoon kosher salt

Freshly ground black pepper

1 teaspoon very finely snipped fresh chives, using scissors

SALAD

2 heads gem or Bibb lettuce, coarsely chopped

1 cup snap peas, sliced thinly on the diagonal

1 handful pea tendrils or shoots

½ cup fresh basil or mint leaves, larger leaves torn

½ cup chopped parsley

Freshly ground black pepper

Pistachio Dukkah (page 64) for sprinkling

Roast the garlic: Preheat the oven to 350°F. Trim the top third of each bulb so that the cloves are exposed. Place them cut sides up in a small oven-safe skillet. Add the thyme, rosemary, chile pepper, and oil, drizzling to coat everything. Turn the garlic bulbs to coat all sides in the oil, replace them upright, and season with salt. Cover the pan with aluminum foil, anchoring it around the pan edges. Roast for 30 minutes or until the garlic is fragrant.

Remove the foil and roast for 10 more minutes, until the tops of the bulbs turn golden. Remove the pan from the oven and set on a wire rack to cool fully. Squeeze the cloves out of their papery sheaths into a small jar and pour infused oil from the pan to submerge the garlic in the jar. Store the roasted garlic sealed in the refrigerator. Submerged in oil, they will keep for up to 1 month. This step can be done a week in advance. Save the remainder of the oil for other preparations, such as for Brown Rice, Pickled Spices, Potatoes (page 275).

Make the dressing: In a small high-speed blender, combine all dressing ingredients except the chives. Pulse until the mixture is emulsified. It will appear thick and silky. If you prefer a looser dressing, add a little water and pulse again until incorporated. Taste and adjust the seasoning as needed. Transfer the dressing to a jar, add chives, and stir until combined. This step can be done up to 3 days in advance. Bring the dressing out from the refrigerator 15 minutes before using.

Combine the salad ingredients: In a salad bowl, combine the lettuce, snap peas, pea tendrils, basil, and parsley. Add 2 or 3 tablespoons of the dressing and toss to thoroughly coat all elements. Add a few grinds of pepper. Taste and add more dressing as needed for a robustly flavored but not overwhelming effect. Toss to coat and liberally sprinkle with dukkah. Eat at once.

NOTE: If you prefer to save a portion of the salad for later, reserve it prior to sprinkling the dukkah, whose texture will suffer if refrigerated.

VARIATIONS: You may add or swap thinly sliced green beans, fresh fava beans, asparagus, shelling peas, even frozen peas thawed in cold water—any fresh, crunchy green veg is good. All soft herbs work nicely in this salad.

MUSSELS FOR BETTY

MAKES 2 SERVINGS

I was brought under the wing of two renowned food experts, Jon Rowley and Betty Fussell in my earliest days as a food photographer. These legends gave me a jump-start to become more discerning, sharing with me incredible quality ingredients, among them, many heirloom foods. Jon taught me how to identify the freshest, plumpest oysters, mussels, and wild fish (ruining me for anything not superlative) along with the best peaches I've ever had (thanks to his Brix refractometer and peaches from Frog Hollow Farm). Betty shared how elemental eating could be undeniably sumptuous and spoke about everything with a riveting zeal. Quality foods at peak ripeness, prepared with love, make for the best eating around. This mussels dish is one Jon would have loved and is a dish I first made for Betty in her kitchen, eaten on her patio in the Santa Barbara sunshine. To make it, you will need a cast-iron pan with a fitted lid.

Sauté the shallots in a cast-iron skillet with 1 tablespoon olive oil over medium heat until beginning to brown, 7 to 9 minutes. Add the lemon peel halfway through and stir occasionally.

Add the celery with half its leaves, the radishes, and half of the butter. Season with salt and pepper. Stir to incorporate as the butter foams. Cook for 3 to 5 minutes, until radishes begin to soften, then add the wine. Turn the radishes, stirring occasionally as the mixture bubbles. After 2 minutes, add the water.

When the mixture comes to a boil again, add the remaining butter and stir to incorporate. Add the mussels and cover with the pan lid. Cook for 6 minutes or until their shells open. Stir in the remaining celery leaves, then serve in shallow bowls, being sure to include the softened lemon peels amidst the broth and veggies. Top with the borage flowers, pea tendrils, or parsley (any one or a mix) and eat at once, slurping the broth and softened peels, plucking briny-sweet mussels from their shells, feasting on spring.

3 to 5 medium shallots, cut into thin rings

Extra-virgin olive oil, for sautéing

3 to 5 strips lemon peel (shave away any white pith)

2 stalks thinly sliced celery and leaves

9 small French breakfast or Easter egg radishes, cut in half lengthwise

2 tablespoons salted butter

Kosher salt and freshly ground black pepper

½ cup dry white wine, such as Grüner Veltliner, White Bordeaux, or Vinho Verde

½ cup water

15 to 20 mussels (larger ones are better), beards removed and scrubbed

TOPPINGS (ANY ONE OR A MIX)

1 handful borage flowers or fresh chervil

3 to 5 pea tendrils

¼ cup fresh parsley leaves, torn

CRISPY PORK + FENNEL MEATBALLS IN UMAMI BROTH

MAKES 4 SERVINGS

When spring arrives at last, I feel freer to dole out the final, coveted batches of the prior season's preserved foods. Bottled bright flavors make all the difference, inspiring a new playfulness, witnessing spring sweetness come back on the scene. This dish borrows from the array of flavors I experienced during travels to Japan. Many elements rally to harmonize: delicate meets rich, umami, and tangy. The Shrimp Umami Stock is a roundly savory layer, pleasurable to sip all on its own. Chewy noodles anchor spice-flecked, burnished meatballs. Each of the other elements is meant to take this-and-that style, one texture followed by another, with a tangle of noodles. It is especially fun to place the various jars in the center of the table, unscrew lids from the precious condiments, and let friends choose which their favorite combinations are as conversations and the meal unfolds. It is easy to make enough melted onions to have extra, so that you may use them for the Sage-Buttermilk-Rye Pot Pies (page 257) or any dish that benefits from a little extra.

ROASTED TOMATOES

3 or 4 heirloom tomatoes, sliced crosswise into medium thick slices

Extra-virgin olive oil, to drizzle

Kosher salt and freshly ground black pepper

MELTED ONIONS

8 to 10 any small onions or a mix of whole cipollini, pearl onions, small shallots

Extra-virgin olive oil, to drizzle

JAPANESISH CUCUMBER PICKLES (MAKES 4 OUNCES)

1 Persian or ½ English cucumber, sliced into ⅛-inch-thick coins on a mandoline

Kosher salt, to sprinkle

Rice vinegar, enough to submerge

Roast the tomatoes and make the melted onions: Preheat the oven to 300°F. Arrange the tomatoes on a sheet pan and generously drizzle with the olive oil. Lightly season with salt and pepper. Roast the tomatoes on the upper rack, checking after 1 hour, rotating or scooting lesser-cooked slices to the perimeter of the pan, swapping for those that are more roasted, their liquid more cooked away. After 2 hours, if any still appear to hold their water, roast them a little longer until dry at their surface. Meanwhile, cook the onions. Arrange unpeeled onions in a single layer in an 8-inch skillet and drizzle lightly with the oil. Agitate the pan to coat all surfaces in the oil. Roast on the lower rack for 45 to 55 minutes, checking halfway through to turn them over. Onions are done when they give when gently pressed with the back of a spoon.

Transfer the roasted tomatoes to a squat jar, keeping the slices intact as you layer them as best you can. Once all are roasted, allow them to cool in the jar. Store the tomatoes sealed in the refrigerator for up to 1 week or pour olive oil to submerge the slices and freeze, leaving enough headspace for expansion, for up to 6 months. This can be made 1 week in advance.

Allow the onions to cool fully in the pan, set on a wire rack. When they are cool to the touch, peel the outermost and tougher layers from the root end, revealing whole, tender onions or shallots underneath. This step can be done up to 1 day in advance.

Make the pickles: Arrange the cucumber slices shingled in layers, lining a colander, sprinkling each layer lightly with salt as you go. Set the colander into the sink as the slices release their juices, 20 to 30 minutes. Rinse them well, then take a few slices into a cluster, squeezing them of most of their liquid. Place the squeezed bunches into a half-pint jar as you go, working in batches until there are no more. Pour enough rice vinegar to cover cucumbers, then press the pile down to submerge fully. Seal and chill. These may be eaten half an hour later but can be made up to 1 day in advance.

Make the meatballs: Warm a large cast-iron skillet over medium heat. When hot, drizzle the olive oil and swirl the pan to coat. Bloom the fennel seeds in the oil and then sauté the onions, stirring occasionally. After 3 minutes add the garlic, stir to incorporate, and sauté the mixture until the garlic is fragrant and the onions are softened and translucent, 3 to 4 minutes more.

Transfer the onion mixture to a large bowl. Add the red pepper flakes, salt, pepper, and bread crumbs and stir to combine. Add the pork, egg, and parsley and mix with your hands until uniform.

Do the fry test—take a small amount of the pork mixture and pan-fry it until browned. Taste for seasoning and adjust as needed.

Gently roll the mixture into 1½-inch meatballs, set onto a small tray after forming. Handle the mixture as you would dough and do not overwork. Refrigerate the meatballs. This can be done 1 day in advance. Bring them out 30 minutes before you plan to cook them.

Put a large cast-iron skillet over medium-high heat and drizzle with olive oil. Cook four or five meatballs at a time so as not to crowd the pan. After 3 minutes undisturbed, roll the meatballs to turn. Continue cooking undisturbed for a minute or so at a stretch, rolling the meatballs to lesser-browned sides, until they are caramelized and crispy in parts, 7 to 8 minutes total. As one batch becomes ready, transfer the meatballs to a bowl and cook the remainder.

Boil a pot of well-salted water and cook the noodles according to the package instructions for al dente. Meanwhile, warm the stock in a saucepan over medium heat. Drizzle a small amount of sesame oil into a mixing bowl, grease the sides, and use tongs to transfer the cooked noodles to the bowl. Add a ladleful of the broth and toss the noodles in it to keep them from sticking. Keep the broth warm as you cook the mushrooms.

Make the shiitakes: In the same pan used to cook the meatballs, over medium-high heat, add the sesame oil and swirl to coat. Add the mushrooms and immediately agitate pan to coat them in the oil. Lower the heat to medium. After 1 minute, add the water and toss the mushrooms as the liquid roils. Season with salt and sauté 1 more minute. Add the rice vinegar, agitate the pan to coat, and sauté 1 more minute. Remove the pan from the heat.

Ladle the broth into shallow bowls. Twist lengths of pasta into piles, divided evenly among the bowls. Nestle in 5 meatballs, some onions, and a few tomatoes per bowl. Add a cluster of mushrooms, pickled cucumbers, and a generous handful of greens to each bowl. Eat at once.

MEATBALLS

Olive oil, for sautéing

2 teaspoons fennel seeds

1 small onion, minced (½ cup)

2 garlic cloves, finely grated on a Microplane

1 teaspoon red pepper flakes

1 teaspoon kosher salt

1 teaspoon freshly ground black pepper

1 tablespoon bread crumbs

1 pound ground pork

1 egg

3 tablespoons chopped parsley

8 ounces udon noodles

1 quart Shrimp Umami Stock (page 84)

Sesame oil

VINEGARED SHIITAKES

1 tablespoon sesame oil

¼ pound small shiitake mushrooms, sliced into halves if small or into thirds if large

1 tablespoon water

Kosher salt

1 tablespoon rice vinegar

4 generous handfuls of tender mixed greens, such as small garlic mustard leaves, ground elder, radish sprouts, parsley, or pea shoots

CRISPY PORK + FENNEL MEATBALLS IN UMAMI BROTH

SEARED SCALLOPS + VEGGIE GRAVEL

MAKES 2 SERVINGS

As our cottage became a destination for travelers near and far, we had a chef from Alaska come for a stay. I created this recipe to make sure she felt both at home and impressed with the caliber of food. The salad is finely chopped into a uniform mixture—hence the name "gravel"—creating a marvelously crunchy, juicy background to the meaty scallops.

Prep the scallops: Rinse and pat the scallops dry, then season with salt. Allow them to come to room temperature while you make the veggie gravel.

Make the veggie gravel: In a medium bowl combine the celery, radishes or cucumber, preserved lemon, mint, olives, and olive oil together until well incorporated. Set aside.

Heat a large cast-iron skillet over high heat. Turn to medium-high once hot, add a tablespoon of the olive oil, and swirl to coat. As soon as it shimmers, add half the scallops, keeping space between them to avoid crowding. Cook for a minute, then add half the butter, dragging it around the scallops using a knife or tongs as it foams.

Sear the scallops, 3 minutes on the first side to develop a golden crust, then turn to the second side and baste with the hot fat, tipping the pan toward you to collect spoonfuls, pouring it over scallops continuously, for about 30 seconds. Scallops are ready when they are firm-bouncy when pressed with the back of a large spoon. Transfer them to a plate and repeat with second batch, adding more oil and butter as you did for the first batch.

Add the green garlic and deglaze the pan with the wine. Reduce until it just coats the pan surface, about 1 minute. Add back any accumulated scallop juices from the plate and bring to bubbling once more, then transfer to a small bowl.

Arrange the veggie gravel on a serving platter. Place the scallops on top, garnish with flowers and sedum, pour the green garlic pan sauce over, and season with pepper. Serve at once.

NOTES: If green garlic is out of season, use 3 garlic cloves, very thinly sliced on a mandoline.

Finely chopped arugula and parsley, or chervil leaves, or other soft herbs, can be used in place of the flowers and sedum tips. If you make this in summer, use edible flowers such as borage or nasturtium for garnishes.

SCALLOPS

10 diver scallops (see headnote, page 173)

Kosher salt

3 tablespoons extra-virgin olive oil

2 tablespoons salted butter

1 stalk green garlic, ends trimmed and sliced thinly on a diagonal (see Note)

2 to 3 tablespoons dry white wine such as Vinho Verde or White Bordeaux, to deglaze pan

VEGGIE GRAVEL

5 stalks from the center of a celery bunch, including their leaves, cut into ¼- to ½-inch-thick slices

4 French breakfast radishes or 2 breakfast radishes and half a large purple radish, finely diced, or half a cucumber, diced

Skin from a quarter of a Preserved Meyer Lemon (page 97), sliced very thinly and finely chopped

3 stalks fresh mint, leaves plucked and sliced into chiffonade

¼ cup wrinkly oil-cured black olives, pitted and finely chopped

1 tablespoon extra-virgin olive oil

Mustard or arugula flowers for garnish (see Note)

Sedum tips for garnish (see Note)

Freshly ground black pepper

WILD SALMON + FRIED SAGE GREMOLATA

MAKES 2 SERVINGS

For a number of years, my friends Nelly and Michael Hand of Drifters Fish have express-shipped whole, wild Alaskan salmon during its season, May to September. Fishing season carefully follows wild salmon's spawning migration in brisk Pacific waters, catching fish on their final swim before they perish. Alaskan fisheries are an example of how all fishing operations should function. They are carefully managed with enforced thresholds for catches, so that each season is bountiful for generations to come. I strive to support family fishermen and sustainable fishing practices. Doing so provides some of the most exquisite salmon to be found since they eat only their natural diet and aren't confined to pens or fed antibiotics or dyed pelleted feed.

This dish combines two late spring/early summer darlings—the sockeye and juicy garlic scapes. A zippy take on gremolata punctuates the buttery fillets. Bright seared lemons and crispy sage leaves send all to new heights. This meal can be thrown together fairly quickly once you've made the gremolata.

GREMOLATA

Finely grated zest from 3 lemons

Zest strips from 1 Meyer lemon, any bitter white pith removed, sliced very thinly

1 tablespoon finely sliced garlic scapes or garlic chives, or 1 teaspoon minced garlic

1 teaspoon finely sliced garlic chives

Sea salt and freshly ground black pepper

SALMON

1 pound wild sockeye salmon, portioned into 2 fillets

Sea salt and freshly ground black pepper

1 tablespoon extra-virgin olive oil

1 tablespoon salted butter

1 Meyer lemon, cut in half horizontally

SAGE

2 tablespoons walnut oil

1 handful fresh sage leaves

Make the gremolata: In a small bowl, toss together the lemon zest and strips, the garlic scapes and chives, and season with salt and pepper.

Prep the salmon: Pat the salmon dry and season with salt and pepper on both sides. Let sit at room temperature while you fry the sage.

Fry the sage leaves: Pour 2 tablespoons walnut oil into a heavy sauté pan set over medium heat and heat until shimmering. Pan-fry the sage leaves—they should sizzle on contact. Cook no more than 3 minutes, turning once. They will turn a vivid green through the process. Tap excess oil from each leaf as you remove them from the pan, then place onto absorbent paper, set on a wire rack.

Heat a large cast-iron skillet over medium-high heat. Add the olive oil and when it shimmers, place the salmon skin side down. Sear for 3 minutes, or until the flesh becomes opaque around the edges.

Turn the fillets skin side up and add the butter, dragging it between the two as it foams. Tilt the pan and baste the salmon with the hot fat, using a long-handled large spoon to avoid being burned; repeat tilting and basting for another minute as it cooks. Transfer the salmon to a serving platter.

Sear the lemon halves on medium heat in the remaining butter-oil mixture, 3 minutes or until charred to your liking.

Pile the fried sage leaves, layering with the gremolata mixture, onto the salmon, and serve the seared lemons alongside. Season with salt and pepper to taste and serve at once.

BUTTERMILK PANNA COTTA

MAKES SIX 4-OUNCE SERVINGS

This luscious dessert appears at the Catbird once days are balmy but spring produce—such as rhubarb—is still available. It's a pretty dreamy mix: roasted rhubarb is sweet-tart, the panna cotta is tangy-creamy, and the nuts add a pleasing sweet-savory crunch. Sometimes I layer macerated strawberries with the rhubarb. On other occasions the custard makes a fine dessert for us at home, plain, gobbled up in seconds.

ROASTED RHUBARB

4 stalks rhubarb (deep red is preferable to green)

2 strips each orange and lemon peel

2 star anise

Half a vanilla bean, split open, seeds scraped

2 teaspoons cane sugar

¼ cup cane sugar

Pinch kosher salt

1½ cups heavy cream

Half a vanilla bean, split open, seeds scraped

2 teaspoons plus ¼ teaspoon powdered gelatin

2 teaspoons cold water

1½ cups plus 2 tablespoons full-fat buttermilk

Spiced Nuts (page 77) for garnish

Roast the rhubarb: Preheat the oven to 375°F. Slice the rhubarb on a bias into 2-inch pieces. In a baking dish, toss the rhubarb with the peels, star anise, vanilla bean and seeds, and the 2 teaspoons sugar. Arrange in a single layer. Bake for 20 minutes, or until the rhubarb is juicy and soft but still holds its shape. Set aside to cool to room temperature. Discard the star anise and vanilla bean. This can be done up to 1 week in advance.

Over medium heat, dissolve the ¼ cup sugar and salt into the cream in a medium saucepan, stirring occasionally. Bring the mixture to a bare simmer and remove from heat. Add the vanilla bean and seeds and steep for 1 hour.

In a small saucepan, bloom the gelatin in the cold water and 2 tablespoons buttermilk. Whisk over medium heat until the gelatin is fully dissolved but do not bring the mixture to a boil. Add the gelatin mixture to the cream mixture and whisk to incorporate. Add the remaining 1½ cups buttermilk and whisk all together.

Arrange serving dishes on a small tray. Strain the cream mixture through a fine-mesh sieve into a large measuring cup with a pour spout. Divide the mixture evenly among the six dishes and chill for at least 4 hours, up to overnight.

Spoon (cooled) roasted rhubarb over the top of the panna cotta, followed by little piles of the spiced nuts.

SOUR CHERRY PIE

Before we moved upstate, Jim and I would take day trips to explore nature preserves and to forage. We were traveling through an unassuming working-class neighborhood in Patterson, New Jersey, and my eyes nearly fell out of my head as we passed a glowing, reflectively bright cherry-laden tree at the end of a particular block. I shouted out and Jim obliged me by stopping. I knew I had to try. I knocked on the door, got permission to harvest from an elderly man, and bounded home with numerous containers filled to their brims. (Side note: The forager's motto is always be prepared, for you never know what you may discover.) I later returned to that kind old man's home with slices of cherry pie made with his fruit, and every year I try to carve some time to make a pie commemorating their short season.

Make the dough: Place the flours, cane sugar, and salt in the bowl of a food processor and pulse to combine. Add the cold butter and pulse until the mixture forms pea-size bits. Combine the ice water and vinegar in a measuring cup. In a slow stream, add the ice water–vinegar mixture while pulsing, stopping once a cohesive dough forms. To test, open the lid and squeeze some of the dough in your hand—if it holds together, it is ready. If the dough still crumbles, add just a bit more of the ice water mixture and pulse a few more times. You may end up not using it all.

Empty the dough out onto a long section of plastic wrap, about 24 inches long. Separate the dough into two mounds roughly 10 inches apart, then flatten each to form a disk. Cut plastic wrap in between the disks and then wrap each snugly. Refrigerate for at least 20 minutes to let the dough mellow.

Make the filling: In a large bowl, combine the cherries, cane sugar, cornstarch, orange zest, whiskey, and bitters, and stir. Marinate for at least 20 minutes, up to overnight.

Remove one pastry disk from the refrigerator 15 minutes before attempting to work it. Place the dough between the plastic wrap and a lightly floured sheet of parchment and roll it into a rough circle, ⅛ inch thick, peeling the plastic wrap or parchment away and reflouring at intervals. If the dough becomes smeary or flabby at any point, transfer to a sheet pan and chill in the refrigerator for 10 to 20 minutes. Use the pie tin as a gauge for the needed size—the dough should exceed the pie tin by ½ inch all the way around.

Remove the plastic wrap from the dough and center the inverted pie tin on it. With one hand underneath the parchment and the other on top of the tin, invert the dough, then peel away the parchment. Work your way around the pastry to lift the

CONTINUED →

PASTRY DOUGH

1½ cups all-purpose flour

1 cup rye flour

1 teaspoon cane sugar

1 teaspoon kosher salt

2 sticks salted butter, cubed and freezer-cold (see Notes, page 261)

½ cup ice water

¼ cup apple cider vinegar

FILLING

4 cups sour cherries, pitted

3 tablespoons cane sugar

1 tablespoon cornstarch

1 tablespoon finely grated orange zest

1 tablespoon rye whiskey

3 dashes angostura bitters

1 egg, beaten, for egg wash

2 or 3 tablespoons demerara sugar

overhang with one hand while the other gently presses the pastry flush with the base and to the edge of the pan. Set the tin on a sheet pan and refrigerate.

Bring the remaining disk out 15 minutes before working, as you did the first. Roll the dough between the plastic wrap it was wrapped in and a layer of floured parchment, to ¼ inch thick, its diameter wide enough to exceed the pie tin. Use a ruler and a pizza wheel or a sharp knife to cut dough into ½-inch-wide (or wider, to your preference) strips. Refrigerate the lattice pieces on a sheet pan 15 minutes before attempting to weave them or lay them as an unwoven lattice for easier work.

Bring the bottom pastry from the refrigerator and fill with the sour cherry mixture, mounding it at the center.

Arrange half the strips parallel across the pie, as tightly spaced or open as preferred. Weave the remaining strips at a right angle to the others, pulling back every other strip to weave over and under the first group of strips, and replacing them as the strips have been woven through. Repeat with the remaining strips until the pie has a complete woven lattice surface. Trim any excess overhang, including the bottom pastry, to exceed pie tin by ½ inch. Use lightly wetted fingertips dipped in cold water to seal lattice to the bottom pastry and tuck pastry under, pressing to seal on the pie tin edge.

Paint a thin slick of egg wash onto the pastry, being sure to cover the latticework seams. Use a shallow tablespoon to sprinkle two or three spoonfuls of demerara sugar to coat the pie, then transfer the pie to the freezer for at least 2 hours, up to overnight.

Preheat the oven to 400°F. Bake the pie on a sheet pan for 45 to 55 minutes, rotating after 35 minutes for even baking, until the crust is deeply golden and the filling bubbles.

Cool the pie fully for the filling to set, at least 1 hour. Serve slices with whipped cream, ice cream, or crème fraîche. Any leftovers can be stored at room temperature, wrapped in aluminum foil, for up to 3 days.

NOTE: For an enviable short-crust pastry, distinct little spots of butter must be suspended in the dough so that when it meets the roaring hot oven, the steam released by the butter melting produces those sought-after flaky layers in the crust. Do not handle the pastry more than absolutely necessary; work it while it is cold, so that the butter does not become smeary. The apple cider vinegar hinders the formation of the gluten strands, producing a more tender pastry. If you overwork the pastry, it may still end up tough, but this is one way to ensure success.

GINGER-PECAN STRAWBERRY STREUSEL CAKE

MAKES 6 TO 8 SERVINGS

This cake sets a cheery tone any way you slice it. It is decadent without being sugary, loaded with fruit and spice. I sometimes have a piece with coffee for a midday treat. You could enjoy the cake with a dollop of crème fraîche for an extra seductive dessert or bring it in tow on a spring picnic. Once you combine the ingredients for each component, simply layer them and bake.

Combine the filling ingredients: In a medium bowl combine the strawberry slices, grated ginger, and cane sugar in a large bowl. Fold to incorporate and set aside.

Preheat the oven to 350°F. Generously grease a 12-inch enameled skillet or 9-inch springform pan with pecan oil.

Make the streusel: Toast the pecans on a rimmed sheet pan until fragrant and slightly darkened, 8 minutes. Let cool, then coarsely chop them. Stir together the all-purpose flour, sugars, and salt in a small bowl. Add the cubed butter and toss to coat. Use your fingers to rub the butter into the dry ingredients until the butter is incorporated and the mixture is chunky. Add the chopped pecans and fold into streusel. Chill for at least 15 minutes before using.

Mix the batter: In a medium bowl, use a fork to stir together the flours, baking powder, baking soda, orange zest, and salt. Set aside. In a large bowl, beat the butter and sugars with an electric mixer until light and fluffy, about 4 minutes. Pause to scrape down the sides of the bowl as needed to reincorporate. Add the eggs one at a time, beating after each addition, followed by the pecan oil. Beat just until uniform. Mix in the kefir on low speed (the mixture may look curdled, which is fine). Gradually add the flour mixture and mix to combine.

Spoon half the batter into the skillet and spread into an even layer. Fold the strawberry filling one more time to evenly distribute the sugar, ginger, and juices, then transfer half to top the batter. Spoon the remaining batter over the berries, smooth again, then add the remaining strawberries, including any juices. Spoon the streusel to top the berries, covering any nooks and crannies.

Place the skillet on a parchment-lined sheet pan and bake 45 to 55 minutes, until a skewer inserted into the center comes out clean. Run a thin butter knife along the perimeter to free the cake from the sides of the skillet, and allow to cool on a wire rack for 15 minutes, then slice into wedges. Store any leftovers wrapped in foil at room temperature for up to 3 days.

FILLING

2 cups strawberries, sliced

2-inch piece ginger, peeled and finely grated using a Microplane

2 teaspoons cane sugar

STREUSEL TOPPING

½ cup pecans

½ cup all-purpose flour

2 tablespoons packed brown sugar

2 tablespoons demerara sugar

¼ teaspoon kosher salt

6 tablespoons cold unsalted butter, cut into small cubes

BATTER

1 cup all-purpose flour

½ cup buckwheat flour

1 teaspoon baking powder

1 teaspoon baking soda

1 teaspoon grated orange zest

½ teaspoon kosher salt

8 tablespoons salted butter, softened

½ cup cane sugar

2 tablespoons packed light brown sugar

2 eggs

2 tablespoons pecan oil, plus more for greasing the pan

½ cup whole milk kefir

summer

Summer manifests in a great pinnacle. The diversity of harvests, wild foods, colors, flavors, sounds, and smells . . . so much reaches its peak. This is a place we long for in the barren days of winter. In real time, it is dizzying to keep up with the garden and its pests, to capture these moments of ripeness and get them on the plate in all their sunshiny glory, and to enshrine the season in sauces, preserves, even suspended in ice cube trays to be relished when our palates (and souls) could use some brightening. It seems fitting that it's the hummingbirds—with their impossibly quick wings—that fill our garden at this time of year, zooming from flower to flower in a flash.

JULY 25

The symphony of frogs arrives just before August. The cicadas began in earnest a week or two earlier, and tomato shoulders are turning their seductive final hues. The house finches seek out the mustard greens seeds at dusk. I haven't had the heart to remove them, though they have gone to seed, instead allowing them to stay put for these sweet birds. It brings me great joy to see them visit: the scarlet male alights, floating on top of the tangle of spindly stems, a vision the color of wine as I look out the window from my writing desk, freeing the tiny round seeds from their pods as part of their evening forage.

Speaking of forage, we scored a great haul of wineberries yesterday. They were impossibly red and at peak ripeness, bursting sweet and juicy. Make sure to harvest them wearing boots in case of poison ivy or mud, and always wear long sleeves if you can remember—they are quite thorny. Yesterday I did not, so I have many shallow scratches that will memorialize our harvest. But it was worth it.

AUGUST 13

The dog days of summer. There is a ubiquitous din of crickets. The hummingbirds are fighting their tiny avian territory battles and the gardens are in their fullest glory, though there is evidence of the first beginnings of dieback. I have entered full-on combat with a chipmunk that has relentlessly committed to gouge small holes into numerous ripe—and now even unripe—tomatoes.

Despite that, this year's tomato harvest is promising. I had an initial bounty harvested just a few days ago, including many of my large Cherokee Purples and the first flush of my new favorite, Santorini. The Santorini came as part of a collection of seeds gifted to me from the amazing fifteen-year-old tomato grower, Emma Biggs in Toronto, who graciously sent an impressive array of heirloom seeds I'd never heard of before. The diversity of this year's tomato plants bears fruits in many tones, shapes, and flavors both rich and bright.

The Santorini tomato is ribbed and a gorgeous bright red. The Cherokee Purples have delivered their customary juiciness and tangy rich flavor. The Sungolds are cheery, reliable, and similar to last year, surpassing the 8-foot-tall frames we installed to support them. They produce abundantly. We treat them as if they're candy, grasping handfuls of the plump fruits to pop into our mouths.

I am going to make a tomato confit to begin preserving the season, once I can pull myself from the ongoing bird and chipmunk dramas playing out on the deck. There is another round of amending the soil for all of the potted plants. That care will boost their production and blooms for a last crucial chapter. Each day in my morning garden walk, I dutifully trim away yellowing squash leaves, snap away suckers, kill tomato fleas, deadhead cosmos and anything else needing it, and protect the zinnias—first time growing these—as best I know how. I have learned they are no match for an intrepid woodchuck.

SEPTEMBER 3

It is late summer on the calendar but it feels like we are greeting fall. I've worked so hard, each day paying attention, relishing the time with a cup of coffee and my scissors in hand, keeping on top of what to harvest, why, and toward what end, as well as doing the daily grooming. There are small but crucial observations, connecting to the changes, good and bad. Everyone is going to meet the end of their timeline sooner than I'd like. As I consider this, I sit and watch Tarzan, one of the tiny red squirrels who visits daily, streak down and back up the big white pine, feasting on his small pile of treats before soaring off into the tree canopy.

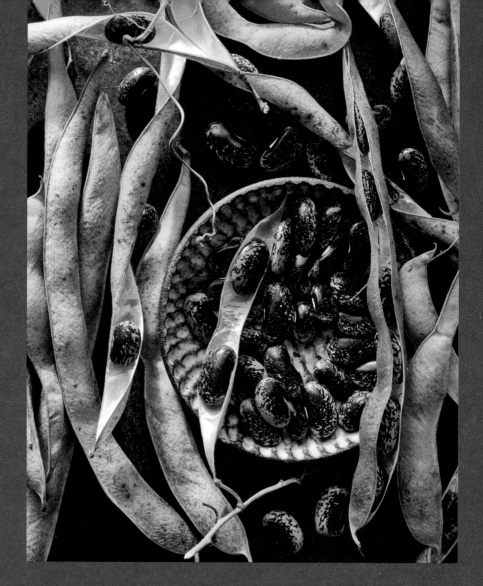

The scarlet runner bean tower is looking majestic. It adds a real beauty to the garden, a wonderful surprise I couldn't have imagined when I made the plant map early in the year. Currently, there are multiple pendulous pods tempting to be harvested. I have done exactly that with many. Young pods offer a surprising juicy crunch. Many of the others will be allowed to mature until the pods become starchy and fibrous, then turn brown and dry to a papery crisp. I will harvest the plump, beautifully patterned beans and devise stews for colder days, shelling them while seated in front of the wood-fired stove.

Today and this weekend the weather is going to be balmy again. But this whole past week, the night has brought with it a chill, a clear reminder that the seasons are changing. All of the hummingbirds will migrate away. They have been one of our greatest joys this season. Many other birds will, too, along with the butterflies. But for now, it is still a dreamscape and I feel quite lucky to live here, participating in the vistas of all garden things.

EAT'CHA GARDEN

MAKES 2 SERVINGS

This dish is an homage to summer produce. I like combining differently hued elements to eat the rainbow as much as possible, dazzling the eyes and ensuring any meal is packed with a range of nutrients. The different kinds of crunch also make a refreshing way to start the day. In this preparation, cooling yogurt offsets the spicy jalapeño, and the punchy dressings and toppings make a zippy foil to mild flavors. Gomasio is a Japanese sesame-salt spice blend, available at specialty markets.

ZUCCHINI NOODLES

1 medium zucchini, sliced finely lengthwise with the julienne attachment on a mandoline

1 tablespoon extra-virgin olive oil

Juice from half a lemon

2 tablespoons chopped parsley

Kosher salt

2 eggs (see Notes)

SALAD

3 to 5 young scarlet runner beans (substitute double the amount of thin green or wax beans if you cannot get fresh scarlet runner beans)

1 cherry or sweet Hungarian pepper, sliced thinly into rings

Half an orange or red jalapeño or other similar medium-heat chile pepper, sliced very thinly on a mandoline, seeds discarded

2 teaspoons extra-virgin olive oil

1 teaspoon fish sauce

¾ teaspoon sherry vinegar

Freshly ground black pepper

½ cup full-fat Greek yogurt

Gomasio or everything bagel sprinkles and crispy fried shallots for garnish (see Notes)

Make the zucchini noodles: Toss the zucchini strands with the olive oil, lemon juice, parsley, and a pinch of salt. Taste, adjust seasoning as needed, and set aside. This step can be prepared up to 1 day in advance.

In a small saucepan, bring enough water to cover eggs to a rolling boil (do not add the eggs yet). Gently lower refrigerator-cold eggs into the water and return to a rolling boil for 30 seconds. Lower the heat to a simmer for 6 minutes. Remove the eggs using a slotted spoon and plunge into an ice bath. Leave them to chill as you do the remaining prep, peeling their shells once cool enough to handle.

Make the salad: In a mixing bowl, combine the runner beans, Hungarian pepper, and chile pepper with the olive oil, fish sauce, sherry vinegar, and black pepper and toss to coat. Taste and adjust the seasoning as needed.

In two shallow bowls, swirl a base layer of Greek yogurt. Add a pile of the zucchini noodles, tossed once more in their dressing before dividing between bowls. Nestle a rainbow salad cluster beside the zucchini, and top each with an egg, cut in half. Finish with gomasio, crispy shallots, and freshly ground pepper.

NOTES: For perfectly peeled custardy eggs, use eggs that are at least 2 weeks old, as they release more easily from their shells.

Keep special sprinkles such as gomasio or everything bagel topping, along with crispy shallots at the ready in your pantry. These flavorful, crispy bits instantly make a humble meal special.

PILLOWY FRENCH TOAST +
WILD BLUEBERRY COMPOTE

MAKES 4 SERVINGS

When I was a child, anytime my Ma made French toast, she would top it with grape jelly and sour cream. Sounds bizarre probably—but playing the game of sweet-versus-tart/savory, it was also delicious. Carrying that tradition forward, I've taken it to the next level with foraged Wild Blueberry Compote, paired with a blend of crème fraîche and thick yogurt. You could opt for one or the other dairy in a pinch. Do not skimp on double soaking the bread, however. This step produces toasts that are lush and moist all the way through, an excellent textural contrast once they are well caramelized in the pan.

In a shallow baking dish, use a fork to whisk together the eggs, buttermilk, half-and-half, orange zest and juice, cinnamon, and salt.

Combine the crème fraîche and yogurt in a bowl and whip together until silky and uniform. Place in the refrigerator while the French toast cooks.

Dip the bread slices, one at a time, into the egg mixture to coat. Puncture the bread a few times with a fork, turn to the second side, and repeat. Transfer the slices to a plate as you work, stacking one on top of the next.

Preheat the oven to 180°F. Place a wire rack on top of a sheet pan on the top rack.

Heat half the grapeseed oil over medium heat in a large nonstick skillet. Add half the butter. As it foams, dip three bread slices into the egg mixture, piercing each with a fork again and turning once, then carefully transferring to the pan to cook, three slices at a time.

Repeat dipping and cooking slices in batches until deeply golden brown on both sides, 5 to 7 minutes total per batch. Add a small additional drizzle of oil or dab of butter if the pan looks dry, tilting the pan to coat as the fats sizzle. Lower the heat as needed so as not to burn the toasts while they cook. Transfer the finished toasts to the oven as you cook the remaining batches.

Divide the French toast among the plates. Dollop the crème fraîche mixture, then swirl the blueberry compote on top.

4 eggs

½ cup full-fat buttermilk

½ cup half-and-half or heavy cream

Finely grated zest from 1 orange, plus 2 tablespoons freshly squeezed juice (see Note)

1 teaspoon ground cinnamon

Pinch kosher salt

½ cup crème fraîche

½ cup full-fat Greek yogurt

Eight ½-inch-thick slices challah, cinnamon, or brioche bread

1 tablespoon grapeseed oil, plus more as needed

1 tablespoon salted butter, plus more as needed for pan and to serve

8 to 10 tablespoons Wild Blueberry Compote (page 100)

NOTE: It may sound obvious, but always zest citrus before you juice it—it is much easier to hold onto the fruit before its juice has been squeezed.

BUTTERY SCRAMBLED EGGS + CHANTERELLES

MAKES 2 SERVINGS

Chanterelle mushrooms impart a fruity, aromatic, meaty quality, excellent when paired with mild foods such as toast, eggs, polenta, or pasta. The magic of these eggs is in cooking them slowly. If they start sticking, turn the heat even lower or remove the pan from the heat altogether as you stir. Cook them not fast, but rather deliberately, to render them into soft, luscious curds.

4 eggs

Kosher salt

2 tablespoons salted butter

½ to 1 cup halved tender chanterelle mushrooms (see Note)

2 slices Sourdough Bread (page 68), toasted

Flake salt

1 tablespoon coarsely chopped garlic chives or finely snipped chives

Freshly ground black pepper

Crack the eggs into a small bowl and use a fork to beat them and a generous pinch of kosher salt until frothy.

Set a small enameled pan over medium-high heat. Add 1 tablespoon of the butter when the pan is hot. Swirl to coat, lower the heat to medium, and when the foaming subsides, add the mushrooms. Vigorously agitate the pan to coat the mushrooms in the butter and season them with a pinch of kosher salt.

Sauté the chanterelles undisturbed for 1 minute. Agitate the pan again and arrange lesser-cooked sides facedown. After another minute, move the remaining lesser-cooked mushrooms toward the hottest part of pan to brown further. Remove the pan from the heat and set aside.

Melt the rest of the butter in the pan over medium heat, then turn to low once the butter foams. Pour the egg mixture in once the foaming has subsided and leave undisturbed for 10 to 15 seconds.

Use a silicone spatula to drag the eggs from the pan edge to the center, repeating in an X pattern, moving some of the eggs from center outward and then outward to center, until you have dragged all of the mixture.

As curds form, swirl around the periphery of the pan in smooth, broad strokes, alternating with dragging the spatula across the bottom to ensure the eggs do not stick. Repeat this process until they resemble wet but fully formed curds, about 3 minutes. Eggs should appear soft and wet but hold their shape.

Remove the pan from the heat. Arrange the toast on plates. Spoon the scrambled eggs onto the toasts and top with the chanterelles. Scatter the flake salt and chives over all. Add a few grinds of pepper, to your taste, and eat at once.

NOTE: This will be delicious no matter what mushrooms you find, so ultimately, use any mushrooms available to you. That said, richer tasting mushrooms produce a more interesting result. If you can't find chanterelles, aim for shiitake, chestnut—even morel or maitake mushrooms—if you have a choice.

SUMMER SKILLET: CRISPY EGGS + SCARLET RUNNER BEANS

MAKES 2 SERVINGS

Scarlet runner beans are one of my favorite crops. Not only do their flowers lure hummingbirds through their extended season but the young pods burst with a juicy crunch, compelling the thought that maybe I'd just eat them all straight from the vine. When allowed to mature, they make an excellent shelled bean (see Stewed Scarlet Runner Beans, page 276) whose pattern is reminiscent of pink and black leopard print. The whole experience is *Gezamkunstwerk,* basically, a total work of art.

This simple but lively breakfast makes use of stale bread, transformed into a crunchy topping you'll want to sprinkle onto everything. To make, I carefully dismantle a small sourdough heel, pressing the tip of a chef's knife to divide it into small chunks, and go gently bashing away using a mortar until it's a mix of chunky and fine crumbs. You'll end up with more herbed bread crumbs than called for—any leftovers can be used for the Puntarelle + Tardivo with Punchy Dress (page 201), or they can be stored at room temperature in a sealed jar for up to a week.

Make the bread crumbs: In a small cast-iron skillet set over medium heat, drizzle the oil. Once the pan is hot, add the bread crumbs and stir until uniformly coated. After cooking 2 to 3 minutes, add the red pepper flakes and kosher salt, stir to combine, and continue cooking until golden and fragrant, stirring occasionally so that the crumbs brown evenly. Transfer to a small bowl to cool. Once they're at room temperature, add the chopped parsley and stir to incorporate.

Crack the eggs into two small shallow bowls and set aside. In a medium heavy skillet over medium heat, sauté the scarlet runner beans in oil until tender but still bright green, 7 to 9 minutes (if using green beans, cook for half as long—no more than 5 minutes). Turn the beans periodically as they cook. Halfway through, add a tablespoon of water to help them along—the steam produced from the vigorous bubbling will soften their membranes.

Using tongs, hold a bean at its center to see if there is a slight droop. If so, they are ready. If not, cook another 1 to 2 minutes, until they pass the droop test. Push the beans to the perimeter of the pan, drizzle a little oil in the center, and add the eggs. They should immediately sizzle upon contact. Cook undisturbed for 3 to 5 minutes. Once the whites closest to the yolk are set, remove the pan from the heat.

Shower the pan with the crispy bread crumbs and season with ground black pepper and flake salt. Bring to the table, set on a trivet, and divide between two plates.

HERBED BREAD CRUMBS

1 teaspoon extra-virgin olive oil

¼ cup coarse bread crumbs

½ teaspoon red pepper flakes

Pinch kosher salt

2 tablespoons chopped parsley

2 eggs

10 to 12 scarlet runner beans or 20 to 24 tender green beans, stem end trimmed

Extra-virgin olive oil, for sautéing

Freshly ground black pepper and flake salt

VEGAN MORNING BOWL

MAKES 4 SERVINGS

This bowl is varied and bright and sets a happy tone for the day. It is also meant to be served at room temperature for less fuss on a warm morning. I like to make batches of beans before I need them, in part to have sustaining food at the ready (I'm one of those people who gets hangry), and in part because I love when bean liquor, the liquid from cooking beans, melds with the aromatics and thickens a bit. The liquor becomes its own sauce when you take care to add aromatics, so even a simple pot of beans can be heavenly. The elements are added in piles, whether plucked from your garden, foraged on a jaunt, or gathered at the market. The many fresh veggies together make a joyful experience, as do the fermented and jarred condiments sprinkled just before serving.

1 cup dried cranberry beans

3 tablespoons extra-virgin olive oil, plus more to drizzle

1 dried chile pepper, such as cayenne or chipotle

1 teaspoon kosher salt

2 heirloom tomatoes, such as Cherokee Purple or Pineapple

5 or 7 smaller tomatoes, such as Sungold, Pink Bumblebee, or Santorini

2 or 3 Persian or Kirby cucumbers (thinner-skinned varieties are best—use 1 English cucumber if you cannot find these)

1 cup curly parsley, chopped

Skin from a third of a Preserved Meyer Lemon (page 97), sliced very thinly crossways

1½ cups lambsquarters, or baby spinach, watercress, or mache

1 avocado

Fermented Green Garlic (page 89) for garnish (see Note)

Ramp Salt (page 63) for garnish

Sedum, purslane tips, or sunflower sprouts for garnish

Pistachio Dukkah (page 64) for garnish

Soak the beans with enough water to cover by 2 inches and let sit overnight on the counter.

The next day, strain the beans in a colander and transfer to a saucepan. Cover them with enough water to submerge by ½ inch and add the olive oil and dried chile. Bring the mixture to a boil, then lower to a simmer and cover. Cook the beans for 30 minutes or until tender. Remove the pan from the heat and season with the salt. Stir to incorporate, taste, and adjust seasoning as needed. Remove the pan lid and allow the beans to cool.

Cut the larger tomatoes into sturdy wedges and the smaller ones in half. Slice the cucumbers in half lengthwise, then horizontally into chunky slices.

Stir the parsley and preserved lemon into the beans. Taste and adjust the seasoning as needed.

Divide the beans among shallow bowls. Nestle piles of cucumbers, tomatoes, whichever greens you're using, and the avocado, cut into bite-size chunks. Drizzle a small bit of olive oil to moisten the tomatoes and cucumbers, then season all with fermented green garlic and ramp salt to taste. Add a cluster of sedum/purslane/sprouts and a shower of dukkah.

NOTE: You may swap the fermented green garlic for many of the other pickles or ferments in this book: pickled pearl onions (see page 165), Juniper + Cumin Meyer Lemon Kraut (page 90), Moroccan Pickled Carrots (page 86), and so on.

BROWN BUTTER + LEMON CECAMARITI

Cecamariti, one of the first recipes I tried from Jenn Louis's superb book *Pasta by Hand*, hails from Lazio and translates to "husband blinders," as they become "blinded" by this marvelous dish. Dressed in brown butter and crispy and bright elements, everyone agrees that this chewy, spindle-shaped pasta is a home run.

Make the dough: In a measuring cup, stir the yeast, tepid water, and wine together to dissolve the yeast. Set it aside until the yeast becomes foamy, about 10 minutes. Add the date syrup and olive oil and stir to combine.

In a large bowl, combine the all-purpose flour and kosher salt. Slowly pour the yeast mixture into the flour mixture, stirring to incorporate as you pour. Once all the liquid is incorporated, knead the mixture on a work surface until a soft, cohesive dough forms. It shouldn't be sticky, dry, or stiff. Grease the bowl with a small amount of oil and place the dough into it. Cover loosely with a damp tea towel or plastic wrap and allow to rise for 1 hour.

Line a sheet pan with parchment and a light dusting of semolina flour. Empty the dough onto a work surface and cut a narrow chunk from it—about the width of two fingers—and cover the remaining dough with the tea towel or plastic wrap. Roll the chunk into an even rope about ½ inch in diameter, dusting the work surface lightly with all-purpose flour if the dough sticks. Use a bench scraper to cut the rope into ½-inch segments, then roll each piece back and forth to create spindle shapes about 3 inches long. Transfer the cecamariti to the semolina-dusted sheet pan as you work, repeating the process to shape the remaining dough. Agitate the sheet pan to lightly coat cecamariti so that they do not stick to each other as the pan fills. Refrigerate the cecamariti, covered in plastic wrap, up to 2 days, or freeze.

Prepare the sauce: In a light-colored 9-inch skillet, sauté the sunflower seeds in 1 teaspoon butter over medium heat until aromatic and golden, about 5 minutes. Transfer them to a small dish. In the same pan, melt the remaining 4 tablespoons butter over medium heat. Once the foaming subsides, swirl the pan. The butter will start to produce a white froth as it toasts—swirl occasionally to prevent burning. Once the butter is the color of honey and nutty smelling, remove the pan from the heat.

Bring a large pot of generously salted water to boil, lower the heat to simmer, and cook a third of the pasta until they float to the surface, 2 to 3 minutes. Immediately transfer them with a slotted spoon to the pan with the brown butter. Toss the dumplings thoroughly in the butter to coat.

Divide the cecamariti and brown butter between two plates. Scatter the sunflower seeds and torn olives, then add the lemon zest. Pluck the basil leaves from their stems, tear the basil leaves over the top, and season with flake salt and freshly ground pepper.

DOUGH

1 tablespoon plus 1 teaspoon active dry yeast

¾ cup tepid water

¼ cup dry white wine, at room temperature

1 tablespoon date syrup

1 tablespoon extra-virgin olive oil

3 cups all-purpose flour, plus more for dusting

1 teaspoon kosher salt

Semolina flour for dusting

SAUCE

¼ cup lightly salted roasted sunflower seeds

4 tablespoons plus 1 teaspoon salted butter

5 to 7 Castelvetrano olives, flattened, pitted, flesh coarsely torn

Finely grated zest from half a lemon

2 or 3 stems fresh basil

Flake salt and freshly ground black pepper

GRAND AIOLI SUMMER FEAST

MAKES 4 SERVINGS AS A MEAL OR 6 SERVINGS AS A SNACK

This nearly no-cook feast highlights colorful early summer bounty, paired with a luscious sauce through which to drag everything. By all appearances, the abundance of elements looks like it takes a good bit of effort to put together, but hooray, it does not. That is the magic of this dish, because who wants to cook when it's hot out? And who also would like to eat outdoors, making minimal ovations to do so, and reap great results? Whole, tender veggies present in piles alongside plump, lightly poached seafood. Use what is peak ripe from your garden or the market and you will eat royally. Use this as a guide and set off to make your own delectable version. I use duck eggs as often as possible when making aioli, as they produce an extra creamy result. If you cannot find duck eggs, chicken eggs work just fine.

AIOLI (MAKES 1 CUP)

2 eggs

Juice from half a lemon

1 tablespoon Dijon mustard

1 teaspoon kosher salt

½ cup grapeseed or sunflower oil

POACHING LIQUID

1 to 2 cups stock (I use corn stock, page 82)

½ cup dry white wine

2 strips lemon peel

1 small stalk fennel with its fronds

1 shallot, quartered

Petals from 2 wild bergamot flowers, or 1 stem fresh oregano

½ to 1 teaspoon kosher salt (season the poaching liquid like the sea)

½ teaspoon cayenne

Make the aioli: With your hand placed over a small bowl, crack an egg and empty it into your palm. Slightly part your fingers to allow the white to fall through into the bowl beneath, passing the egg from one hand to the other until all the egg white has slipped through, leaving you with only the yolk. Place the yolk in a medium high-sided bowl. Repeat the process with the second egg (save the egg whites for My Mother's Gruyère Soufflé, page 246).

Add the lemon juice, mustard, and salt. Using an immersion blender, blend them together until uniform.

Add the oil in a bare drizzle, blending continuously, until emulsified. It's okay to occasionally pause adding the oil so you can incorporate the mixture fully.

Once the mixture is emulsified, it will appear uniform, thick, and silky. Taste and adjust the seasoning as needed and pulse to blend. Transfer the aioli to a squat jar and seal. Refrigerate for at least 4 hours, or up to overnight, to set. This step can be done 3 days in advance.

Poach the seafood: Combine the poaching liquid ingredients in a medium saucepan and bring to a boil. Add the mussels and cover the pan with its lid, cooking the mussels until their shells have opened, about 6 minutes. Use a slotted spoon or julep strainer to transfer the mussels to another large plate as you poach the remaining elements.

Lower the heat to simmer and poach the shrimp until opaque, 4 or 5 minutes. Strain and set the shrimp aside with the mussels.

Gently poach the fish pieces until opaque, 3 to 5 minutes. Salmon can be cooked medium rare, whereas the others should be cooked fully, until the meat flakes but retains its tenderness. Carefully remove the pieces using the slotted spoon or julep strainer and add the fish segments to the plate with the other seafood.

Strain any solids from the poaching liquid and compost them—the poaching liquid will be a delicious elixir for yet another meal. Freeze or use for cooking beans or grains.

Arrange the asparagus spears in a steamer basket, placed inside a saucepan with 1 inch of water. Place the lid on and steam over high heat until the asparagus turns bright green and the stems become just tender, 4 to 6 minutes, then shock in an ice bath until cool to the touch. Pat dry and set aside. Boil potatoes in salted water until tender when pierced with a sharp knife. Drain them in a colander and allow to cool to room temperature.

Arrange the veggies into piles on a serving platter around a bowl placed in the center to accommodate the aioli. Alternate cooked and raw elements—and variety in color—as you plate. Peel the eggs, slice them in half, and add them to the platter. Nestle in the seafood and fish as you add everything to the platter. Dollop the aioli into a bowl in the center and bring to the table. Keep flake salt and freshly ground black pepper nearby to season to taste. Eat at once.

SEAFOOD

8 to 12 mussels, scrubbed and beards removed

4 to 6 jumbo wild shrimp, shell on and deveined

8 ounces buttery fish such as cod, halibut, sable, or wild salmon, cut into 1 by 3-inch segments

1 bunch asparagus, woody ends snapped off (save for stock, pages 79, 80, and 82)

5 to 7 small waxy potatoes, such as new potatoes or Yukon gold potatoes

2 handfuls slender wax beans, green beans, scarlet runner beans, or a mix

3 small pattypan or summer squash, cut into bite-size wedges or spears

2 or 3 Persian or Kirby cucumbers, cut into spears

Half a bunch of French breakfast or Easter egg radishes and their greens, trimmed

2 custardy eggs (page 148)

Flake salt and freshly ground black pepper

GRAND AIOLI SUMMER FEAST

OAXACA-MEETS-THE-MEDITERRANEAN, TOMATOES, CORN

MAKES 4 SERVINGS

This no-cook dish bursts with summer's stars: raw corn is sweet and refreshing, as are lambsquarters and succulent purslane. Just-picked tomatoes seduce with their juicy forms. The sauce is sublime. It straddles the beloved Italian bagna cauda and a garden pesto, sans the cheese. Additions of fresh mint and tender carrot tops make a lust-worthy experience out of simple vegetables in a bowl.

½ cup Oaxaca-Meets-the-Mediterranean sauce (recipe follows)

7 to 10 different sizes of colorful heirloom tomatoes, such as Cherokee Purple, Green Zebra, Sungold, Blush, Santorini, and Pink Berkeley Tie-Dye

3 to 5 stems lambsquarters

Kernels cut from 2 ears of corn (save the cobs for stock, page 82)

5 to 8 stems purslane, cut into bite-size sprigs

Extra-virgin olive oil, for drizzling

Flake salt, such as Maldon, for garnish

Freshly ground black pepper

If you refrigerated the sauce, bring it to room temperature 30 minutes prior to using.

Cut the larger tomatoes into chunky wedges, the smaller ones into halves. Spread the sauce as a base layer in shallow bowls to coat the bottom of each bowl. Scatter the lambsquarter leaves, stripped from their stems, followed by the corn. Nestle the tomatoes into the mixture. Finish with the purslane sprigs. Drizzle all lightly with oil, season with flake salt and ground pepper.

OAXACA-MEETS-THE-MEDITERRANEAN
MAKES 1½ CUPS

1½ cups extra-virgin olive oil

1 cup almonds, toasted (walnuts also work nicely)

2 garlic cloves

8 anchovies

2 cups tender carrot tops

¾ cup fresh mint leaves

4 stems pipicha

¼ cup fresh parsley

¼ teaspoon sherry vinegar

I started growing pipicha after discovering it at Solid Ground Farm at the Kingston farmers' market. They had an ambitious herb program going, and this unusual thing immediately seized me. Pipicha, a Oaxacan herb, is not messing around. It appears delicate but delivers sabor fuerte, sort of a gasoline flavor (in a good way, like epazote) crossed with cilantro. I experimented with ways to capture its essence and landed on this umami-packed paste. To retain its brightness, either consume the batch within a couple days, or freeze extra into small containers the same day you make it.

In a food processor, blitz the olive oil, almonds, and garlic until the mixture resembles a loose paste. Add the anchovies and blend until incorporated. Add the carrot tops, mint, pipicha leaves plucked from their stems, parsley, and vinegar and blitz until combined, scraping down the sides with a rubber spatula as needed. Taste and adjust the seasoning. Sealed in a jar, the sauce can be refrigerated for 1 week and frozen for up to 6 months.

SCALLOP-SHISO CEVICHE

MAKES 2 SERVINGS

My husband, Jim, and I met while working at competing high-end Nuevo Latino restaurants in the 1990s, run by chefs Guillermo Pernot and Douglas Rodriguez, respectively. Given that seminal period, this book would not be complete without a take on ceviche. Ceviches at their best are explosions of flavor interwoven with contrasting textures, and a refreshing experience. Originally from Peru, ceviche is a simple affair: the day's catch thrown into a bucket with citrus juice and eaten promptly seaside.

This recipe is quite simple even if at first glance it appears exotic. Aside from prepping the pickled pearl onions, it comes together in an instant. While some cookbooks will have ceviche marinate for 20 or 30 minutes, it is my belief that seafood remains its most tender just dressed, then brought to the table to eat at once. If you source the freshest, highest-quality ingredients, you don't need anything more.

Pickle the pearl onions: Shave the pearl onions crosswise into rings on a mandoline. They should be so thin you can nearly see through them, like a windowpane. Place the coriander seeds and peppercorns in the jar, then pack in the onion rings. Add enough rice vinegar to submerge. This should be done at least 1 hour in advance and can be done up to 1 week in advance. Store in a sealed container in the refrigerator.

Toast the buckwheat in a dry skillet over medium-low heat until lightly brown and slightly aromatic, about 3 minutes. Set aside to cool to room temperature.

Shingle the sliced scallops in a circle formation on plates. Combine the citrus juices into a small vessel with a pour spout. Arrange the plum wedges, chile, and 12 to 14 rings of pickled onion around the scallops. Spoon or pour the citrus juice over the scallop slices, enough for a very small pool to form in the bottom of the dish. Scatter the buckwheat and shiso leaves, then sprinkle with flake salt. Eat at once.

PICKLED PEARL ONIONS

3 pearl onions or enough to pack a 2-ounce jar, peeled

½ teaspoon coriander seeds

½ teaspoon black peppercorns

Rice vinegar, to submerge

2 teaspoons buckwheat groats

4 diver scallops (see headnote, page 173), sliced very thinly, about ⅛ inch thick

2 tablespoons freshly squeezed orange juice

2 teaspoons freshly squeezed lemon juice (half a lemon)

1 plum, sliced into thin wedges (use the ripest plum you can find)

Half a serrano chile, sliced very thinly on a mandoline

2 stems fresh purple shiso, larger leaves torn, or equal parts torn fresh mint and Thai basil

Flake salt for garnish

ROASTED SALMON +
SPICY CUCUMBER-ORANGE SALSA

My Noni's feasts were seminal. She and her husband traveled to far corners of the world and spent years living in Mexico. Their travels, of course, influenced her food. As I've refined the food in my own kitchen, I regret she always had her cooking completed by the time we'd arrive. To see her process would have meant everything. She was a smart lady and wanted to be present for us, rather than toil in the kitchen during our precious visits. This dish is a nod to one she made several times. It can be prepared in advance, is delicious served hot or cold, and only asks for a small bit of your time so you can be with those you love.

Make the salsa: In a medium bowl, combine the cucumbers, dill, scapes, olive oil, avocado oil, vinegar, fish sauce, jalapeño, and orange zest. Toss to incorporate, taste, and add kosher salt and freshly ground pepper as needed. Set aside.

Roast the salmon: Lightly grease a sheet pan with olive oil and lay the salmon skin side down onto it. Drizzle with more oil, spread to coat, and season with kosher salt and freshly ground black pepper. Preheat the oven to 400°F. The fish should warm to room temperature while the oven heats for even cooking.

Roast the fillet until the surface is opaque and the center is still translucent. Check after 8 to 10 minutes for doneness. Chances are some eaters will prefer greater doneness, and some medium-rare: the varied thickness in a portion of salmon will contain parts to please everyone.

Carefully transfer the fillet to a serving platter and spoon the salsa to top the salmon. Garnish with torn fresh cilantro and scatter flake salt to taste.

NOTE: Find garlic scapes late spring or early summer at farmers' markets. If you're unable to source scapes, you may use 2 scallions or a small bunch of chives.

SALSA

3 Persian cucumbers, diced

1 small bunch dill, chopped (½ to ¾ cup)

2 or 3 garlic scapes, finely chopped (see Note)

2 tablespoons extra-virgin olive oil

1 tablespoon avocado oil

3 teaspoons white wine vinegar

2 teaspoons fish sauce

Half a jalapeño, seeds and ribs removed if you prefer less spicy, very thinly sliced on a mandoline

Zest from 1 orange

Kosher salt and freshly ground black pepper

SALMON

Extra-virgin olive oil

2 pounds wild sockeye or coho salmon fillet

Kosher salt and freshly ground black pepper

¼ cup fresh cilantro leaves—bonus if it is flowering—for garnish

Flake salt

MAPLE-GOCHUJANG RIBS, PICKLE PLATTER, CORNBREAD

MAKES 4 TO 6 SERVINGS

Picnics and cookouts have always been cherished celebrations in my family. Socializing, the great outdoors, and foods you can get messy with—what could be better? I loved the Southern-influenced, blended Appalachian and African-American barbecues at my father's union local: there were barrel smokers and grills, folks tending ribs or chicken at different stations—sometimes even a whole pig—large foil pans of corn on the cob, collard greens, and all manner of junk food, including chips galore and cotton candy (which my brother and I loved, because our mother wouldn't keep the stuff at home).

Fast-forward years later, I wanted to recreate a version of the ribs my mother made in her slow cooker. She cooked hers in beer until the meat would fall off the bones and then painted a glaze to finish them. This version pays homage to these fond memories: the ribs get rubbed all over with spices and a kick-butt glaze is painted on before a last kiss under the broiler to char the meat in spots. There's a whole variety of pickles to eat with the juicy meat. One includes a way to minimize waste and uses watermelon scraps—another nod to Southern food—and another uses foraged wild blueberries, a new favorite. While not traditional by any stretch, the fresh-corn cornbread is creamy and wonderful and made even better with a slather of butter and a drizzle of date syrup. Make the pickles at least a few days in advance so the flavors can meld. Ribs can be made a day or two ahead and chilled, then brought to room temperature, painted, and broiled just before eating.

PICKLED BLUEBERRIES (MAKES I HALF-PINT)

3 tablespoons cane sugar

1 teaspoon kosher salt

⅓ cup white vinegar

1 cup blueberries (smaller and firmer berries are better here)

½ teaspoon coriander seeds

Filtered water, to top

ingredients continued →

Make the pickled blueberries: Dissolve the cane sugar and salt in a small amount of the vinegar, heated in a small saucepan, whisking to expedite the process. Set the liquid aside to cool.

Pack the blueberries in the jar, followed by the coriander seeds. Pour the sugar-salt mixture in. Add more vinegar to fill the jar two-thirds full. Add filtered water to top off, seal, invert the jar, then turn it upright, repeating a couple times to incorporate. Refrigerate for at least 3 days to allow the flavors to meld. Blueberry pickles keep refrigerated, up to 3 months.

Make the pickled watermelon rinds: Slice the skin off the rinds and discard, leaving the white flesh of the rind intact, along with the barest stripe of watermelon flesh. Slice the rinds into 2-inch-long strips, about ¼ inch wide. Pack into a jar surrounding the cinnamon stick fragment. Add the allspice and peppercorns. Dissolve the sugar and salt, heated in a small saucepan with just enough of the water to readily dissolve them, whisking to expedite the process.

CONTINUED →

MAPLE-GOCHUJANG RIBS, PICKLE PLATTER, CORNBREAD CONTINUED

PICKLED WATERMELON RIND (MAKES 1 HALF-PINT)

Rinds from a quarter of a small watermelon

Small fragment of a cinnamon stick, approximately ¼ stick

3 allspice berries

¼ teaspoon black peppercorns

1 teaspoon cane sugar

½ teaspoon kosher salt

¼ cup filtered water

¼ cup white vinegar

MAPLE-GOCHUJANG RIBS

1 packed tablespoon brown sugar

2 teaspoons cumin seeds, toasted and ground in a mortar and pestle

2 teaspoons coriander seeds, toasted and ground in a mortar and pestle

2 teaspoons kosher salt

1½ teaspoons paprika

1 teaspoon freshly ground black pepper

1 teaspoon granulated onion

½ teaspoon cayenne

½ teaspoon smoked paprika

6 pounds pork spareribs

1½ cups stock (I use corn stock, page 82) or water

RIB GLAZE

⅓ cup tomato passata or roasted tomatoes (page 128)

1 clove garlic

3 anchovies

1 tablespoon plus 2 teaspoons maple syrup

1 tablespoon plus ½ teaspoon soy sauce

Pour into the jar, followed by the remaining water and vinegar. Seal and invert the jar, then turn it upright, repeating a couple times to incorporate. Chill, sealed in the refrigerator for at least 4 days for the flavors to meld. Watermelon rind pickles keep refrigerated for up to 3 weeks.

Make the ribs: Combine the brown sugar, cumin, coriander, salt, paprika, black pepper, onion, cayenne, and smoked paprika in a shallow bowl, stirring and mashing any clumps with a fork to break them up. Pat the spice rub on both sides of the ribs and arrange all with the rib tips facing up in a slow cooker. Slowly pour the stock or water in on one side to avoid washing the spice rub off the ribs. Cook on the low setting for 8 hours.

Make the glaze: In the meantime, add the tomatoes, garlic, anchovies, maple syrup, soy sauce, gochujang, molasses, fish sauce, and smoked paprika to a blender and purée until uniform. Taste and adjust the seasoning as needed. Refrigerate the sauce, bringing it out 30 minutes before using to reach room temperature.

Make the cornbread: Preheat the oven to 400°F. Generously grease a heavy 9-inch enameled or cast-iron skillet with coconut oil.

Whisk together the flours, cornmeal, baking powder, and kosher salt in a medium bowl.

Using two knives, cut the coconut oil into the flour mixture until crumblike. Add the eggs, one at a time, mixing with a silicone spatula to incorporate fully. Pause at intervals to scrape any accumulated dough off the spatula using one of the knives. Add the honey and mix to combine. Add the buttermilk and fold in with the spatula until it is just combined. The mixture will be thick, more like a dough than a batter.

Fold in the corn and sliced jalapeños, reserving 6 to 10 chile slices to top. Spoon the batter into the skillet, swirling to push it to the pan edge, though handling it as minimally as you can so as not to overwork it.

Paint some buttermilk over the surface. Arrange the jalapeño slices and sprinkle with flake salt and freshly ground pepper. Bake until the surface is golden, about 40 minutes, rotating the pan halfway through for even baking. Cool in the pan for 10 minutes.

Use potholders to move the oven rack to the topmost position and set the oven to broil. The ribs will be quite tender, so use two sets of tongs to carefully transfer them to a sheet pan in a single layer. Generously baste with the glaze. Broil for 3 to 5 minutes, until crispy and burnished in parts.

Transfer the ribs to a serving platter. Serve alongside the array of seasonal pickles. Slice the cornbread into wedges with a serrated knife and serve warm slathered with butter and drizzled with date syrup.

1 tablespoon gochujang

½ teaspoon molasses

½ teaspoon fish sauce

⅛ teaspoon smoked paprika

JALAPEÑO CORNBREAD

8 ounces coconut oil at room temperature, plus extra to grease the pan

1 cup whole-wheat pastry flour

½ cup all-purpose flour

½ cup rye flour

½ cup fine cornmeal

2 teaspoons baking powder

½ teaspoon kosher salt

2 duck eggs

1 tablespoon buckwheat honey

½ cup full-fat buttermilk, plus extra for brushing

1½ cups fresh corn kernels, cut off the cob (save the cobs for stock, page 82)

Half or a whole thinly sliced jalapeño pepper—remove the seeds if you prefer less heat

Flake salt for sprinkling

Freshly ground black pepper for sprinkling

Salted butter and date syrup for serving

⅔ to 1 cup Tarragon-Shallot Summer Squash Pickles (page 98)

8 to 16 Moroccan Pickled Carrots (page 86)

VEGAN UMAMI UDON

MAKES 2 SERVINGS

Attending an international elementary and middle school in Detroit, I was exposed to foods from Bangladesh, Pakistan, Ecuador, Guatemala, the Philippines, the Ukraine, Poland, Iran, and more at school-wide potlucks. The complex flavors of these dishes piqued my palate. This dish is more a mash-up of elements than from one particular culture. Creamy roasted eggplant feels equally Asian and Mediterranean. Japanese udon are silky, meaty noodles I use often. The Spanish-Portuguese "escabeche" is originally a Persian technique. Once the punchy dressing, Fermented Green Garlic, and Wild Mushroom Escabeche are made, there isn't much left to endeavor. The eggplant can even be roasted a day in advance if you're short on time.

DRESSING

¼ teaspoon Marmite

2½ teaspoons white wine vinegar

2 garlic cloves, finely grated on a Microplane

2 tablespoons avocado oil

1 teaspoon Dijon mustard

1 teaspoon pickle brine

½ teaspoon soy sauce

Freshly ground black pepper

1 fairy tale, graffiti, or Japanese eggplant, sliced crosswise into ½-inch-thick slices

Extra-virgin olive oil, for roasting and wilting

2 bundles udon pasta (about 5 ounces)

½ to ⅔ cup Wild Mushroom Escabeche (page 93)

1 bunch dandelion greens, root end trimmed

Half a serrano chile, sliced very thinly on a mandoline

2 tablespoons coarsely chopped fresh parsley for garnish

Fermented Green Garlic (page 89) for garnish

Make the dressing: In a small mixing bowl, smear the Marmite into a thin film and whisk ½ teaspoon of the vinegar into it until uniform. Add the remaining 2 teaspoons vinegar, the garlic, avocado oil, mustard, pickle brine, soy sauce, and pepper and whisk until emulsified. Set aside.

Preheat the oven to 400°F. Toss the eggplant in 2 tablespoons of oil to coat all sides, then arrange in a single layer on a sheet pan. Roast for 20 to 30 minutes, until they are burnished and golden, checking halfway through to rotate the pan. Transfer the pan to a wire rack to cool slightly.

Bring a pot of water to boil and cook the noodles according to the package instructions for al dente. Transfer the cooked pasta to a medium bowl with tongs (saving a tablespoon of pasta water for the dandelions) and fold in 2 tablespoons of the dressing to fully coat. Save the remaining dressing for another use (salad, grains, beans, and so on; see Note). Add the escabeche and eggplant to the pasta and toss together.

Wilt the dandelion greens in a medium skillet over medium heat, drizzling in a small amount of oil when the pan is hot. Once they sizzle, add a tablespoon of pasta water to the greens to help them soften. Cook just until bright green and wilted, then transfer to the bowl with pasta. Serve the pasta in bowls and finish tableside with shaved serrano, parsley, and fermented green garlic to taste.

NOTE: The dressing makes an excellent swap for the Punchy Garlic Anchovy Dressing (page 58) when you want bold flavors but also want to honor vegan eating.

SCALLOPS, CORN CONFIT, MILKWEED

MAKES 2 SERVINGS

This dish is a celebration of summer, each element lovely on its own. When layered together, it is sheer bliss. The velvety sauce asks for everything to be dragged through it. Scallions and asparagus impart silky textures, a good match for sea-sweet, meaty scallops. If possible, choose diver scallops, and ones that are truly fresh, not previously frozen. Diver scallops are the most sustainable choice: in choosing them, you can be confident your food won't contribute to bycatch collateral, inevitable in most larger fishing operations. If you can find the peppery nasturtiums, they add a whole new layer to the experience: floral and sweet-spicy. Tempura milkweed buds (see "Foraging," page 21) add a delightful, crispy finish—good enough to munch all on their own by the bowlful, showered in flake salt. Substitute squash blossoms if you cannot find milkweed and choose organic cornstarch to ensure it is not derived from GMO corn.

Prep the scallops: Rinse and pat the scallops dry, then season with kosher salt. Allow them to come to room temperature while you make the confit sauce.

Make the confit sauce: Warm the olive oil over medium heat in a small saucepan and add the shallots, stirring to coat all in the oil. Bring the mixture to a simmer, then lower the heat to medium-low or low and gently poach the shallots in the olive oil, stirring occasionally, until translucent and very soft, 10 to 12 minutes. Season with salt and pepper.

Add ⅓ cup of the white wine and bring back to simmer. Reduce by half, about 3 minutes. Add the corn and fold into the shallots to incorporate. Bring back to a simmer and cook, softly bubbling, until the corn is translucent and softened, 5 minutes. Remove from the heat and allow the mixture to cool to room temperature.

Purée the shallot-corn mixture using a high-speed blender until uniform and creamy. Taste and adjust seasoning as needed. Add the remaining 1 tablespoon wine, followed by 1 tablespoon water to loosen the mixture if it resembles a paste more than a sauce. Transfer back to the saucepan and keep warm over the lowest heat until the rest of the meal is ready.

Fry the milkweed buds: Combine the cornstarch, flour, and ice water in a shallow bowl and mix until uniform. Allow the mixture to thicken for 10 minutes.

In a small heavy skillet, heat ¼ inch grapeseed oil until hot over medium-high heat. Test by adding a drop of the batter: it should sizzle on contact. Dredge the milkweed blossoms in the flour, then the batter. Allow any excess to drip off, then transfer to the hot oil. Cook buds in two batches, 3 to 5 minutes each,

CONTINUED →

SCALLOPS

10 diver scallops

Kosher salt

1 tablespoon salted butter

SWEET CORN SHALLOT CONFIT

⅓ cup extra-virgin olive oil

3 shallots, thinly sliced

⅓ cup plus 1 tablespoon dry white wine, such as Sauvignon Blanc, White Bordeaux, or Vinho Verde

Kernels from 2 small ears of corn

Kosher salt and freshly ground black pepper

MILKWEED BUDS

½ cup cornstarch

¼ cup self-rising flour, plus extra for dredging

¾ cup ice water

Grapeseed or canola oil, for frying

6 to 8 milkweed buds

Kosher salt

ingredients continued →

ASPARAGUS

Extra-virgin olive oil, for sautéing

1 bunch thin scallions

Half a bunch of thin asparagus, woody ends snapped off (save for stock, pages 79, 80, and 82)

6 nasturtium flowers (see Note)

10 to 12 purslane tips or wood sorrel leaves

Freshly ground black pepper and flake salt

rotating every minute or two for even crisping. Lower the heat as needed so as not to burn the oil or the flower buds. Transfer the fried milkweed to absorbent paper set on a wire rack and dust with a pinch of kosher salt.

Sauté the asparagus and scallions: Over medium-high heat, warm a large cast-iron pan until it is hot. Drizzle with olive oil and swirl to coat. Sauté the scallions and asparagus until they have softened and turned bright green and caramelized in parts, turning them periodically so that the white ends cook evenly and the asparagus spears become just tender, about 5 minutes. Transfer the lot to a plate.

With the pan well hot now, add a tablespoon more of oil and swirl to coat. As soon as it shimmers, add half the scallops, keeping space between them to avoid crowding. Cook for a minute, then add half the butter, dragging it around the scallops using a knife or tongs as it foams.

Sear the scallops in two batches, 3 minutes undisturbed on the first side to develop a golden crust, then turn over and baste with the hot fat, tipping the pan toward you to collect spoonfuls, pouring over the scallops continuously, for about 30 seconds. Lower the heat as needed to prevent them from burning. Scallops are ready when they are firm-bouncy when pressed with the back of a large spoon. Transfer them to a plate and repeat with the second batch, adding more oil and butter as you did for the first batch.

Swirl a few spoonfuls of the confit sauce onto plates. Arrange a pile of the scallion-asparagus mixture in the center, flanked by the scallops. Top with milkweed and add the nasturtium flowers and purslane or wood sorrel to surround, plus a few grinds of freshly ground pepper and flake salt to taste. Eat at once.

NOTE: If you cannot find nasturtium flowers, use 2 tablespoons chopped fresh parsley and baby arugula.

LAMB SKEWERS WITH ALLIUMS THREE WAYS

This is dressed-up picnic food. Though it feels special, this dish is made with elements that either don't take long to prepare or can be prepped in advance, so you can spend your time enjoying the beautiful summer evening. Three kinds of alliums—garlic chive flowers, Ramp Salt, and pickled red onions—plus a shower of fresh herbs, produce a range in flavors and make this a bright, nourishing summer meal. Labneh, or yogurt cheese, imparts a custardy, sour richness and happens to be good for you. Paired with the juicy, spice- and herb-flecked lamb, they make great companions and a real feast.

Make the labneh: Line a medium sieve with muslin or finely woven cheesecloth and place atop a container large enough to catch any drips. Transfer the yogurt to the muslin and place the whole thing in the refrigerator overnight. The liquid that separates is whey and can be saved for another use, such as baking sourdough, adding to salad dressings, or fermenting. Store the labneh refrigerated in a sealed container for up to 10 days.

Make the lamb mixture: Grind the coriander and cumin seeds with a mortar and pestle. Combine the lamb, mint, parsley, coriander, cumin, ½ teaspoon kosher salt, and pepper in a medium bowl. Mix with your hands until evenly incorporated. Loosely form the mixture into six 2 by 2 ½-inch ovals and thread three each onto skewers that can fit inside a large cast-iron skillet.

In a medium saucepan, add the 1 tablespoon kosher salt to enough water to cover the potatoes. Bring to a boil, then simmer potatoes over medium-low heat until they are tender when pierced with a small sharp knife (check after 5 to 7 minutes). Drain and set aside.

Pour the tablespoon of extra-virgin olive oil into a cast-iron skillet set on medium-high heat. When it shimmers, swirl to coat and sear the skewers undisturbed for 2 minutes. Turn a few times to brown evenly on all sides, cooking 6 to 7 minutes for medium or medium-rare.

Divide the labneh between two plates, swirling dollops on the plate surface. Arrange a small cluster of potatoes beside it. Arrange a lamb skewer on top of the labneh and nestle small piles of Japanesish pickles and pickled onions on either side. Add a generous amount of fresh basil leaves and snipped garlic chive blossoms to top the skewers, and sprinkle the potatoes with Ramp Salt. Eat at once.

LABNEH
1 cup full-fat Greek yogurt

LAMB SKEWERS
1 teaspoon coriander seeds, toasted

1 teaspoon cumin seeds, toasted

1 pound ground lamb

⅓ cup mint leaves, finely chopped

¼ cup packed fresh parsley leaves, finely chopped

½ teaspoon kosher salt

¼ teaspoon freshly ground black pepper

1 tablespoon extra-virgin olive oil

1 tablespoon kosher salt

7 to 10 small Carola, Yukon gold, or new potatoes, scrubbed

Japanesish cucumber pickles for garnish (page 128)

Quick Pickled Red Onions for garnish (page 85)

Purple or regular basil leaves for garnish

2 garlic chive flower heads

Ramp Salt (page 63) for garnish

PINEAPPLE, TEQUILA GRANITA, BRITTLE

MAKES 4 SERVINGS

During one particular summer swelter, I improvised what became a stunning dessert, largely because I wanted to avoid using the oven. An extra bonus, this creation satisfies both vegan and gluten-free lifestyles. This dessert hits high marks, wowing with its layers: sweet-tart lime-flecked tequila granita foiled by buttery, juicy pineapple, offset by crunchy, sweet-salty cashew brittle. Chile salt centers it all, pulling the elements back from feeling too sweet. I use smooth and earthy Corralejo tequila, a reposado we regularly stock at our bar.

TEQUILA GRANITA

1¼ cups water

½ cup cane sugar

Pinch kosher salt

½ cup tequila

Zest from 1 lime

½ cup fresh lime juice (2 or 3 limes)

CASHEW BRITTLE

Scant ½ cup cane sugar

½ cup salted cashews

Half a ripe pineapple (cut in half lengthwise)

Extra-virgin olive oil, for searing

¼ teaspoon Aleppo chile flakes

½ teaspoon flake salt

Make the granita: Heat the water, sugar, and salt in a small saucepan over medium heat, stirring until the solids are fully dissolved. Remove the pan from the heat, add the tequila, and allow the mixture to cool fully. Add the lime zest and juice, stir to combine, and pour the mixture into a small metal (accelerates the rate of freezing) baking pan, 8 by 8 inches.

Freeze for 45 minutes or until beginning to freeze, then use a fork to rake the frozen areas fluffy. Return the granita to freezer for another 30 minutes. Bring out to rake again, paying special attention to the edges of the pan. Repeat raking and breaking the mixture up until fluffy, every 30 minutes until fully frozen (2½ to 3 hours). Granita can be made up to 3 days in advance, covered, and kept frozen. Scrape the surface to refluff it when serving.

Make the cashew brittle: Over medium heat, transfer the sugar to a small sauté pan and warm until it begins to melt. Once the sugar is nearly melted, about 5 minutes, add the cashews. When the sugar has fully melted, quickly stir to thoroughly coat the cashews using a silicone spatula, turning the heat down as needed so the cashews do not burn. The sugar will turn deep golden and caramelize: scrape the mixture out of the pan onto a parchment-lined tray. It will immediately solidify, so work swiftly to get it all out and in one piece. Set aside to harden while you sear the pineapple. This step can be done 1 day in advance and kept on its tray in the refrigerator.

Trim the skin and fibrous core of the pineapple and slice it crossways into ½ by 2-inch segments. In a small nonstick pan set over medium-high heat, drizzle the oil once the pan is hot. Swirl the pan to coat, then arrange the pineapple and sear undisturbed for 2 minutes. Turn once the first side is burnished in parts, then sear for another 1 to 2 minutes. Turn the pieces onto their ends and sear for another minute, then transfer to a plate to cool.

Combine the Aleppo chile flakes and flake salt in a small bowl and stir together until uniform. Divide the pineapple evenly among the plates. Break the cashew brittle into shards. Spoon the granita into the center and arrange the brittle toward the edge of each plate. Sprinkle the chile salt across the pineapple and granita and serve.

STONE FRUIT, PECAN + PISTACHIO CRISPS

MAKES 4 SERVINGS

When our farmers' market is in full swing, abundant summer fare in saturated reds, purples, and oranges demands you cart away armfuls, if for no other reason than feeling dazzled by their juiciness. This indulgent-feeling dessert uses little sugar and has no gluten, and the extra brightness of pink peppercorns scattered on top just before bringing to the table adds a bit of extra "oooooh." It is so good, sometimes we eat it for breakfast.

STREUSEL TOPPING

½ cup gluten-free rolled oats

½ cup almond flour

3 packed tablespoons brown sugar

½ teaspoon ground cinnamon

½ teaspoon kosher salt

¼ teaspoon ground ginger

¼ teaspoon freshly grated nutmeg

4 tablespoons cold salted butter, cubed

⅓ cup pecans, toasted 5 to 7 minutes or until fragrant in a 350°F oven, transferred to a plate to cool

⅓ cup pistachios, toasted 5 minutes or until fragrant in a 350°F oven, transferred to a plate to cool

FRUIT

5 mixed stone fruits, such as nectarines, plums, and peaches, sliced into thin wedges

2 tablespoons brown sugar

2 teaspoons cornstarch

2 teaspoons fresh lemon juice

Finely grated zest from half a lemon

¼ teaspoon kosher salt

Labneh (page 177) for garnish

Pink peppercorns for sprinkling

Make the streusel topping: In a medium bowl, combine the oats, almond flour, brown sugar, cinnamon, salt, ginger, and nutmeg and stir with a fork to combine. Add the butter and toss to coat. Working quickly so the butter doesn't become warm and smeary, use your fingers to squeeze the butter cubes flat, coating them with the dry ingredients.

Coarsely chop the pecans and pistachios once they are cooled to room temperature and then add them to the streusel mixture. Press the butter and dry ingredients together once more, rendering the largest pieces of butter into blueberry-size bits amidst the rest. Chill in the refrigerator until ready to use. This step can be done up to 1 day in advance.

Preheat the oven to 375°F.

Make the fruit filling: In a medium bowl, mix together the fruit, brown sugar, cornstarch, lemon juice and zest, and salt until well combined. Cover loosely with plastic wrap or a silicone lid and allow the flavors to meld for at least 15 minutes or up to 1 hour.

Divide the fruit mixture evenly among four shallow ovenproof bowls or small gratin pans, placed on a rimmed sheet pan. Scatter the streusel topping to completely cover the fruit, evenly dispersing the butter pieces and nuts between all. Bake for 25 to 35 minutes, until the fruit bubbles and the streusel top is golden. Cool for 10 minutes.

Arrange the bowls on dessert plates to serve while still slightly warm. Dollop 1 or 2 tablespoons of labneh onto each crisp. Rub the pink peppercorns between your fingers until the papery sheaths slough off and sprinkle the sheaths and peppercorns over all, 2 or so teaspoons divided among the four desserts.

NOTE: If you're allergic to the nuts, pine nuts, sunflower seeds, or pepitas make fine substitutions.

KAHLÚA CHOCOLATE MOUSSE

MAKES 6 SERVINGS

This recipe was originally a page torn out of a *Playboy* magazine, circa 1990. My high school covaledictorian gave it to me, but there are no other clues held in my memory. It was a serendipitous moment meant for something good down the road, I like to think. After rediscovering it in a folder of recipe clippings, I've been making a take on this mousse for more than twenty years. My mother swears it is the best dessert ever, and after chilling overnight in the fridge, the mousse is a definite crowd-pleaser no matter the season. Tart, gemlike red currants offer a contrasting brightness. If you cannot find red currants, use cherries, raspberries, or tart red plums. Don't skip on the scatter of flake salt—it brings more flavor to the whole experience.

In a large bowl, whisk together the sugar, egg yolks, Kahlúa, and coffee.

Melt the chocolate and butter in a pot set into another that is partially filled with simmering water, also known as a double boiler. Once melted, stir the chocolate and butter together and remove from the heat, wiping the base of the pan dry so as not to drip any water as you combine the ingredients.

Fold the chocolate mixture into the sugar-yolk mixture until incorporated. Add a third of the cream and stir until uniform. This helps prevent the chocolate from seizing up once the whipped cream is added.

In the bowl of a food processor, add the rest of the cream. Run it for 10 to 15 seconds to thicken it, then pulse until the cream holds stiff peaks, pausing at intervals to scrape down the sides of the bowl with a spatula.

Transfer to the chocolate mixture and fold in until there are no streaks and the mixture is silky and uniform.

In a small but tall stainless bowl, whip the egg whites with an electric mixer until soft peaks hold. Gently fold this into the chocolate mixture until fully incorporated.

Gently but working quickly, transfer the mousse into individual shallow glasses. Cover tautly with plastic wrap so as not to disturb the swirled surfaces and chill in the refrigerator for at least 8 hours, or overnight. Serve cold, topped with a pinch of flake salt and fresh currants.

¼ cup confectioners' sugar, sifted

2 eggs, separated

3 tablespoons Kahlúa

½ teaspoon finely ground coffee

8 ounces dark chocolate wafers or chips

1½ ounces salted butter, cubed

1 cup heavy cream

Flake salt, such as Maldon

½ pint fresh red currants

DOUBLE RYE BUCKWHEAT PLUM CAKE

MAKES 8 SERVINGS

This short cake makes up for in flavor what it lacks in height. Sweet-tart, juicy, earthy and a little boozy, it feels like a real indulgence. The bones of this recipe belong to Clair Safftiz of *Bon Appétit* cake fame. Over the years I've riffed on it many times, landed on this version, and now lust for it when plum season arrives. Use very ripe plums: once the cake is ready, they're basically rendered into jam, in the best possible way. The almonds and sprinkled sugar make a superb textural contrast to the moist cake and fall-apart fruit. Though it is richly sensuous tasting, this cake is virtuous enough that you could begin the day with it.

½ cup all-purpose flour, plus more for dusting the pan

¼ cup rye flour

¼ cup buckwheat flour

¾ teaspoon baking powder

½ teaspoon kosher salt

⅓ cup rye whiskey

¼ cup full-fat Greek yogurt

¼ cup melted salted butter, slightly cooled, plus more for greasing the pan

1½ tablespoons lemon zest (from 2 small lemons)

2 eggs

1 duck egg, or 1 additional chicken egg

¾ cup cane sugar

5 or 6 elephant heart or mix of plums, pitted and cut into halves (see Notes)

2 to 3 tablespoons slivered almonds, for scattering

3 to 4 tablespoons demerara sugar, for sprinkling

Preheat the oven to 375°F. Grease the sides and base of a 9-inch springform pan, then tap the flour to coat the surface thinly, emptying out any extra flour.

In a medium bowl, use a fork to mix together the flours, baking powder, and salt. In a small bowl, whisk together the rye whiskey, yogurt, melted butter, and zest.

Use an electric mixer to beat the cane sugar and eggs in a large bowl until pale and fluffy, about 45 seconds. Add the yogurt mixture to the egg mixture and whisk to combine. Use a sieve to sift the dry mixture into the wet a little at a time, folding the dry mixture in fully to ensure there are no lumps. Pause occasionally to scrape down the sides of the bowl. This step takes about 5 minutes. Once fully incorporated, refrigerate the batter for 10 minutes.

Pour half of the batter into the pan and bake for 10 minutes. This is so that the plums don't sink to the base of your pan, and you can see their cheery faces once the cake is done. Chill the remaining batter until needed.

Pour the remaining batter on top of the already baked batter, then nestle the plums cut sides up. Scatter with the almonds and sprinkle with the demerara sugar, being sure to emphasize the periphery (the cake will become nice and crispy at the edges).

Bake 25 to 35 minutes more, until a toothpick comes out nearly clean when inserted into the center. Allow to cool for 5 minutes, then run a thin offset spatula or butter knife around the edge to separate the tacky surface from the cake pan. Allow the cake to cool fully, remove the collar, and serve. Keeps for 2 days wrapped in parchment or foil at room temperature.

NOTES: Always sift dry ingredients as they are incorporated—it is no fun to discover a lump of baking powder or flour as you take a bite.

If it isn't summer but you long to bake this cake, it can be made with fruit from any season—use sturdy fruit, cut in a similar size as the plums for best effect. I have made this using Seckel pears, poached quince, and rhubarb. All are a delight.

BLACK RASPBERRY–BOURBON MASCARPONE TARTLETS

MAKES FOUR 5-INCH FLUTED TARTLETS

To commemorate berry season, I like extracting their magic via jams and drinking vinegars, aka shrubs, and baking them into pastries. Subtly sweet mascarpone cream is an excellent canvas in this dessert. Crunchy, rustic praline and ephemeral, peppery flower petals complement juicy, sweet "black caps," memorializing the harvest I have—no matter how great or small (I'm looking at you, wily catbirds and chipmunks)—in a stunning dessert. Blind-bake the tart cases the same day for best texture, especially if it is a humid day.

Make the maple mascarpone base: Vigorously whip the mascarpone, yogurt, maple syrup, rye whiskey, and salt together in a small bowl until uniform and fluffy. Chill for 20 minutes before using. This can be made up to 3 days in advance, stored in the refrigerator sealed with a lid or plastic wrap. Rewhip prior to using if prepared in advance.

Make the pastry: Place the flours, sugar, and salt in the bowl of a food processor and pulse to combine. Add the cold butter and pulse, until the mixture forms pea-size bits. Combine the ice water and vinegar in a measuring cup. In a slow stream, add the ice water–vinegar mixture while pulsing, stopping once the dough holds together. To test, open the lid and squeeze some of the dough in your hand—if it holds together, it is ready. If the dough still crumbles, add just a bit more of the ice water mixture and pulse a few more times. You may end up using slightly less than the full amount.

Empty the dough out onto a long section of plastic wrap. Separate it into two mounds, then divide one mound into four smaller balls. Flatten each to form a disk. Place plastic wrap in between the disks and wrap each, saving the larger one for a galette. Refrigerate for at least 20 minutes to let the dough mellow. This can be made up to 3 days in advance.

Make the pistachio praline: Heat the sugar in a small sauté pan over medium heat. When the sugar begins to melt, add the pistachios. As it turns into liquid, stir the mixture with a rubber spatula, coating the pistachios fully. When the mixture is completely liquid and coating the nuts, quickly and carefully scrape the mixture onto a parchment- or Silpat-lined sheet pan. Allow the mixture to set until hard and brittle. If it is warm on the day you make this, the pan can be placed in the refrigerator to accelerate the process.

CONTINUED →

MAPLE RYE MASCARPONE

1 cup mascarpone

⅓ cup thick plain yogurt

2 tablespoons maple syrup

1 tablespoon rye whiskey

Pinch kosher salt

PASTRY

1½ cups all-purpose flour

1 cup rye flour

1 teaspoon cane sugar

1 teaspoon kosher salt

2 sticks salted butter, cubed and freezer-cold (see Notes, page 261)

½ cup ice water

¼ cup apple cider vinegar

PISTACHIO PRALINE

Scant ½ cup cane sugar

½ cup lightly salted pistachios

1 cup heavy cream

2 cups black or red raspberries

Petals from wild bergamot/ monarda flowers or very small fresh oregano leaves or flowers for garnish

Bring one of the four small pastry disks from the refrigerator, giving it 10 minutes to warm up so you may roll it without splitting it at the edges.

Roll the dough between lightly floured parchment and the plastic wrap it was wrapped in, peeling the wrap away and reflouring at intervals. Roll the dough roughly in the shape of a circle, ⅛ inch thick. If the dough becomes smeary or flabby at any point, transfer to a sheet pan and chill in the refrigerator for 10 to 20 minutes. Place a removable-bottom tartlet pan over the dough to ensure there is 1-inch overhang; if not, roll it again until it is wide enough to accommodate it.

Remove the plastic wrap from the dough and center the inverted tartlet pan on it. With one hand underneath the parchment and the other on top of the pan, invert the dough, then peel away the parchment.

Working your way around the pastry, lift the overhang with one hand while the other gently presses the pastry flush with the base and into the corners of the pan. Hold along the outside pan edge as you press the dough into the fluting. Place the tartlet shell back in the refrigerator and repeat rolling, transferring, and lining the pans with the remaining disks.

Use a rolling pin over the top edge of each pan to trim any overhang and use the scraps to repair any tears or thin areas. Save the scraps for another use or make a cook's treat of them. Dock the pastry bases all over with the tines of a fork. Return them to the refrigerator to chill for at least 20 minutes.

Preheat oven to 400°F. Place the tartlets on a sheet pan. Cut squares of parchment larger than the tart pans and lay them over each pastry, filling them with pie weights, rice, or dry beans, especially at the corners.

Blind-bake for 15 minutes or until the edges turn golden. Gather the parchment corners to remove the pie weights and bake for a further 12 to 15 minutes, until the shells are golden all over. Keep an eye on the edges—if they start to darken too much, cover them with lengths of foil as the rest of the pastry finishes baking. Cool the tartlets completely on a wire rack.

While the pastry shells cool, chop the pistachio brittle into a coarse praline.

In a food processor, combine the mascarpone and heavy cream. Pulse until fluffy and the cream holds soft peaks, pausing at intervals to scrape down the sides of the bowl.

Arrange the pastry shells on small plates or a serving platter. Divide the cream evenly among each shell, swirling it to the edges. Nestle the berries into the fluffy cream and shower with the pistachio praline. Sprinkle with wild bergamot petals or oregano leaves to top and eat at once.

fall

Fall is the season of dieback. Before I tended a garden, I loved the beautiful leaves turning. Now that I grow food, so eagerly anticipated through the season, seeing the garden fade away elicits a melancholy. I am not good at saying goodbye, especially to things I have built, poured myself into. I must reconcile this loss and forge something in its place to provide new momentum.

Then, there are some fall days that feel like the best in the world. Radiant hues everywhere provide much to reflect on. The air is crisp and sweet, and carried by a warm breeze, it brings a most peaceful vibe. A precious hummingbird has arrived on the scene. We're seeing only females now. I changed the nectar once more. These are the final days before they make their way on an impossibly long flight (nearly 3,000 miles!) to the equator. Today, the first fuchsia morning glories are showing off their ruffled petals. It is another of the many small changes that, when beholding them together, feel profound.

SEPTEMBER 15

I'm not sure what there is to be gained from the loss of all things green, the withering away of the gardens, other than reacquainting myself with the ebb and flow of life. It does provide an opportunity for certain contemplation. But if I had a choice, I just might trade changing seasons for the constant of colorful blooms and fruiting abundance that a warmer climate gives. There is a wellspring in that. But no, I live on the East Coast in the Hudson Valley, and winter is something we must bear. Given that, we have both expressed a few times now that our newly installed wood-fired stove will provide a great comfort as temperatures plummet.

OCTOBER 3

I can't say I'm enthralled with the colder days to come—though, we have debuted the wood-fired stove and it IS amazing to curl up next to. The kitties think we installed it for them—both are sprawled, luxuriating in their respective basket beds. Occasions to go foraging or on a bike ride fill my well with ideas that'll be a reserve, for days when there is a paucity of living things to harvest, less ability to meander without first bundling in umpteen layers, stark skies, and a landscape absent of color.

I am bottling sunshine—preserving all manner of herbs, still harvesting an array of tomatoes, and saving all kinds of seeds in a messy corner on the counter, next to my workstation. I'll consider what to do with them, with thoughts toward next year and what it might bear.

I will harvest much of the dandelion for fall braises. That is a cold weather joy. And soon, I'll begin the daily snip-snip of hoary bittercress, that punchy, resilient green. It is a wild plant with a flavor not unlike arugula. With the recent much-needed rains, I will set out shortly on a hunt for one of fall's great stars, *Grifola frondosa*, aka hen of the woods mushrooms.

OCTOBER 31

A harsh chill washed into the region after two and a half days of nonstop rain. Which turned to snow and sleet. It was 24 degrees when we woke today. Jim has begun a daily routine of starting the fire in the morning. Kitties and I migrate from the bed to sit in front of the hearth, but not before I go tend to the birds outside, filling their feeders and affixing them to the lowest limbs of the eastern white pine out back. And today for the first time, I needed to thaw the birdbath. Delicate frost framed every leaf edge, every blade of grass, as if glass was poured onto all, glittery with the sunrise.

WILD MUSHROOM–POTATO–ONION TART

MAKES 4 SERVINGS

This versatile dish makes good use of meaty mushrooms, like the unexpected porcini I discovered on an afternoon bike ride. Sautéing the onions and mushrooms beforehand intensifies their character for a proper savory affair. This tart can serve as breakfast, lunch, or dinner and can be eaten hot or room temperature. Good all-butter store-bought puff pastry is something I keep in my freezer as a matter of course, so I can throw together a meal just like this without much notice.

1 package prepared puff pastry, such as Dufour, thawed in the refrigerator

All-purpose flour, for dusting

12 ounces any fresh wild mushrooms, or a mix of hen of the woods, oyster mushrooms, king boletes, or chanterelles

Extra-virgin olive oil

Kosher salt

Full-fat buttermilk, to paint the crust

3 ounces Gruyère, grated

4 medium Yukon gold potatoes, sliced ⅛ inch thick on a mandoline

½ to 1 cup caramelized onions (page 116)

Leaves from 5 to 9 sprigs fresh thyme

Freshly ground black pepper and flake salt

3 stems fresh tarragon

Unfold the pastry onto a lightly floured sheet of parchment and roll to a rough rectangle. With a sharp paring knife, hold the knife edge perpendicular to the pastry and score a border 1 inch in from the edge, all the way around (see Note). Transfer to a sheet pan and chill in the refrigerator.

Preheat the oven to 400°F.

Slice the mushrooms into ¼-inch pieces. In a large cast-iron skillet, cook the mushrooms with a drizzle of oil and a pinch of salt until they begin to collapse and brown, 5 to 7 minutes, turning occasionally. Remove the pan from the heat and set aside.

Bring the pastry out from the fridge. Paint the buttermilk onto the border. Sprinkle the Gruyère in an even layer onto the pastry, inside the border. Arrange the potato slices like shingles, followed by the caramelized onions, scattered around. Sprinkle half the thyme leaves, then add the mushrooms, followed by the remaining thyme leaves. Season with pepper and drizzle a very small amount of oil, just enough to kiss the surface in places.

Bake the tart on the sheet pan for 30 minutes or until the pastry is golden and the cheese is melted, rotating the pan after 20 minutes for even baking. Set the tart on a wire rack and cool for 5 minutes.

Cut into slices, season with flake salt and freshly ground pepper to taste, and sprinkle with fresh tarragon leaves plucked from their stems for garnish. Store any leftovers between layers of parchment, sealed in a container in the refrigerator, for up to 3 days. Reheat slices in a moderate oven or toaster oven for best results.

NOTE: Scoring a border helps puff up the crust as the butter within the laminated pastry melts, expanding the layers in the roaring hot oven.

QUINOA + QUINCE PORRIDGE

Don't let the monochrome palette fool you. This breakfast feels like a big hug—an aromatic, juicy hug. When we were young, my mom prepared Filipino champorado on special occasions for breakfast, passed on from close family friends, a huge Filipino family who threw legendary, colorful, and abundant feasts. We knew the breakfast as "sticky rice" and loved it. The porridge was rich and sweet, made with cocoa and sweetened condensed milk. As I developed this recipe, I was brought back to those fond memories. The quinoa is substantial and creamy like champorado, but more delicately sweetened. Fleshy Rosé + Spiced Poached Quince enhances the quinoa with a lingering of wine and spice. The crunchy buckwheat bits and lemon peel are enlivening layers, perfect for morning. Served warm on a brisk day, this porridge is nourishing and unexpectedly luxurious.

Toast the buckwheat groats in a dry skillet over medium-low heat until lightly brown and slightly fragrant, about 3 minutes. Transfer to a small dish and set aside to cool to room temperature. This can be done up to 3 days in advance and stored sealed in a jar on the counter.

Make the quinoa: Mix ½ cup of the heavy cream, 1 cup of the water, the honey, and salt together in a medium bowl until uniform. Add the quinoa and cinnamon and stir to incorporate. Cover loosely with plastic wrap and leave at room temperature for 4 to 6 hours. Place it in the refrigerator before going to bed.

The next day, bring the quinoa and quince out of the refrigerator. Give the quinoa mixture a thorough stir, then transfer it to a small saucepan, and warm over medium heat for 10 minutes, or until the seeds turn translucent, stirring occasionally to prevent scorching. Turn the heat off and add the remaining ¼ cup cream and ½ cup water for more porridge consistency (if preferred), stirring again until uniform. Warm it once more over low heat if the consistency is too thin.

While the quinoa warms, transfer the quince-poaching liquid into a small saucepan set over medium heat and reduce by half. Add two quince quarters per serving along with the lemon peels to the hot liquid, gently stirring to coat all and set aside.

Spoon the porridge into bowls. Top with the quince, lemon peels, and some of their poaching liquid. Sprinkle with the toasted buckwheat and spiced nuts, a drizzle of honey to taste, and eat at once.

NOTE: To make this dish vegan, simply swap oat milk or soy milk in place of the cream, and swap maple syrup for the honey.

2 tablespoons buckwheat groats

QUINOA

¾ cup heavy cream

1½ cups water

1 teaspoon honey

Pinch kosher salt

1 cup quinoa

½ teaspoon ground cinnamon

¾ cup poaching liquid, 2 to 3 poached quinces, and 6 strips lemon peel from Rosé + Spice Poached Quince (page 101)

Spiced Nuts (page 77), coarsely chopped, for garnish

Honey for topping (optional)

FALL SKILLET: PUMPKIN + BRUSSELS LEAVES

MAKES 2 SERVINGS

Brussels greens impart a unique sweetness akin to the better-known sprouts, but in a different format I quite love. Though substantial like other brassica varieties, Brussels' fanlike leaves soften easily, rendering a tender result. If you cannot find Brussels greens, you may substitute those of collards, broccoli, or cauliflower: halve the number of leaves, cut them in half lengthwise, chop the stems, and add 3 minutes to the cooking time.

GREEN GODDESS SAUCE

¾ cup full-fat Greek yogurt

2 tablespoons full-fat buttermilk

2 tablespoons fresh lemon juice

3 or 4 anchovies

1 large clove garlic

½ cup fresh parsley leaves, coarsely chopped

2 tablespoons fresh tarragon leaves, coarsely chopped

1 tablespoon plus 1 teaspoon fresh chives, coarsely sliced

¼ teaspoon kosher salt

1½ pounds pumpkin (see Note), seeds and stringy bits scraped out, cut into wedges

Extra-virgin olive oil

Kosher salt

1 large shallot, thinly sliced

7 Brussels leaves, stems trimmed

½ cup stock (chicken, corn, or mushroom, pages 79, 80, and 82)

1 tablespoon tomato paste

1 teaspoon Harissa (page 59) or chile paste

2 eggs

Flake salt and freshly ground black pepper

Make the sauce: Blend the yogurt, buttermilk, lemon juice, anchovies, garlic, parsley, tarragon, chives, and salt in a high-speed blender until creamy and uniform. Taste and adjust seasoning as needed. Refrigerate at least 2 hours before using. This step can be done up to 3 days in advance.

Preheat the oven to 400°F. Place the pumpkin wedges on a sheet pan, drizzle with oil, and rub all over to coat. Season with salt and roast for 20 minutes or until wedges begin to brown on the bottom sides. After checking, drizzle with a small additional amount of oil, then turn over and roast until tender, about 15 minutes more. Remove from the oven and set aside. This step can be done a day in advance and left at room temperature.

In a large cast-iron skillet warmed over medium heat until hot, drizzle with oil and add the shallots. Sauté, stirring occasionally until the shallots have softened, 5 to 7 minutes. Add the Brussels leaves and another drizzle of oil, dragging them around the pan to coat. Add half the stock, the tomato paste, and harissa and stir to dissolve, coating all in the savory mixture. Add the remainder of the stock, stir, and cook the Brussels leaves until they have collapsed and turned bright green, another 5 to 7 minutes.

Add the pumpkin wedges to the skillet a minute or two before all is ready, then make space at the hottest part of the pan for the eggs. Drizzle with oil and crack the eggs into the pan, frying until the edges become crispy and the whites are fully set, 3 to 5 minutes.

Bring the skillet to the table, set on a trivet. Serve with spoonfuls of the green goddess sauce on top and season with flake salt and freshly ground pepper to taste.

NOTE: You may substitute butternut squash, kabocha, or other winter squash cut in similar sizes to roast if pumpkin is not available.

PUNTARELLE + TARDIVO WITH PUNCHY DRESS

MAKES 4 SERVINGS

These two alien-looking greens in the chicory family make good friends. Juicy, crunchy, and slightly bitter, they are complemented perfectly by the robust flavors of this classic Roman vinaigrette. Cicoria di catalogna, otherwise known as puntarelle, has dense elongated sawtooth leaves similar in appearance to dandelion. The leaves envelop clusters of paler segments that grow from a connected base. Puntarelle is one of the more bitter among the chicories—it's an acquired taste that mellows considerably with a simple soak in cold water prior to consuming. Tardivo is an Italian heirloom radicchio variety known as Fiori d'Inverno, which is Italian for "winter flower." It has unique fingerlike, long, slender burgundy leaves with white ribs, often tinged with green.

Years ago, you couldn't pay me to eat bitter greens such as these. Now I crave them and have been known to eat an entire mixing bowl's worth in a single sitting. Long Season Farm at our great Hudson Valley Kingston farmers' market grows stunning heads of both in late fall. Any time they are available, I leap to bring multiple heads home. Pairing these chicories with a punchy vinaigrette balances them out. It is helpful to dress them generously 10 minutes before you plan to eat them to soften their structure. At a glance all the flavors read as strong, perhaps even intimidating, it's true. But . . . this salad is a joy to eat: enlivening, juicy, and refreshing (see photo, page 218). See that you don't devour every last leaf and crumb.

DRESSING

3 garlic cloves

4 or 5 anchovy fillets
(see Notes)

1 tablespoon Dijon mustard

2 teaspoons white wine
vinegar

Freshly ground black pepper

¼ cup extra-virgin olive oil

SALAD

1 head puntarelle

Half a head Treviso tardivo,
or other radicchio, leaves
cut into 3-inch sections

Herbed bread crumbs
(page 155) for sprinkling

Flake salt and freshly ground
black pepper

Make the dressing: Mash the garlic and anchovies in a mortar and pestle (see Note) to make a thick paste. Add the mustard, vinegar, and freshly ground black pepper and whisk to combine. At a bare drizzle, whisk in the olive oil to emulsify. If you are unsure about the consistency or if the dressing is in fact emulsifying, drizzle the oil more slowly or stop altogether and look at the whisked mixture— if there is a film of oil on top, it needs further whisking. The end result will be a savory-tangy, velvety dressing that coats the puntarelle once tossed together in a large bowl. Taste the dressing and adjust the seasoning as needed. The dressing can be made up to 1 day in advance and stored in the refrigerator.

Prep the salad: Strip puntarelle's outermost green leaves and save for braises or soup. Separate the inner stalks from their cluster, then work on one at a time to slice them into thin vertical strips, ⅛ to ¼ inch wide. Place the strips into a large bowl filled with cold water.

Repeat with all remaining segments, slicing them thinly into the vertical strips. They should sit in the cold-water bath for at least 1 hour and will curl as they do so. This step can be done up to 1 day in advance.

Empty the bowl with puntarelle into a colander to drain. After allowing it to sit for a minute or two, shake the colander of excess water. Lay a tea towel on a work surface and arrange the puntarelle in a single layer. Lay another tea towel on top and roll the puntarelle up in a cylinder, short end to opposite short end, to absorb remaining moisture. This step can be done 1 hour in advance and the puntarelle can be stored rolled, in a plastic bag in the refrigerator.

Rinse the tardivo leaves under cold running water. Drain in a colander and pat dry. In a large salad bowl, combine the tardivo and puntarelle. Use 3 or 4 tablespoons dressing and toss to coat all evenly. Season with freshly ground black pepper. Taste, and adjust the dressing or seasoning as needed.

Transfer to a serving platter and bring to the table with the herbed bread crumbs in a bowl served alongside. Add a shower of bread crumbs and a small scatter of flake salt and freshly ground black pepper, and eat at once. Any leftovers not dressed in the crumbs can be stored in a sealed container in the refrigerator for up to 1 day.

NOTES: Buy jarred anchovies so you can see if they are still pink, a sign of freshness.

You may alternatively place all dressing ingredients except the oil into a small blender vessel and whizz until uniform. Add the oil, then run on high speed until emulsified. Taste and adjust the seasoning as needed.

To make a heartier salad and to add a further nod to Rome, add toasted pine nuts.

TWO TOASTS: LABNEH + THE WHOLE BEET, TOMATOES + SAUCE

This hearty appetizer is a delectable way to incorporate various staples from earlier in the book. Mellow, sweet beets and their greens and tangy yogurt cheese complement each other, piled onto crunchy toast. The robust tomato confit and earthy Oaxaca-Meets-the-Mediterranean sauce impart a silky indulgence. The two are a satisfying marriage of contrasts, and nearly fully plant-based.

Preheat the oven to 400°F.

Make the whole beet toasts: Scrub the beets and trim the greens stems ½ inch up from the roots. Rinse the greens under cold running water. Shake them of excess water, then pat dry. Set the greens toward the center-back of a sheet pan (or wherever your oven isn't its hottest), toss them in olive oil to coat, and season with kosher salt.

Set the beets onto a segment of aluminum foil at the front of the sheet pan, large enough to wrap them loosely. Generously drizzle them with olive oil, toss to coat, add 2 tablespoons water, and season with kosher salt. Bring the foil ends to touch. Fold to tent the beet parcel and seal so they initially steam as they roast.

Roast the beet greens until soft and collapsed, 15 to 20 minutes. You should be able to easily twirl the stems. Check halfway through, rearranging them with tongs as needed. It's okay if some leaves become crispy. The texture will provide good contrast to the juicy, softened stems. Transfer the greens to a dish once they're done as the beets continue roasting.

Beets will need an additional 30 to 40 minutes to roast. Open the aluminum-foil parcel carefully so as not to get hit with hot steam and add another tablespoon or two of water if the liquid has evaporated. Beets are ready when they give easily when pierced with a sharp knife. Allow them to cool, then rub the skins off and cut into quarters or bite-size wedges. This step can be done up to 2 days in advance.

Assemble the toasts: Slather the labneh onto two toasts. Snip the cooked beet greens into bite-size lengths with scissors, directly onto the labneh. Top with a few beet wedges apiece, then add the Toasted Seeds. Slather the Oaxaca-Meets-the-Mediterranean sauce onto the other two slices. Spoon the tomato confit to top, reserving most of the infused oil for another use. Drizzle olive oil onto the beet toasts and add a few grinds of freshly ground pepper and a scatter of flake salt onto all.

LABNEH + THE WHOLE BEET TOASTS

2 small beets and their greens

Extra-virgin olive oil, for drizzling

Kosher salt

½ cup labneh (page 177)

2 slices Sourdough Bread (page 68), toasted

Toasted Seeds (variation of Spiced Nuts, page 77)

TOMATOES + SAUCE TOASTS

½ cup Oaxaca-Meets-the-Mediterranean sauce (page 162)

2 slices Sourdough Bread toasted

½ to 1 cup Tomato Confit (page 60)

Freshly ground black pepper and flake salt

SUNCHOKE SOUP + CRISPY MUSHROOMS

MAKES 2 QUARTS

My neighbor Ruthie is blessed with a prolific yearly sunchoke harvest. She would beg to differ, saying instead she is cursed, and she enthusiastically uproots the tubers with a pitchfork. She has shared bucketloads with me, and so I have experimented, looking for delicious new ways to showcase this uncommon vegetable. This soup is quite soothing when the weather has turned cold, can feed a crowd, and freezes well. Salty, crispy mushrooms balance out the creamy subtle sweetness. A drizzle of thinned sour cream and fresh green shoots add brightness, whether you enjoy this as a small plate or serve wide, warming bowls as the main attraction alongside wedges of crusty bread to dunk. This soup is an emblem of fall.

1 medium onion, thinly sliced

Extra-virgin olive oil, for sautéing

2 garlic cloves, finely grated on a Microplane

4 cups cubed sunchokes

1 tablespoon salted butter

¾ teaspoon kosher salt

Freshly ground black pepper

2 small bay leaves

3 to 5 sprigs thyme

¼ teaspoon cayenne

2 cups chicken stock or mushroom stock (pages 79 and 80)

½ pint heavy cream

3 shiitake mushrooms, stems trimmed (save for stock, page 80), sliced thinly

1 tablespoon water

½ teaspoon tamari

2 tablespoons sour cream, thinned with a little water so it can be drizzled

1 cup fresh pea shoots

3 to 5 stems garlic chives

In a Dutch oven or other heavy, wide pot, sauté the onions in 1 tablespoon olive oil over medium heat until translucent and softened, 7 minutes. Add the garlic and stir to incorporate. Cook for a few minutes, adding another small drizzle of oil as needed, should the garlic stick to the pan.

Add the cubed sunchokes and the butter and stir mixture to incorporate as the butter melts. Season with the salt and black pepper and add the bay leaves, thyme, and cayenne. Sauté until the sunchokes give when pressed with the back of a fork, 5 to 7 minutes, stirring occasionally.

Add the stock and bring to a boil, then place the lid on the pot, lower the heat, and simmer covered for 10 minutes, or until the sunchokes give easily when pierced with a sharp knife. Remove the lid and set the pot on a wire rack to cool for at least 5 minutes.

Remove the bay leaf and thyme stems from the soup and carefully transfer it to a high-speed blender. Add in the heavy cream and purée until uniform and velvety. Be mindful to keep the lid sealed as you blend to avoid being burned by the hot soup. Taste and adjust the seasoning as needed.

Drizzle 1 tablespoon olive oil into a medium cast-iron skillet set over medium-high heat. Once hot, swirl to coat and sauté the mushrooms undisturbed for 3 minutes. Add the water and agitate the pan so all mushrooms get some of the liquid.

Add another drizzle of oil, turn the slices over, and sauté for 2 more minutes. Add the tamari and agitate the pan so all the slices get some of the liquid, then add a final drizzle of oil, and sauté for another minute until all are deeply golden and crispy. Transfer the mushrooms to a dish and set aside.

Ladle the soup into bowls. Drizzle the sour cream onto the soup, nestle in a pile of mushrooms, and top with pea shoots and thinly snipped garlic chives. Finish with freshly ground black pepper and eat at once.

ROASTED WHOLE CAULIFLOWER WITH HARISSA + YOGURT

MAKES 2 TO 4 SERVINGS

While cauliflower is a blank canvas of sorts, when roasted until caramelized in parts and soft to its core, it is a thing of beauty I could eat in its entirety in a single sitting. See if you aren't tempted to as well, slicing chunky florets and dragging them through robust harissa and cooling yogurt.

Preheat the oven to 400°F. Trim the tough end of a cauliflower stem and any yellowing leaves. Rinse the cauliflower well under cold running water. Place it florets side down in a large cast-iron skillet, allowing some of the droplets to travel to the pan. Drizzle the head all over with olive oil, 1 to 2 tablespoons. Season generously with salt and roast for 20 minutes.

Check the cauliflower and invert it so the stem side faces down. Drizzle the water over the head, drizzle additional oil, and return to the oven to roast for 15 minutes more.

Drizzle it again with olive oil, then lean the cauliflower against one edge of the pan so that one side tilts up as it rests against the hot pan surface. Roast for 15 more minutes. Repeat this process for one to three more rounds, moving its position to get exposure to both the hot air and hot pan, cooking at 15-minute intervals and drizzling a small bit of olive oil until the head feels soft and collapsing and is caramelized in places. The entire roasting time from start to finish takes 65 to 95 minutes.

Remove the pan from the oven. Carefully transfer the cauliflower to a serving plate, florets facing down. Bring to the table with a bowl each of the yogurt and harissa. Dollop some yogurt and harissa onto the plates. Use a serrated knife to cut chunks of the cauliflower, divide onto plates, and drag the cauliflower through the sauces as you eat. Serve with finely sliced preserved lemon for an extra lemony-salty hit.

1 large head of cauliflower

Extra-virgin olive oil

Kosher salt

2 tablespoons water

1 cup full-fat Greek yogurt

½ to 1 cup Harissa (page 59)

Skin from a quarter of a Preserved Meyer Lemon (page 97), finely sliced

ULTIMATE NIBBLES PLATTER

When I assemble this bountiful platter for guests, I feel giddy. In part because I get to open precious jars, having patiently waited for this moment to debut their special verve. There is a symphony of elements that get to meet one another, meld, dance, play—a "greater than the sum of its parts" harmonizing moment. As guests experience the array, their eyes and grins widening as I describe what's been placed in front of them, it's extra exciting. They are niche ingredients from my gardens or experiments I'm exploring, each a time capsule of the season. The cherry-on-top in serving it all is choosing the vintage or handmade dishes on which the preserves, pickles, and local fare will be presented. I have long adored the unapologetically rich triple-cream cheese from Burgundy, Délice de Bourgogne. It is excellent paired with tart flavors such as Autumn Olive Jam or the "jelly" of a very ripe persimmon. The cheesy-savory quality the miso imparts to mugwort shortbreads pairs wonderfully with many pickles. Mix and match whatever you have on hand. Include rich-bright, sweet-savory, and crunchy and lush texture pairings, and you can't go wrong. Make the pickled beans 5 days in advance for the flavors to meld and chill the shortbread dough 1 hour before baking.

PICKLED SCARLET RUNNER BEANS (MAKES 1 PINT)

½ teaspoon peppercorns

1 teaspoon coriander seeds

1 bunch tender scarlet runner beans (or other snap bean such as romano, wax, or green beans) that can fit upright in your jar

2 garlic cloves

Peel from half a lemon, any bitter white pith removed

1 bay leaf

¾ cup water

1 tablespoon cane sugar

1 teaspoon kosher salt

¾ cup white vinegar

ingredients continued →

Make the pickled beans: Place the peppercorns and coriander seeds into the jar. Pack the beans in, stem end facing up, until there is no room left, setting the jar on its side as you add them to help keep them organized. Nestle in the garlic cloves and slide the lemon peels and bay leaf in as you add the beans.

In a small saucepan, heat half the needed amount of water with the sugar and salt, stirring until they completely dissolve. Pour the vinegar halfway up the jar, followed by the sugar-salt water and remaining room temperature water, so that you end up with a 1:1 ratio of vinegar to water. Press down to submerge all, seal, and refrigerate. Pickled beans need 5 days to meld. They keep for up to 3 months, refrigerated.

Make the shortbread: Combine the flour, salt, chile flakes, black pepper, and cheeses in a food processor. Pulse until combined.

Add the cubed butter and process until the mixture resembles coarse crumbs. Add the mugwort and egg yolk and process in a few bursts, until incorporated throughout. Follow with the miso-water, pulsing as you drizzle it in, until dough holds together when squeezed with your fingers.

Roll the dough into a log about 2 inches in diameter on a piece of parchment, using the parchment to pat the shortbread together at first so the warmth of your hands does not melt the butter. Use a bench scraper to free up any bits stuck to your hands or the parchment. Turn the log on its end to tamp it even, then repeat with the other end. Twist the ends closed and chill until firm, at least 1 hour.

CONTINUED →

MISO-MUGWORT SHORTBREAD (MAKES 18 TO 20 SHORTBREADS)

1⅓ cups all-purpose flour

1 teaspoon kosher salt

1 teaspoon Aleppo chile pepper

½ teaspoon freshly ground black pepper

3 ounces Gruyère, grated

1 ounce Parmesan cheese, finely grated

8 tablespoons salted butter, cubed and cold

2 tablespoons fresh mugwort leaves, finely chopped

1 egg yolk

1 tablespoon chickpea miso, dissolved in scant ¼ cup warm water

Autumn Olive Jam (page 99)

Bloomy rind/triple-cream cheese, such as Délice de Bourgogne or Robiola

Fourme D'Ambert blue cheese

Ash rind goat cheese

Hachiya persimmon(s), extremely ripe

Fresh figs

Walnuts or hazelnuts in their shells or Spiced Nuts (page 77)

Moroccan Pickled Carrots (page 86) or Tarragon-Shallot Summer Squash Pickles (page 98)

Sourdough Crackers (page 75)

Preheat the oven to 400°F. Cut the dough into ¼-inch-thick coins, press the edges to keep them even, and place close but not touching on parchment-lined sheet pans. Bake for 15 minutes, until golden at their centers and slightly darker around the edges. Rotate the pans halfway through for even baking as needed. Transfer the shortbread to a wire rack to cool completely. Store in an airtight container at room temperature for up to 1 week.

Arrange small dishes of jams and cheeses that pair well together. Place the persimmon on its own dish, puncture the skin, and serve it with a spoon. Add the figs, nuts (and a nutcracker), pickles to surround, and a tray of crackers and shortbreads.

BOUILLABAISSE + ROUILLE-SLATHERED TOASTS

MAKES 2 SERVINGS

When I was a child, seafood was too extravagant for our household budget, save for excellent fried smelts or marinated perch. We knew if we went out to dine and were allowed to order seafood, it was a very special occasion. Not long ago when my parents came to visit, I crafted a plan to make them a bouillabaisse I'd developed and had fallen in love with. It was achingly delicious, replete with a whole lobster I had steamed at the fishmonger's. We each sat with individual trays, brimming wide bowls, seafood crackers, and a large communal bowl for shells. To this day it is one of the special meals I make for people I love. Served with rouille, a traditional herby roasted red pepper sauce, generously spread onto toast, this is hands-down a favorite meal. Make the rouille and stock at least 1 day in advance. They will taste better if you do.

Make the stock: In a Dutch oven or large saucepan, heat the oil over medium heat. Add the onion and fennel. Cook until translucent, stirring occasionally, 5 to 7 minutes. Stir in the mashed garlic and cook 2 minutes more or until fragrant.

Add the tomatoes, along with the fish heads, bones, and trimmings, the fresh herbs, salt, star anise, saffron, coriander seeds, and water.

Bring to a boil, cover, and lower to simmer. Cook, simmering, for 30 minutes to infuse the flavors. Use a sieve to strain the stock into a large bowl or another pot, squeezing excess liquids from the solids once they are cool enough to handle, and discard. This step should be done at least 1 day in advance for the flavors to meld, and it can be done up to 4 days in advance and refrigerated or frozen until ready to use.

Make the rouille: Place bell and chile peppers on a sheet pan on the top oven rack in a preheated broiler, or lay peppers on a bare burner with flame set to medium-high. Turn when they are blackened on one side, and repeat until the entire surface of each is blackened and charred. Place them into a stainless bowl and seal with plastic wrap. After 20 minutes, once peppers are cool to the touch and skins have puckered, slough skins off with your fingers over another bowl, to catch the pepper liquor. Discard skins, stems, and seeds, keeping the pepper flesh and liquor together. Wear plastic gloves when peeling the chile pepper. Use an immersion blender or food processor to purée the bell pepper, chile pepper, lemon juice, garlic, bread crumbs, parsley, and salt until smooth. Slowly add the olive oil as you purée to emulsify. The result will be a thick paste. Transfer to a small bowl for serving (or to a sealed container and refrigerate until ready to use). This step can be done up to 1 day in advance.

CONTINUED →

STOCK

2 tablespoons extra-virgin olive oil

1 cup chopped onion

1 cup sliced fennel bulb

5 garlic cloves, mashed with the flat of a knife

2 large tomatoes, coarsely chopped—if not using summer tomatoes, use whole canned

2 to 3 pounds of a mixture of fish heads, skeletons, trimmings

5 stems fresh parsley, fennel fronds, and cilantro (in any combination)

3 sprigs fresh thyme

1 tablespoon kosher salt

1 star anise

½ teaspoon saffron threads

½ teaspoon coriander seeds

2½ quarts water

ingredients continued →

BOUILLABAISSE + ROUILLE-SLATHERED TOASTS

Make the stew: Add the onion and fennel to a Dutch oven, heated over medium-high heat and drizzled with oil once hot. Sauté the mixture until translucent, stirring occasionally, 7 to 9 minutes.

Meanwhile, in a cast-iron skillet set over medium-high heat, drizzle enough oil to coat the pan once hot. Add the prawn halves, flesh side down. Cook until opaque and beginning to caramelize, 4 to 5 minutes. Transfer to a shallow bowl.

Drizzle oil into the skillet once more and add the scallops, keeping space in between them to avoid crowding. Sear them undisturbed for 2 minutes or until burnished and golden. Turn to the second side and baste their surfaces with the hot oil for 10 to 15 seconds, cooking for another minute or so total. Transfer the scallops to the plate with the prawns.

Add the tomato to the onion-fennel mixture. Add the stock to the pot and bring the mixture to a boil. Reduce the heat and simmer for 5 minutes. Add the fish pieces and any accumulated juices from the scallop bowl, and cook until the fish is just opaque, 5 minutes or so. Season to taste.

Gently ladle the bouillabaisse into shallow bowls. Nestle the scallops and prawns into each and finish with a shower of fennel fronds and fresh herbs. Serve with toasted bread slathered with the rouille.

NOTES: Evaluate what fish or seafood looks good the day you go to market: swap for the freshest, most plump versions to make your bouillabaisse sing. Mussels make an excellent addition and are often more widely available.

If you cannot find large head-on prawns, U16/20 shrimp are a fine substitute. If lobster is available, use claws and tail meat: claws left whole, tail meat pulled from the shell and cut into generous chunks. Whether you use lobster, prawns, or shrimp, use the carapaces toward making the stock.

ROUILLE

1 red bell pepper

1 hot chile pepper, such as aji, Calabrian, or chile de arbol

1 tablespoon fresh lemon juice

1 garlic clove

¼ cup fresh bread crumbs

¼ cup fresh parsley leaves

½ teaspoon kosher salt

⅓ cup extra-virgin olive oil

STEW

½ cup chopped onion

½ cup sliced fennel bulb

Extra-virgin olive oil, for drizzling

1 large head-on prawn, cut it in half lengthwise (in its shell) and seasoned with salt (see Note)

4 sea scallops, patted dry and seasoned with salt

1 large tomato, coarsely chopped—if not using a summer tomato, use whole canned

6 ounces cod or halibut, cut into 3-inch chunks, seasoned with salt

½ cup any combination fennel fronds, parsley, or cilantro

Toasted crusty bread for serving

BRAISED LAMB SHANKS + MELTED ONIONS

MAKES 6 SERVINGS

When brisk days bear down, this is the food I want to eat. Humble ingredients turn to bliss via a slow braise. Onions and lemons melt. Turnips become like candy. Lean meat is rendered so tender you can eat it with a spoon. Happy faces lean over big bowls. It's soulful food like this that makes everything feel right. Sautéing the veggies and browning the meat prior to braising them deepens their flavors, enhancing their savoriness before getting tucked into a flavorsome liquid for a good slow cook. If you can exert restraint and refrigerate the mixture in its pot overnight once it has cooled, then the following day, scrape any solidified fat away and reheat, the stew will give even more oomph.

LAMB SHANKS

6 small to medium lamb shanks—they should all be about the same size

Kosher salt and freshly ground black pepper

Extra-virgin olive oil, for sautéing

7 small onions, halved lengthwise or quartered if they are larger, root end trimmed with just enough left intact to hold each wedge together

12 to 14 small hakurei turnips, scrubbed, stems and root ends trimmed

6 small carrots, scrubbed, stem and root ends trimmed

2 garlic bulbs, cloves separated and peeled

2½ cups dry red wine

2 cups canned whole tomatoes

4 lemons, cut into wedges, seeds removed

3 bay leaves

4 cups chicken stock, preferably homemade (page 79)

ingredients continued →

Prepare the lamb shanks: Pat the lamb dry and arrange on a rimmed sheet pan. Generously season with kosher salt and freshly ground pepper and allow the shanks to come to room temperature while you prep the other ingredients.

Drizzle a tablespoon of oil into a Dutch oven or large, deep enameled cast-iron pot over medium heat. In two batches, so as not to crowd the pan, brown the shanks on all sides, about 10 minutes or so per batch. Transfer the browned shanks to a platter as you cook the remainder.

Place the onions in the hot fat cut sides down—add more oil as needed—and sear them in batches undisturbed until nicely browned, 5 to 8 minutes per side. Transfer the cooked onions to the platter with the lamb to make room for the remaining wedges, adding the turnips and carrots to the pot along with them. Brown the carrots and turnips, turning to brown all sides, 5 to 7 minutes. Add the garlic cloves and sear until fragrant, about 2 minutes per side.

Add the wine and bring to a boil, then cook for 1 minute to reduce. Stir in the tomatoes. Place the shanks and any accumulated juices on the platter back into the pot, nestling them in with the turnips and carrots, along with the lemon wedges and onions above, below, and around the shanks. Tuck in the bay leaves. Anything at the top will become more caramelized, while all submerged elements will become fall-apart soft. It's nice to have both textures, so I alternate ingredients for some with each outcome. Season with kosher salt and freshly ground pepper.

Preheat the oven to 325°F. Place a sheet pan on a rack in the lowest position to catch any bubbling liquid as the braise cooks, with another rack placed in the lower third to accommodate the pot with its lid on.

CONTINUED →

MASHED POTATOES

3 russet potatoes, peeled and cubed

2 medium Yukon gold potatoes, peeled and cubed

2 tablespoons salted butter

½ cup sour cream

½ cup milk

Kosher salt and freshly ground black pepper

ROUGH GREMOLATA

Finely grated lemon zest from 3 lemons

1½ teaspoon field garlic bulbs, crushed into a paste

6 tablespoons chopped parsley

2 cups hoary bittercress, stems trimmed from roots, or chopped arugula

Flake salt

Pour in the stock and bring to a boil. Cover the pot and transfer to the oven. Braise the shanks until they are tender, about 2½ hours. Uncover the pot and continue to cook in the oven until the shanks are so tender that the meat nearly falls off the bone and the braising liquid has reduced some, about 45 minutes.

Make the mashed potatoes: During the last 30 minutes of cooking the braise, simmer the potatoes in just enough salted water to cover. Bring them to a boil, then lower to simmer and cook until the potatoes are tender when pierced with a sharp knife.

Strain the potatoes into a colander. Carefully transfer them in batches to a potato ricer, passing them through to a medium bowl. Add the butter to the riced potatoes as you work—the residual heat will melt it. Dollop the sour cream onto potatoes just before finishing and add the milk once all potatoes are riced. Season with ½ teaspoon kosher salt, or more to taste, and freshly ground black pepper. Fold in to incorporate, taste again, and adjust the seasoning as needed. Replace the lid until the lamb is ready.

Remove the braise from the oven and allow to cool on a wire rack for 10 minutes. Alternatively, plan ahead to cool the braise, as the flavors of this dish deepen meaningfully on the second day. Discard solidified fat and reheat before serving.

Make the gremolata: As the braise cools, mix together the lemon zest, field garlic paste, and parsley (and arugula, if not using bittercress) in a bowl.

Serve the lamb shanks, veggies, and flavorful liquid ladled atop the mashed potatoes. Finish each dish with a couple spoonfuls of the gremolata and tender bittercress, and a sprinkle of flake salt to taste.

PASTA PUTTANESCA

Simple, flavorful puttanesca originates in Naples. Among various legends as to the origins of its name is the tale of a 1950s chef, whose hungry diners near closing time pleaded "Facci una puttanata qualsiasi," meaning, "throw together whatever." Pasta puttanesca is a perfect pantry meal. If you keep salt-packed capers, oil-packed anchovy fillets, jarred or refrigerated olives, dry pasta, and whole canned tomatoes in your cupboards, you have everything for this delectable meal. While the traditional preparation is made with Gaeta olives, I love the slight smokiness wrinkled, salt-cured Moroccan olives add, along with their denser, somewhat meaty texture. A little tomato paste, garlic, and red pepper flakes make this dish an even greater powerhouse, producing a remarkable and fast meal. To make this vegetarian, add a splash or two of soy sauce in place of the anchovies.

In a 9-inch enameled sauté pan, heat the anchovies over medium heat in half the oil until they sizzle. Break them up with a spatula or wooden spoon to help them dissolve. Add the garlic and stir to incorporate, stirring frequently until fragrant, 2 to 3 minutes.

Add the remaining oil, the olives, and capers and stir to combine. Cook for a minute or two to bind the anchovy mixture to the olive-caper mixture.

Add in the tomatoes, tomato paste, red pepper flakes, and a few grinds of freshly ground black pepper and stir to incorporate. Stir occasionally. Once bubbling, break the tomatoes up into coarse chunks.

Lower the heat to simmer and reduce the liquid until the sauce has thickened, 7 to 10 minutes, lowering the heat as needed so it doesn't splatter as it cooks. Taste. Adjust the seasoning as needed. Turn off the heat and set aside while the pasta cooks.

Cook the noodles in well-salted water according to the package instructions for al dente. Use tongs to transfer the pasta to a serving platter, top with the sauce, and toss to coat. Use the tongs and a large spoon to pile generous sauce and noodles onto plates.

4 or 5 anchovies

2 tablespoons extra-virgin olive oil

2 or 3 garlic cloves, finely grated on a Microplane

⅓ cup black oil-cured olives, pits removed and coarsely chopped

2 tablespoons salt-packed capers, rinsed and drained

1 28-ounce can (or homemade canned) whole tomatoes

1 teaspoon tomato paste

1 teaspoon red pepper flakes, more if you like spicy

Freshly ground black pepper

8 ounces linguine or fettuccine or other long, flat noodle

PASTA PUTTANESCA • PUNTARELLE +
TARDIVO WITH PUNCHY DRESS (PAGE 200)

CHICKEN THIGHS, QUINCE, CIPOLLINI, PRESERVED LEMON

This one-pan dish feels like an embrace, keeping you cozy when it's cold out. Mellow, earthy flavors are complemented by preserved lemon and poached quince. Soak up the pan sauce with couscous, rice, or a good crusty bread. You may use any kind of small onion or swap tart, firm apples for the quinces.

Pat the chicken thighs dry and place on a small tray. Season both sides with salt and pepper and let sit at room temperature for 30 minutes before cooking.

Warm a large cast-iron skillet over medium heat. When hot, add 2 teaspoons olive oil. Sauté the onions and any larger carrots until they begin to show a little color, about 5 minutes. Add the remaining smaller carrots, agitate the pan to coat, and cook for 2 more minutes, turning once.

Preheat the oven to 400°F.

Scoot the veggies to the periphery of the skillet and add the chicken thighs skin side down. Reposition the vegetables, fitting them between and around the chicken, placing lesser-cooked sides on the hot pan surface. Cook undisturbed for 7 minutes, rotating the pan halfway through to ensure even browning.

Turn the thighs skin side up. Add the sage and quince, rearranging other vegetables to lay the quince slices flat on the pan surface, and cook for 3 minutes or until the quince slightly browns.

Turn the quince slices and add the wine; reduce by half. Add the stock, along with the preserved lemon skin, and bring back to a boil. Transfer the skillet to the oven to cook for 12 minutes, or until the juices run clear from the thighs when pierced with a sharp knife.

Divide onto plates, giving each serving equal portions of carrots, onion, quinces, and their liquid. Finish with freshly ground pepper. Serve with crusty bread and eat at once.

4 skin-on bone-in chicken thighs (about 1½ pounds)

Kosher salt and freshly ground black pepper

Olive oil, for sautéing

12 cipollini onions

10 small carrots, peeled and ends trimmed (save for stock, pages 79 and 80)

12 to 15 sage leaves (about 3 tablespoons)

4 quarters Rosé + Spice Poached Quince (page 101), each sliced in half (see Note)

1 cup dry white wine

1½ cups mushroom or chicken stock (pages 79 and 80)

Skin from a third of a Preserved Meyer Lemon (page 97), sliced very thinly on a diagonal

Crusty bread, to sop up any juices

NOTE: You may use poached apples in place of the quince if you cannot find quince. See the Note on page 101 for the best apple types.

HALIBUT + POACHED VEGETABLES WITH AIOLI SLATHER

MAKES 2 SERVINGS

Aromatic-infused veggies appear in spring and fall menus at the cottage, sometimes as an appetizer including our own radishes pulled that day from the garden and finished with crispy bread crumbs (page 155). Burnished halibut has become a regular feature, too. It is delicate, satiny, and when pan-fried for a crispy skin, is some of the best fish to be found. I can trace the sustainability of these ingredients through my relationships with family fishermen and local fishmongers, ensuring I support smartly managed fisheries. This warming dish marks the change in seasons.

HALIBUT

2 6-ounce skin-on halibut fillets

Kosher salt

POACHED VEGETABLES

2 to 3 cups corn stock (page 82)

1 cup dry white wine

¼ cup extra-virgin olive oil

4 strips lemon peel, bitter white pith removed

4 strips orange peel

1 medium fennel bulb, stems trimmed, reserve a small handful of fronds—trim root, leaving enough intact to keep its shape when sliced lengthwise into thin wedges

4 to 8 small radishes—French breakfast, watermelon, or Easter egg are good choices—cut in halves lengthwise

6 shallots, cut in half lengthwise

1 bay leaf

¾ teaspoon kosher salt

½ teaspoon red pepper flakes

Extra-virgin olive oil, for sautéing

2 tablespoons salted butter

2 slices Sourdough Bread (page 68), toasted

Aioli (page 158) for serving

Prep the halibut: Pat the halibut dry and place the fillets skin side up on a small sheet pan. Generously season with kosher salt and allow to come to room temperature while you poach the vegetables.

Poach the vegetables: Place the stock, wine, olive oil, lemon and orange peels, fennel, radishes, shallots, bay leaf, salt, and red pepper flakes in a 9-inch Dutch oven or other heavy pot, tucking the smaller elements between and around the large so the liquid submerges all. Bring the mixture to a simmer. Cut a parchment cartouche, aka a parchment lid, and place flush to the surface. Gently simmer until all the vegetables are tender, 15 to 20 minutes. Timing will vary based on the size of the vegetable. Check the radishes and shallots first: if they give when pierced with a sharp knife, they are ready. Use a slotted spoon to transfer them to a plate or bowl as they become ready. Replace the cartouche to finish cooking the remainder. Remove the pot from the heat and discard the cartouche. This step can be done up to 3 days in advance, with the vegetables stored in their poaching liquid, refrigerated, in a sealed container.

Heat a large cast-iron skillet over high heat. Turn to medium-high once hot, add a tablespoon of oil, and swirl to coat. Once it shimmers, add the fillets, skin side down, keeping space between them to avoid crowding. Cook for a minute, then add half the butter, dragging it around and between the fillets as it foams.

Sear the halibut 3 to 5 minutes on the first side or until the edges become opaque, turning the heat down to medium as needed. Turn them over, drizzle a small bit of oil, and add the remaining butter to the pan, tilting the pan as the butter foams to coat. Tip the pan toward you to collect a spoonful of the cooking liquid and baste the fillets with the hot fat. Repeat the tilt-baste process for 20 to 30 seconds to render the skin crispy. Continue cooking for 1 to 2 more minutes, depending on the thickness of your fillets. They are ready when they feel firm but give slightly when pushed with the back of a spoon. The flesh should be opaque and silky.

Ladle the aromatic vegetables, including the citrus peels and some of the liquid into shallow bowls. Top with fennel fronds and nestle the halibut onto the vegetables. Serve with crusty bread slathered with aioli and eat at once.

PERSIMMON-DATE ICE CREAM + SPICED NUTS

MAKES 1 QUART

As soon as I see persimmons at the market, I jump at the fortune and cart armfuls home. When buying either Fuyu or Hachiya persimmons, look for fruits with a smooth surface, free of any blemishes or tears. They will usually be hard—fine for the Fuyu—but the Hachiya require time to ripen before you may consume them. This is serendipitous, because it gives a stretch of days so you may strategize the myriad things you'll create, growing ever desirous as you watch them transform. Sitting on my kitchen sideboard piled into a bowl, they make a perfect Dutch masters still life. After a couple weeks of patiently waiting, the longer, more acorn-shaped Hachiya persimmons ripen. These must be nearly falling-apart-ripe to be enjoyed, as they are highly astringent otherwise, and will make you think they are terrible if eaten prematurely. When eaten at the proper moment, this fruit is the epitome of sensuality. Once Hachiya persimmons are ripe, make this ice cream. It is earthy-sweet and a favorite way to use the beloved fruit. The spiced nuts bring delectable texture and should be added as generously as you like.

In a medium saucepan, combine the half-and-half and cream. Bring the mixture to a simmer, stirring occasionally. Add the sugar and salt and stir until the sugar dissolves, 3 to 4 minutes. Taste and add more sugar and salt as needed to balance the flavors. It should taste slightly too sweet when warm, as the sweetness will be muted once the ice cream is frozen. Refrigerate at least 4 hours, or overnight.

Cut the stem from the persimmons and slice each in half lengthwise. Examine if there is a distinct seed in either and remove it if so. Scoop the persimmon flesh from the skin and discard the skins.

Transfer the cream mixture to an ice cream maker. Churn the cream according to the manufacturer's instructions. Five minutes before the ice cream is ready, add the persimmon flesh and date syrup. Churn until incorporated. Transfer to an airtight container and freeze until solid.

Serve the persimmon-date ice cream with spiced nuts in shallow bowls.

2 cups half-and-half

2 cups heavy cream, not ultra-pasteurized

1 cup cane sugar, plus more as needed

½ teaspoon kosher salt, plus more as needed

2 small very ripe Hachiya persimmons

2 to 4 tablespoons date syrup

Spiced Nuts (page 77) for garnish

QUINCE TARTE TATIN

MAKES 6 TO 8 SERVINGS

The characteristically apple dessert is said to have originated in the late 1880s in the Loire Valley, France. By accident or folly, the tart was served upside down in a hotel run by the Tatin sisters, and that is how it got its name. However it occurred, we can all be grateful for the melding of caramelized butter and sugar cooked onto fruit and pastry, making a pretty fine treat from a rather simple process. In this recipe I use quince. I prefer less sugar and have swapped it for the aromatic liquid they're poached in, reduced to a thin syrup. Once the quince are poached, this dessert comes together easily. Be sure to include one or two lemon peels from the poaching mixture, as their chewy brightness adds even more interest.

1 package all-butter puff pastry, such as Dufour brand

1 tablespoon cane sugar

9 poached quince quarters and 1 cup poaching liquid from Rosé + Spice Poached Quince (page 101)

2 tablespoons unsalted butter, cubed

All-purpose flour for dusting

Ice cream or crème fraîche for serving

Pink peppercorns for garnish

Unfold the puff pastry fully, then fold it flush back onto itself along a natural fold line most closely resembling a square. Roll the puff pastry into a square about ¼ inch thick, just large enough to exceed the edges of a 9-inch pan. Use a pan to score a circle just larger than the pan. Separate the scraps (flatten and reroll for another use later), then cut an X in the center of the pastry, so that while baking, steam can escape. Chill on a tray in the refrigerator.

Preheat the oven to 425°F.

In a heavy enameled or cast-iron 9-inch pan, dissolve the sugar in the poaching liquid, set over medium-high heat. Reduce the liquid by three-quarters, five to seven minutes, leaving ¼ cup once brought to a boil. Add the cubed butter and allow to bubble undisturbed for 30 seconds or so. Swirl to incorporate.

Remove from the heat and place the quince cut sides facing up into the reduced syrup (keep in mind the rounded sides will be what you see once the pan is inverted). Lay the pastry on top, tucking the edges in around the perimeter.

Bake for 45 minutes or until crust is deeply golden and cooked through (examine at the scored X to confirm) and the caramel is bubbling. Check after 35 minutes and fold a short length of aluminum foil over any edges that may be extra dark, to allow the other areas to catch up.

Allow the tart to cool in the pan for 5 minutes before inverting, so the caramel can set and be less likely to run out of the pan (careful, it is quite hot). Press a serving plate onto the pan with one hand, and holding a potholder with the other, invert the pan swiftly and smoothly. If any quince stick to the pan, use a butter knife to release and replace onto the tart.

Cut into wedges. Serve with ice cream or crème fraîche and pink peppercorns, sloughing the papery bits between your fingers and sprinkling a pinch of the papery sheaths and peppercorns onto each slice.

AUTUMN OLIVE LINZER TART

MAKES 8 TO 10 SERVINGS

This festive tart is one I love to pair with coffee. It is earthy and not too sweet: think midday, curl-up-by-the-fire, elevenses momentum snack. It is also perfect to take to neighbors as a holiday gift—it travels well in its fluted pan—or as part of a late-season potluck. You could substitute any tart jam such as raspberry, lingonberry, or red currant, but the autumn olive version is rosy, round, and a conversation starter—who wouldn't be impressed you made jam without spending a nickel, from an invasive shrub? It is best served once completely cooled, or even the following day. Another make-ahead pantry staple stunner.

Make the pastry: Toast the hazelnut flour in a large nonstick dry skillet over medium heat until fragrant, stirring regularly to avoid burning, 3 to 5 minutes (see Notes, page 230).Transfer the toasted mixture to the bowl of a food processor. Repeat with the almond flour, agitating the pan to disperse it evenly and stirring to avoid burning. Once it's fragrant and slightly golden, add to the hazelnut flour.

Add the all-purpose flour, spelt flour, sugar, citrus zests, cinnamon, baking powder, cloves, and salt and pulse the mixture to incorporate. Add the butter and pulse until the mixture resembles coarse sand, with a few slightly larger pieces of butter remaining. Add the whole egg and yolk and pulse to combine until the dough comes together.

Divide the dough onto two segments of plastic wrap, one mound slightly larger than the other. Working with one, gather opposite ends of the plastic wrap to bring the dough together, using the plastic wrap as a barrier to limit how much you directly handle it. Flatten the dough into a disk, wrap securely, and compress it further, pressing around the circumference with one hand and flattening it in the center with the other. Repeat with remaining mound. Refrigerate the pastry for at least 20 minutes to allow it to mellow. This step can be done up to 3 days in advance.

Butter a fluted 9-inch tart pan with a removable bottom. Roll the dough about ¼ inch thick to exceed the pan edges by ¾ inch all around, sandwiched between a layer of lightly floured plastic wrap and parchment. Roll incrementally from the center out, so that dough edge does not split.

Once it is the correct size, remove the plastic wrap from the dough and center the inverted tart pan on it. With one hand underneath the parchment and the other on top of the pan, invert the dough. Place the pan onto the work surface and peel away the parchment. If the dough sticks to the paper, refrigerate it for 10 to 15 minutes until the parchment easily comes free.

CONTINUED →

PASTRY

¾ cup hazelnut flour

¾ cup almond flour

1 cup all-purpose flour

½ cup spelt flour

½ cup cane sugar

1 tablespoon finely grated lemon zest (1 lemon)

1 tablespoon finely grated orange zest (half an orange)

1 teaspoon ground cinnamon

½ teaspoon baking powder

¼ teaspoon whole cloves, ground into a powder with a mortar and pestle (see Notes, page 230)

¼ teaspoon kosher salt

14 tablespoons salted butter, cubed and freezer-cold (see Notes, page 261)

1 egg plus 1 yolk

1⅓ cups Autumn Olive Jam (page 99)

Unsalted butter for greasing

Confectioners' sugar for dusting, or crème fraîche for serving

Working your way around the pastry, lift the overhang with one hand while the other gently presses the pastry flush with the base and into the corners of the pan. Secure the pan along the outside edge as you press the dough into the fluting.

Working from the center outward, use a rolling pin over the top edge of the tart pan to trim away any overhang. Save scraps to repair any tears or thinner areas and for the rolled edge to finish the tart. Refrigerate the pastry as you work on the lattice.

Bring the smaller disk out 10 to 15 minutes before planning to roll, to allow the dough to warm slightly. Roll the dough in between a layer of floured parchment and the plastic wrap it was wrapped in, to ¼ to ⅛ inch thick and long enough to exceed the tart pan. Use a ruler and pizza wheel or sharp knife to cut the dough into 1-inch-wide strips. Refrigerate or freeze the lattice pieces on a sheet pan 15 minutes before attempting to lace them, or lay them as an unwoven lattice for easier work.

Spread the jam in an even layer on the base of the tart, all the way to the edges. Arrange strips into a lattice design, then trim the lattice ends flush with the inner edge of the tart base. Roll the remaining scraps together into a ¼-inch-thick rope. Arrange it along the circumference to unite the lattice and fluted edge. Mend any breaks in the rope using the back of your fingernail, smoothening the seams into a continuous circle. Refrigerate the tart for 20 minutes, or up to overnight.

Preheat the oven to 350°F. Bake the tart on a parchment-lined sheet pan 40 to 45 minutes, until the jam bubbles and the pastry is puffed and golden. Arrange lengths of foil along any part of the crust to protect it from becoming too dark, as needed.

Cool the linzer tart on a wire rack completely, 45 to 60 minutes. Lift it out of the fluted ring and slide it from its base onto a cake plate. Serve dusted with confectioners' sugar or with crème fraîche.

NOTES: I prefer to use whole spices, particularly the cloves used here. Whenever I need them, I grind cloves using a mortar and pestle. They last longer and release an incredible aroma that makes me love cloves more than I ever did when I used them in powder form.

Always toast nuts and nut flours before using them. Doing so unlocks their fragrance and delicate oils.

PAWPAW CRÈME BRÛLÉE

MAKES 4 CUSTARDS

Also known as the custard apple, pawpaws have an ardent following by anyone who has tasted them. Their flavor is a cross between banana and mango, with texture of pear-pineapple. Their fragrant flesh imparts a special sweetness to this divine custard. Once the sugar glass has hardened, a scattering of delicate herbs or flowers adds important contrast to the sweetness—they are not just pretty leaves and petals. They assert a peppery punch that requires you pay attention. This dessert readily scales up or down and freezes well, too, so you can entertain grandly without working yourself to the bone. Just wait to add the final sugar for brûléeing for once they have been thawed in the refrigerator.

¾ cup ripe pawpaw flesh (from about 2 pawpaws; page 34)

2 cups heavy cream

3 tablespoons cane sugar, plus additional to brûlée

Pinch kosher salt

Finely grated zest from 1 lemon

4 duck eggs, or 5 chicken eggs

1 tablespoon leaves or flowers from strawberry mint, calamintha, or lemon thyme

Set four ¾-cup heatproof ramekins, shallow porcelain bowls, or small gratin pans in a baking pan large enough to hold them.

Place the pawpaw flesh into a small high-speed blender. Blend into a smooth purée.

In a saucepan over medium heat, combine the cream, sugar, and salt, stirring until the sugar dissolves and small bubbles appear around the edges of the cream, 4 to 5 minutes. Add the zest and allow the mixture to sit for 30 minutes to infuse. Strain the mixture through muslin draped inside a sieve or a fine-mesh wire strainer into a bowl. While the cream infuses, preheat the oven to 325°F.

Crack open one of the eggs and transfer it to your palm. Gently pass it back and forth between your hands, allowing the white to slip through your fingers and into a bowl placed underneath. Place the yolk into a separate medium bowl. Repeat with remaining eggs. Save the egg whites for My Mother's Gruyère Soufflé (page 246).

Whisk the yolks in a medium bowl until thickened, just past the 1-minute mark, when your arm starts to ache. Gradually whisk the cream mixture into the beaten yolks. Whisk in the pawpaw purée until fully blended, then strain the mixture once more.

Set the baking pan with the ramekins near the oven. Boil a large kettle of water. Divide the custard equally between each dish. Carefully transfer the pan with the custards into the oven. Gently but swiftly pour the hot water into the baking dish to create a bain marie, so that the water reaches halfway up the sides of the ramekins.

Bake until the custards are set but still tremble slightly in the center when shaken. I use shallow enameled gratin pans. They conduct excellent heat and were ready in 20 minutes. Ceramic or Pyrex vessels may take 30 to 35 minutes. Begin checking at 25 minutes, using the wobble test at 5-minute intervals.

Using tongs and a potholder, carefully lift the custards out one at a time and place them on a wire rack. Cool on the rack for 25 minutes. Wrap each ramekin tightly with plastic wrap and refrigerate until well chilled, at least 4 hours, or up to overnight.

Remove the custards from the refrigerator. Sprinkle a layer of sugar to coat the surface. Using a small kitchen torch, heat the sugar until bubbling and deeply caramelized. Repeat with the remaining custards. Allow the sugar glass to harden. Garnish with tiny sprigs or the pulled leaves from your chosen herb. Shatter the surface with a spoon and enjoy!

winter

It is sunny out. I'm grateful for that. The temps will rise and I'll take a walk, perhaps even remove the cold frame for overwintering greens, if it feels temperate. My kitties are lazybones who bask by the fire. That enviable toasty fire, which I'd like very much to transport into the considerably chillier kitchen, to keep me company doing the roasting and sizzling prep work, for guests who arrive tomorrow. The oven will be my warming friend, soon enough.

DECEMBER 5

I have developed a clear rapport feeding the birds. They skitter to the windowsill just outside the sunroom in the morning as I gather seed cups and fill the feeders. I am beside myself with imploring peeps and cheep-instructions—they have gotten bossy!

This routine started when we ran out of seed bags, and due to COVID-19, we weren't in a rush to run to our garden center to restock. A month prior, a neighbor we met on a bike ride asked if we liked feeding birds. This was an exciting, leading proposition. She offered the dried sunflower heads lining her husband's plowed cornfields for us to harvest. Her generous offer merited a reciprocal delivery of homemade sourdough bread, one of those food things that feels like an expression of gratitude.

After a couple weeks installing the glorious heads and watching birds pluck prized seeds and race away, I witnessed the smallest, braver birds hopping onto the flower head before I'd even placed it onto the feeder. I began holding the sturdy, dry stems to encourage their visits. When we restocked seed bags, I spontaneously offered them the cup of treats that I usually whisked out to Tarzan, our resident red squirrel. Sure enough, bold, trusting chickadees soon came to perch, choose a treat, examine me, and fly off. They now wait for us as we exit the house, and it feels like something out of a Mary Poppins movie, if I'm honest.

The featherweight of chickadees landing on my finger is so precious. The somehow even lighter weight of red-breasted nuthatches is impossibly cute, their delicate claws holding onto me as they peer at my face, alternating with an eye to the cup. They are as demure with their cute little "peep" toward me as they are bossy with the other birds that visit: a rather squawking horn sound. They chase others off with great purpose, nose around in the treat cup for a choice morsel and make off. Only then do the numerous other birds take their turns diving, swooping in, alight, snatch, flee. As winter wore on, I established a self-serve treat cup, where intrepid birds dove and collected mostly peanuts, the favorite among everyone, all day until dusk. We even have a few brave cardinal couples who visit in the wee hours of evening, aware of special treats made available for them.

JANUARY 12

Winter is a quieter time in so many ways. And so what few sounds there are become etched into our days. At the cottage, the song of white-throated sparrows is a lullaby in the quiet. They are wistful songs, sung as if the sparrows are not sure someone will know who they are, or wondering who will hear them. It is solemn and very sweet.

Though the gardens are all brown faded stems, my relationship with the outdoors keeps me returning to witness, to connect to the animals'

daily exercise of survival and perseverance. And in turn this has piqued curiosities, such as how do chickadees sleep, anyhow? I am learning more all the time about the natural world around me. Many birds in fact hide—cache—seeds for later on. I have observed birds tucking seeds into the seams in our cedar gate, then honing their beaks and scuttering off for the next score. They use their thin beaks to deftly bury nuts inside stiffened flower stems, in our woodpile, or even into the seams of our raised beds. Many hundred times over, they must have an excellent recall to retrace where this or that has been stowed. This enchants me and gives cold days new purpose.

It's also made me realize the value in leaving all the dead matter just as it is, so they can use them to alight onto, cache their bounty, and even use them as protection from wind or predators. I can and will cut back the dead matter once it's early spring. I'll be hankering for work like this, assurance that spring's crowning shoots are arriving. I marvel at the bravado of birds in their relentless survival dance—tiny, perfect, paranoid creatures.

WILD SALMON RILLETTES + SEEDED RYE LAVASH

MAKES ENOUGH RILLETTES FOR THREE OR FOUR 4-OUNCE JELLY JARS

I've been a pickle lover my whole life—my mom has proudly recounted that I ate pickled pearl onions straight from the jar as young as the age of two. I love their salty brightness and pairing them with rich foods. I also love pâtés and rillettes. They reinvent leftovers or scraps, refashioning them into lush, somehow luxurious-feeling fare. In a waste-not-want-not fashion, sometimes I roast a salmon frame so I can comb the last bits of meat from the bones. I use this to make rillettes. Perhaps there's a leftover piece from spring sockeye (with Fried Sage Gremolata, page 134) or summer's roasted side (with Spicy Cucumber-Orange Salsa, page 167). Leftover meat from either can be frozen, then thawed and incorporated into this dish. Fennel seeds are a natural choice added to the lavash, but you could just as easily use sesame seeds, ground pepper, or just flake salt. Mind how much salt you add to top the lavash so you strike a balance when eaten with the rillettes.

Combine the room temperature butter with the chives in a shallow bowl and use a fork to mash them together until combined. Add the mayo, horseradish, mustard, smoked paprika, lemon zest and juice and stir together until uniform. Use a spatula to drag any remaining butter solids against the bowl to make them easier to incorporate and use a fork to render any larger clumps uniform.

Add the capers, both cooked and cured salmon, the dill, and a generous amount of ground pepper and fold in until combined. Taste and adjust the seasoning as necessary. Pack the rillettes mixture into jars, then smooth the surfaces. Pour the 2 tablespoons of slightly cooled melted butter on top, divided equally among the jars. Gently smooth any high points on the rillettes, leveling the surface so that the butter fully submerges the rillettes. Once the butter solidifies, this layer of fat serves as an additional means of preserving the mixture, extending how long you may use it.

Refrigerate the rillettes for at least 4 hours before eating. Spread the rillettes on the lavash and sprinkle herb leaves and fronds on top. Any leftover rillettes keep, sealed in the refrigerator, for up to 1 week or frozen for up to 6 months.

NOTE: If you cannot find garlic chives, scallions or chives work just as well.

4 tablespoons salted butter, half at room temperature and half melted and cooled slightly

1½ teaspoons garlic chives, minced (see Note)

2 tablespoons mayonnaise

1 tablespoon prepared horseradish

2 teaspoons Dijon mustard

1 teaspoon smoked paprika

Zest and juice from half a lemon

1 tablespoon salt-packed capers, rinsed well and finely chopped

6 ounces cooked salmon, flaked with a fork

4 ounces cured salmon, chopped

½ cup fresh dill, chopped, or a mix of dill and parsley

Freshly ground black pepper

Seeded Rye Lavash (page 67) for serving

Herbs or foraged greens such as bittercress, garlic mustard, ground elder, parsley, or dill, to garnish

WINTER SKILLET: FRIED DUCK EGGS, WILTED GREENS, FURIKAKE

MAKES 2 SERVINGS

I always ate royally when hosted by my friend Aya in Japan. Tiny, unseen restaurants became our regular destinations, as Aya knew what to look for and could decipher the scrolled banners that swayed in their doorways. She shared many kinds of Japanese foods and with each, I was struck by the array of flavors and textures included in each meal. It has shaped how I eat to this day. To add crunch and umami to a simple breakfast, I reach for a favorite Japanese sprinkle, furikake. Its elements are simple: crunchy, briny, smoky, and herbaceous. If you decide to add bonito flakes and seaweed to your pantry, you can throw this condiment together immediately. They may feel like niche ingredients, but if you already love Japanese—or deeply savory—flavors, they store infinitely and are quite versatile. I have made furikake with dried sumac and mint leaves, as well as with purple shiso from my garden. They are both great, so I have included how to make each below. Scatter the furikake onto fried duck eggs (their yolks are like liquid gold) and juicy wilted greens. The layers bring decadence to something otherwise simple. And that is a nice luxury to lace into a day.

FURIKAKE

2 tablespoons finely chopped dried shiso leaves (see Note)

1 tablespoon plus 1 teaspoon bonito flakes, rubbed into a coarse powder between your fingers

1 sheet nori seaweed, cut into ¼-inch squares

1 tablespoon sesame seeds, toasted

1 teaspoon black sesame seeds, toasted

Extra-virgin olive oil for sautéing

1 bunch scallions, ends trimmed, cut in half to make shorter stalks

14 leaves escarole, including a few smaller, more tender leaves near the heart

Kosher salt and freshly ground black pepper

2 duck eggs

Make the furikake: Combine the shiso leaves, bonito flakes, nori, and both sesame seeds in a medium bowl and stir to combine. Furikake will keep up to 2 months sealed in a jar at room temperature.

Over medium-high heat, warm a large cast-iron pan until it is hot. Lower the heat to medium, drizzle the olive oil, and swirl to coat. Sauté the scallions until they have softened and turned bright green and caramelized in parts, turning them periodically so that the white ends cook evenly, about 5 minutes.

Move the scallions to the cool side of the pan and repeat sautéing with the escarole, turning them so that the thick white ribs get contact with the hot pan. Add another drizzle of oil to help them along and season all with salt and pepper. When the escarole has cooked for 3 to 5 minutes, it should appear soft and translucent. Scoot all to the edge of pan and place the scallions on top of the escarole.

Add another drizzle of oil and add the eggs to the pan. While the eggs fry, arrange the escarole and scallions around them. Cook the eggs until they are crispy at their edges and the whites have fully set, 3 minutes or so. Season with freshly ground pepper.

Transfer the pan to the table, set on a trivet, and serve onto plates. Top with a shower of the furikake and eat at once.

NOTE: If you cannot find shiso, use 1 teaspoon sumac powder and 1 teaspoon dried mint, rubbed between your fingertips into a coarse powder.

APPLE + POMEGRANATE FLOGNARDE

MAKES 2 TO 4 SERVINGS

This custard goes by different names based on the region in which it is made and which fruit is used. Flognarde originates in the Auvergne region of France. Few ingredients, whisked vigorously together, produce a substantial custard. There is little sugar so it's a dish I most often serve as an indulgent breakfast for guests, featuring the season's fruits. When made with sour cherries, it's called a clafoutis. Peaches are a sublime summer version. Made with caramelized Seckel pears, it is as charming to behold as it is delicious. Glittery pomegranate is a welcome sight strewn onto the puffy custard in winter. Use the ripest fruit you can find, in whatever season it is, and the custard will turn out beautifully.

Preheat the oven with a heavy enameled 9-inch pan or Pyrex baking dish placed inside it to 425°F.

In a medium bowl, mix together the flour, cane sugar, zest, and milk. Add the eggs and beat vigorously until frothy.

Carefully remove the hot pan from the oven and add half the cubed butter. It should sizzle immediately on contact. Gently and quickly replace it in the oven to finish melting. Bring the pan back out from the oven, swirl the melted butter along the sides to coat, then carefully but swiftly pour the egg mixture into the pan. Fan the apple wedges onto the batter. It's okay if they slide around a little as you place them.

Dot the surface with the remaining cubed butter and return to the oven, baking until the custard puffs and has turned golden brown at the edges, 20 to 25 minutes. Do not open the oven at any point except to remove the pan from the oven when the flognarde is done, as the hot air required for it to puff will dissipate, hampering its rise.

Arrange small bowls filled with the pomegranate arils and slivered almonds at the table. Once the flognarde is ready, carefully bring it to the table, set on a trivet. Scatter the almonds on top, then shower with 1 to 2 tablespoons confectioners' sugar, sifted through a sieve. Cut into wedges, sprinkle with pomegranate arils, and serve.

NOTE: You may substitute sliced pears for the apples or include a scattering of raisins before baking as an alternative to pomegranates.

5 tablespoons all-purpose flour

4 tablespoons cane sugar

Zest from 2 or 3 Meyer lemons

⅔ cup whole milk

4 eggs

2 tablespoons salted butter, cubed

3 tart, firm apples, such as Braeburn, Evercrisp, or Arkansas Black, peeled (save for jam making) and cut into ½-inch wedges (see Note)

Arils from half a pomegranate, for sprinkling (see Note)

¼ cup slivered almonds, toasted, for sprinkling

Confectioners' sugar for dusting

MY MOTHER'S GRUYÈRE SOUFFLÉ

MAKES 2 GENEROUS SERVINGS

In our day-to-day, my Ma didn't have time for extra flourishes. She did, however, make clear delineations for special occasion foods, and how fondly we each regarded the special occasions! My Ma makes this soufflé on holidays in the angel food cake tin she baked many a birthday cake, rushing around to spoon the puffed treat onto our plates, just before it deflates. I've adapted this soufflé with buttermilk for extra zip and more spice for a warming effect. Serve this with the radish salad from the Spanish Tortilla (page 115), Spring Fling Salad in Green (page 124), or the crunchy salad from Eat'cha Garden (page 148). Save the leftover yolks for making aioli for Asparagus + Artichokes (page 123) or the Grand Aioli Summer Feast (page 158).

3 tablespoons salted butter, plus more for greasing the pan

1 ounce finely shredded Parmesan

3 tablespoons all-purpose flour

1 cup full-fat buttermilk

½ teaspoon kosher salt

½ teaspoon freshly ground black pepper

¼ teaspoon freshly grated nutmeg

¼ teaspoon chili powder

¼ teaspoon cayenne

6 egg whites

¼ teaspoon cream of tartar

4 ounces grated Gruyère

Butter a soufflé dish or two pint-size ramekins (see Note). Butter the top half of a 3-inch-wide piece of parchment, as long as the circumference of your vessel. Secure it in place by wrapping it around the dish and tying with kitchen twine, so it can act as a collar for the soufflé to climb. Sprinkle a quarter of the Parmesan cheese to lightly coat the dish and collar.

Preheat the oven to 375°F. Melt the butter in a medium saucepan over medium heat. Once foaming subsides, add the flour and whisk to fully incorporate. Lower the heat to medium-low as needed, whisking the roux constantly until golden and toasted smelling, 3 to 4 minutes. Add the buttermilk and whisk to combine. Whisk occasionally until the mixture is thickened and steaming, about 3 minutes. Turn the heat down slightly, add the salt, black pepper, nutmeg, chili powder, and cayenne and whisk to combine. Transfer the béchamel to a large mixing bowl to cool slightly.

Beat the egg whites with an electric mixer on high speed until frothy. Add the cream of tartar and whip until stiff peaks hold. Fold in a quarter of the egg whites and half the remaining Parmesan into the béchamel, working to minimize deflating the air you just whipped into the whites. Add the Gruyère and half the remaining egg whites, folding in gently until uniform. Fold in the last of the egg whites, then carefully transfer the mixture to the prepared dish.

Scatter the remaining Parmesan on top and bake on a rimmed sheet pan for 30 minutes or until puffed and golden. Do not open the oven while it bakes, or you will diminish the heat needed to give the soufflé its loft. Untie the collar, serve alongside salad, and eat at once.

NOTE: If you don't have a soufflé dish or ramekins, butter the bottom of a straight-sided metal saucepan, adhere a parchment circle, and press flush with the base. Butter it, then sprinkle the cheese as you would otherwise.

BEET, MANDARINQUAT, CELERY SALAD

MAKES 2 SERVINGS

A popular Lower East Side boîte in the early 2000s, 'Inoteca introduced me to the first beet salad worth remembering. Jewel-like orange segments, salty shaved Parmigiano-Reggiano, torn mint, and toasted hazelnuts brought humble beets to new heights. When I discovered mandarinquats at lovely Laura Ramirez's stand (JJ's Lone Daughter Ranch) at the Santa Monica farmers' market some years ago, I was gobsmacked with how incredible they tasted and wanted to use them in as many dishes as I could. A hybrid of kumquats and mandarins, they have juicy sweet-tart flesh, and the whole thing is edible, skin and all. If you cannot find mandarinquats, kumquats are charming and beautiful, or you can use blood orange segments. Make the spiced nuts in advance so you can scatter them on top to finish the dish.

If using mandarinquats, slice the fruit lengthwise into four to six wedges apiece, removing any particularly large seeds. If you are using kumquats, slice the fruit widthwise into three or four wheels each, removing their seeds. Place the citrus in a salad bowl.

Add the beets, celery, and mint. Squeeze the additional orange juice over the salad, add a drizzle of oil and ground black pepper, and toss to combine. Season once more with ground pepper.

Divide the salad between two plates. Shave the Parmesan generously on top and scatter with spiced nuts. Sprinkle flake salt for garnish and eat at once.

6 mandarinquats or kumquats

2 medium-large beets, roasted, skins rubbed off (page 203), and cut into bite-size wedges

2 stalks celery and their leaves, sliced thinly

10 to 14 fresh mint leaves, torn

Juice from half a blood orange, mandarin, or small Cara Cara orange

Extra-virgin olive oil, to drizzle

Freshly ground black pepper

Parmesan, shaved with a vegetable peeler

1 generous handful Spiced Nuts (page 77), coarsely chopped

Flake salt

CURED KING SALMON, PERSIMMON, PICKLES

MAKES 2 SERVINGS

I dreamt up this recipe when a guest shared her love for all things unusual, briny, and raved about the cured fish she'd seen me make on Instagram. Once I anchored the dish with cured king salmon, the other winter-themed elements jumped out at me: meaty persimmon, crunchy buckwheat, clacking trout roe, and finger lime—I knew the combination would be divine. Finger lime, endemic to Aboriginal peoples in Australia, is a delicacy worth seeking out. Its vesicles burst as you chew, earning it the appropriate moniker "lime caviar." If you cannot find finger limes, just use a small squeeze of regular lime wedge as garnish.

2 tablespoons buckwheat groats

8 to 10 slices Wild Salmon Gravlax made with king salmon (page 94)

1 Fuyu persimmon, sliced into bite-size wedges

3 or 4 rings pickled pearl onions (see page 165) or Pickled Ramps (page 85)

1 to 2 tablespoons pickled magnolia petals (recipe follows; see Note)

1 tablespoon trout roe

1 small finger lime

⅓ cup radish and cilantro microgreens, or any micro mix

In a dry skillet over medium-low heat, toast the groats until lightly brown and slightly fragrant, about 3 minutes. Transfer to a small dish and set aside to cool to room temperature. This can be done up to 3 days in advance and stored sealed in a jar at room temperature.

Arrange the cured salmon on two plates. Nestle the persimmon and pickled onions to frame it. Arrange a few clusters of magnolia petals, followed by trout roe. Slice a finger lime in half and squeeze the vesicles into little piles, using the whole of it between the two plates. Scatter the buckwheat and the greens on top and eat at once.

NOTE: You may use store-bought pickled ginger if you cannot find magnolia petals.

PICKLED MAGNOLIA PETALS
MAKES ONE 4-OUNCE JAR

This dish gives purpose to foraged, pickled magnolia petals, which I dared not use until the right dish presented itself. They resemble ginger in a slightly more floral way.

½ cup rice wine vinegar

1 tablespoon cane sugar

1 teaspoon kosher salt

½ cup young magnolia flowers or enough to pack a 4-ounce jar, petals cut from their base

Combine the vinegar, sugar, and salt in a small saucepan and warm over medium heat. Stir to dissolve the solids. Once they are fully dissolved, remove the pan from the heat and allow to cool slightly. Pack the magnolia petals into a jar. Pour the vinegar mixture in, pressing petals down to submerge. Taste the pickling liquid to check if the balance between sweet and sharp is to your taste and adjust the seasoning as needed. Allow the flavors to meld at least 1 day in before using. This can be made months ahead and keeps, refrigerated, up to 8 months.

A ROSY SALAD FOR DARKER DAYS

When monochrome winter won't let go, this is the salad to cure the blues. The punchy vinaigrette is a combination of miso and tahini, fresh ginger, garlic, and turmeric. It is a health booster all on its own. Use it with abandon! Dressing the prettiest pink radicchio, Rosa del Veneto cultivar—less bitter than its crimson cousin—the ingredients blend in a terrifically round way. If you cannot find the wild ground elder, use a half-and-half mixture of very thinly sliced celery and torn fresh mint leaves. Don't leave the persimmon out if you can help it—its lushness is a unique treat folded into the layers.

Make the dressing: Combine the orange juice, tahini, miso, and vinegar in a small bowl and smear or whisk all together until a loose paste forms. Add the garlic, ginger, turmeric, and orange zest and fold in. Add the olive oil and whisk until emulsified. Add the date syrup, whisk again, taste, and season with salt as needed. Thin with a small amount of water, to your preference (I add 1 tablespoon water to make it slightly looser). This step can be done up to 3 days in advance, sealed, and chilled in the refrigerator, then brought to room temperature before using.

Assemble the salad: Cut any particularly large radicchio leaves in half. In a large serving bowl, combine the radicchio, persimmon slices, and ground elder and spoon 3 to 4 tablespoons of the dressing, tossing thoroughly to coat. Top with the lemon curls and Bûcheron, sprinkle with flake salt and freshly ground pepper, and divide onto plates to eat.

NOTE: Rosa del Veneto radicchio is milder than its cousin, the radicchio we're most familiar with. If you cannot find this variety, use half escarole leaves and half radicchio to offset any extra bitterness.

GINGER-TURMERIC-MISO DRESSING

1 tablespoon orange juice

1 tablespoon tahini

2¼ teaspoons chickpea miso

1¼ teaspoons sherry vinegar

1 small clove garlic, finely grated on a Microplane

1 tablespoon finely grated fresh ginger, using a Microplane

1 teaspoon finely grated fresh turmeric, using a Microplane

Zest from half an orange

2 tablespoons extra-virgin olive oil

½ teaspoon date syrup

Kosher salt to taste

SALAD

1 head Rosa del Veneto radicchio (see Note)

1 or 2 Fuyu persimmons, thinly sliced parallel to stem end

1 cup tender ground elder shoots

Very thinly sliced curls from 2 strips lemon peel

5 ounces Bûcheron-style cheese, sliced into generous chunks

Freshly ground black pepper

Flake salt

SPICY TOMATO CLAMS + THICK SOURDOUGH TOAST

MAKES 2 SERVINGS

Whenever I bring bowls of these juicy, sauce-lashed clams and thick toast to the table, there is an audible "ooooh." It is a dish you fully commit to eating, slurping the spicy sauce and plucking the juicy meats from their shells. This is a real winter-brightening dish, and there is no question you must drag torn toast through any remaining sauce.

Clams must be purged of any sand remaining in their tightly closed shells before cooking. Fresh water will kill clams, so it is important to make a salt/water mixture that emulates seawater. Use sea salt—not regular salt—and dissolve it into cool water at 3½ percent by volume: 35 grams, or 2 tablespoons plus an additional teaspoon salt, into 1 liter (4 cups) of nonchlorinated water, or enough to submerge the clams. Adjust the proportion of salt accordingly to scale up or down. Purge them for about 1 hour in the refrigerator. If you leave them any longer than that, check from time to time and change the water so they do not die from loss of oxygen. Transfer the clams to a colander by plucking them with your hands from the brine. This will ensure you're not pouring purged sand back onto them. This process is best done right before they will be cooked.

2 shallots, sliced into thin rings

1 cup Tomato Confit (page 60), plus 2 tablespoons confit oil

2 garlic cloves, thinly sliced

1 tablespoon tomato paste

¾ to 1 teaspoon red pepper flakes

¼ teaspoon smoked paprika

Small pinch kosher salt

½ cup dry white wine

1 cup canned whole tomatoes, sliced into chunky coins

18 littleneck clams

Coarsely chopped fresh parsley for garnish

Thick slices of Sourdough Bread (page 68), toasted, to sop up the sauce

In a 10-inch heavy skillet set over medium heat, sauté the shallots in 1 tablespoon of the confit oil until translucent, 5 to 7 minutes. Stir occasionally to prevent browning. Add the garlic slices and the remaining confit oil, stir to combine, and cook 2 to 3 minutes more, until fragrant.

Add the tomato paste, red pepper flakes, paprika, and a small pinch of salt (see Note) and stir to combine. Add the wine to deglaze the pan and reduce by one-third, stirring once or twice as the mixture bubbles. Add the canned tomatoes and tomato confit, stir all together, and bring to a boil.

Add the clams, briefly pressing them into the sauce to get all in a single layer, then cover. Cook, covered, for 7 minutes or until all the shells have opened, lowering the heat to medium while they cook if the sauce threatens to spatter.

Transfer the clams and sauce to wide shallow bowls, scatter with the parsley, and serve with the toast.

NOTE: Clams' natural salinity makes it especially important to avoid oversalting as you cook. Season less than you would otherwise early in the cooking process. You can always add more at the end if needed.

ROAST CHICKEN, HEN OF THE WOODS, LEEKS, PAN SAUCE

MAKES 4 SERVINGS

Long ago, I interviewed chef Galen Zamarra of Mas Farmhouse and the Lambs Club. Even though he was known for "haute" food, he noted that there is unquestionable perfection in a well-roasted chicken. It's a thing that stayed with me all these years, particularly since my own views about what makes good food have shifted, thanks in no small part to chef Joel Hough, who many years ago opened NYC Cookshop. I used to think great food meant feats in molecular gastronomy, but after repeatedly eating Joel's food, I realized I'd sold short simple-seeming, beautifully cooked food. We should all aspire to make a phenomenal roast chicken.

When temperatures plummet, I hike to my mushroom spots, hopeful to discover a choice specimen. This dish was birthed after finding a particularly amazing hen of the woods mushroom (page 40). I produced a stock from its drier parts and added it in making the pan sauce. In a cast-iron skillet, I seared the more choice clusters to accompany the roast. Leeks are a wonderful allium I use in waves. I love them, but since they're large and crowd the refrigerator, I bring them home only on occasion. Do not mistake my rationale for any judgment. Their sweetness makes this meal complete. As a food stylist I go to great lengths to achieve the perfect bronzed roast bird, propping it up along the side of the pan so all parts connect with the hot surface. While it is admittedly a bit of effort, the results are an evenly golden roast chicken, which everyone loves.

Place four thyme sprigs inside the chicken cavity and season the cavity with salt. Set the chicken on a plate or sheet pan, pat dry, and season with salt and freshly ground pepper all over. Tuck the wing tips underneath the bird and tie the drumstick ends into a tidy bundle with kitchen twine. Set the chicken aside to come to room temperature as you prep the other ingredients.

Set a large cast-iron skillet hot over medium-high heat. When the pan is hot, drizzle half the oil in and swirl, then prop the chicken against one edge of pan to brown one outer breast and drumstick.

Add the mushrooms and leeks in a pile on the other side of the pan. Drizzle them with half of the remaining oil and season with salt and freshly ground pepper. After a few minutes, turn the vegetables so that the sides yet untouched get contact with the hot skillet. The mushrooms and leeks will become well seared in parts, deepening the overall flavor of the dish.

After browning along one edge for about 7 minutes, grasp at either end of the chicken—work carefully to avoid being burned—and flip it so the other outer

CONTINUED →

9 sprigs fresh thyme

A 3- to 4-pound pasture-raised whole chicken

Flake salt and freshly ground black pepper

2 tablespoons extra-virgin olive oil, plus more as needed

½ pound hen of the woods mushrooms, torn or sliced into large strips

1 leek, cut in half lengthwise, sand rinsed out, then chopped into 3-inch segments

10 very small potatoes, such as Carola or German Butterball (Yukon gold if you can't get those), sliced in half

7 garlic cloves, lightly smashed

½ cup dry white wine

1½ cups mushroom stock (page 80)

breast and drumstick sit against the pan, leaning it just as you did with the first side against the pan edge.

After cooking like so until golden along that side, 3 to 5 minutes, turn the chicken breastside down onto the base of the pan. Add the potatoes cut sides down around the chicken, scooting the leeks and mushrooms aside and piling them on top of the potatoes as needed.

Preheat the oven to 400°F.

After 3 more minutes, turn the chicken breastside up. Add more oil to the vegetables as needed, and repeat turning the leeks, mushrooms, and potatoes so that lesser cooked elements get their turn. Add the garlic cloves, tucking them in toward the pan base to get direct contact with the hot surface. Season all with ground pepper.

After 4 or so minutes, add the wine. It will bubble vigorously. After reducing it by half, add the stock and remaining thyme sprigs. Give one last turn of the vegetables nestling all around the chicken, lifting caramelized veggies up and placing those lesser cooked down, then carefully transfer the pan to the oven to finish cooking.

Check after 25 to 30 minutes. Pierce the meat in between the breast and the thigh—juices should run clear—or use a meat thermometer for a temperature of 160°F (breast meat should be 155°F, overall temperature should be 165°F). Allow the meat to rest for 10 minutes before serving.

Serve a generous pile of mushrooms, leeks, and potatoes onto each plate, along with choice pieces of chicken. Spoon the pan sauce over the top and eat at once. Save the carcass for making stock (page 79).

SAGE-BUTTERMILK-RYE POT PIES

MAKES FOUR 4½-INCH POT PIES

When I was a child we ate frozen Swanson pot pies, which I loved, particularly because they were packaged food, something my mom rarely indulged. In the decades since, the notion of pot pies still conjures a nostalgia, something I think resonates for many people. When made from scratch, pot pies are a quintessential comfort food. This one uses leftover chicken. Harkening to the romance of English meat pies, these are threaded with sage leaves and adorned with a trio of pastry spheres.

Make the pastry: Combine the water and vinegar in a measuring cup and add a few ice cubes. Pulse the flours, sugar, and salt together in the bowl of a food processor to combine. Add the butter and pulse at intervals, until pea-size bits form. Run the processor at intervals while drizzling in the ice water-vinegar mixture, until a cohesive dough forms, 10 to 15 seconds. Test to see if dough holds by squeezing a clump between your fingers. If so, it is ready. If not, drizzle a little more of the cold liquid and pulse again.

Divide the dough evenly onto two segments of plastic wrap. Use the plastic wrap as a barrier to limit how much you handle the dough: hold opposite ends and press to form the dough into a mass. Flatten it into a disk, wrap securely, and repeat with the remaining dough. Refrigerate the pastry for at least 20 minutes to allow it to mellow. This step can be done up to 3 days in advance.

Prepare the filling: Heat 1 tablespoon of the butter in a large cast-iron skillet over medium heat until foaming. When the foaming subsides, add the carrots and radishes and sauté for 3 minutes, turning once. Add the mushrooms, remaining 1 teaspoon butter, sage leaves, and thyme leaves, and cook for 3 to 5 more minutes, until the mushrooms have softened and begin to brown. Turn the heat off and allow to cook residually as you prep the next step.

Make the béchamel: In a medium saucepan set over medium heat, melt the butter for a roux. Once it has foamed, add the flour and whisk continuously to incorporate it fully, then continue whisking until the roux turns a deep golden color and imparts a nutty aroma, about 2 minutes.

Add the buttermilk and whisk until uniform. Lower the heat to medium-low, then whisk periodically until thickened and the sauce coats the back of a spoon. Add the cayenne, nutmeg, salt, and black pepper, whisking between each addition.

Add the stock in two batches, whisking in between. Warm the mixture for 5 minutes or until thickened, whisking occasionally, and bring to bubbling. Cook like so for 3 to 5 minutes until the mixture is silky. Remove from the heat and allow to cool slightly.

CONTINUED →

RYE PASTRY

½ cup ice water

¼ cup apple cider vinegar

1½ cups all-purpose flour

1 cup rye flour

1 teaspoon cane sugar

1 teaspoon kosher salt

2 sticks salted butter, cubed and freezer-cold (see Notes, page 261)

FILLING

1 tablespoon plus 1 teaspoon salted butter

2 carrots, peeled (save for stock, pages 79 or 80) and cut into coins

2 small or medium watermelon radishes, ends trimmed and each cut into 6 to 8 wedges

10 small mushrooms, cremini or shiitake or a mix, cut into halves, larger ones cut into quarters

8 to 10 fresh sage leaves

½ teaspoon fresh thyme leaves

6 to 8 melted onions (page 128)

3 cups coarsely shredded leftover chicken

1 cup frozen peas

ingredients continued →

In a large bowl combine the sautéed veggies, melted onions, shredded chicken, and peas and stir to combine. Stir the hot sauce into the béchamel, then pour onto the filling mixture, folding in to combine. Divide the fillings evenly among four mini-cocottes or ramekins and set aside.

Remove the pastry from the refrigerator 15 minutes before attempting to work it. Roll one disk placed between the plastic wrap and a lightly floured sheet of parchment to ¼ inch thick. Use one of the cocottes to trace and score a circle just larger than it into the pastry. If your rolled-out pastry is large enough to allow two lids to be cut out side-by-side, do so. Otherwise combine the scraps until a span large enough to accommodate the next lid is possible and reroll. Repeat with the remaining disk, making four lids in all. Chill them on a tray, each separated by a layer of plastic wrap or parchment once they have been formed.

Using the remaining dough scraps, pinch a piece of dough just smaller than the size of a cranberry and roll into a sphere between your palms. Make three per lid. Save any remaining scraps for another use.

Bring the pastry lids out one at a time. Position a sage leaf on top of a lid to gauge where to make a slit, centering it so that it doesn't exceed the pastry edge. With a thin sharp knife, score a 1-inch-long cut, followed by another one parallel to it, ¼ to ½ inch apart. As you work, it is helpful to chill the pastry periodically to avoid it becoming flabby or smeary: return it to the refrigerator to chill for at least 10 minutes before continuing.

Assign which side of the lid is to face up. Lay a sage leaf at the slit. Tuck the stem through one cut, flip the pastry over, then using tweezers or small tongs, pull it through the second cut and return it face up. The sage leaf is now anchored in place by the pastry "tab." Thread a second sage leaf as you did the first. Repeat this process to thread sage for the remaining pastry lids, chilling as needed.

Wet your fingertips with a small bit of water, then press the dough spheres onto the pastry lid, arranging them in a triangle formation to conceal the ends of the sage stems. With wetted fingers, lightly trace the underside circumference of the lid, then position it onto a cocotte. Gently press the lid along the circumference to secure it to the vessel. Repeat with remaining lids. Paint the pastries and spheres with egg wash, carefully lifting the sage leaves to paint the whole pastry surface. Paint sage leaves with olive oil. Refrigerate for a minimum of 1 hour, or overnight.

CONTINUED →

BÉCHAMEL

3 tablespoons salted butter

2 tablespoons plus 1 teaspoon all-purpose flour

1 cup full-fat buttermilk

¼ teaspoon cayenne

¼ teaspoon freshly grated nutmeg

Kosher salt and freshly ground black pepper

1½ cups mushroom stock (page 80) or chicken stock (page 79)

1 teaspoon sriracha—use less if you prefer less spicy

8 medium fresh sage leaves with their stems to thread into the pastry lids

1 egg, lightly beaten, for egg wash

Extra-virgin olive oil, for brushing sage

SAGE-BUTTERMILK-RYE POT PIES CONTINUED

Preheat the oven to 400°F. Bake the pies on a sheet pan for 25 minutes, then rotate the cocottes and the pan for even browning. Fold short segments of aluminum foil to conceal any extra dark pastry (see Notes). Bake for 7 more minutes, check, and lay another length of foil or rotate cocottes as needed. Repeat in this way until the pies are deeply golden and fillings bubble, 45 to 50 minutes in all.

Carefully transfer the pies to a wire rack and cool for at least 5 minutes. Serve the pot pies on their own plates, lined with a napkin or potholder to keep them from sliding. Serve alongside a bright salad mix, such as the garnishes that top the Braised Short Ribs + Creamy Beans (page 263).

NOTES: Cube cold butter and then place in a container into the freezer for 15 minutes for best short-crust results.

I use small segments of foil to inhibit excessive browning while baking pastry and store these sections in their own bag in a drawer and reuse, so that all baked pastries end up evenly deep golden, no matter their size or design.

To make this pastry even more traditional, try blending the pastry by hand: Place dry ingredients in a large bowl and stir to incorporate with a fork. Use a pastry blender to cut the butter into the dry ingredients, until only pea-size bits remain. Drizzle the water-vinegar mixture in a little at a time, cutting the liquid into the dough, pausing to check and see if dough holds together when squeezed between your fingers. Use only as much as needed for the dough to come together without crumbling. Then transfer the dough onto plastic wrap to form into disks as you would using the method on page 257.

BRAISED SHORT RIBS + CREAMY BEANS

This stewish meal is a recipe I return to again and again. Like bourguignon, this is a quintessential meal, but it offers a contemporary flair, while amplifying humble ingredients. The creamy beans are a wonderful meal unto themselves and would make a fine vegetarian feast. Braised ribs marry with gochujang (a substitution for tomato paste I'm fond of—see also the ribs on page 168), anchovies, and fennel. The elements mount to some of the most anticipated eating all winter. Make this one day ahead if you can: the flavors will meaningfully deepen, and it is easier to skim the fat once the braise has been refrigerated. Don't skip the bright garnishes. They offset the richness in an essential way.

Cook the beans: Soak the beans in enough cold water to cover by a few inches for 8 hours or overnight. Drain the beans in a colander. Transfer them to a medium saucepan and fill with water to cover by 1 inch. Add the Parmesan heels. Bring the pot to boil, then cover and lower the heat to simmer. Simmer for 55 minutes or until the beans are tender. Season with kosher salt and ground pepper to taste. This can be done up to 2 days in advance, and the beans will be creamier for it.

Prepare the short ribs: Pat the short ribs dry, lay them out on a rimmed sheet pan, and generously salt them on all sides. Allow them to come to room temperature while you prep the other ingredients.

Over medium heat, swirl 1 tablespoon olive oil in a 7-quart Dutch oven once it is hot. Brown the meat in batches so as not to crowd the pan, until well browned on all sides. Transfer the ribs back to the sheet pan once they're browned sufficiently, adding the remaining ribs to the pot for their turn.

Once all the ribs are browned, drain all but 1 tablespoon of the fat from the pot (save it to be added to the Brown Rice, Pickled Spices, Potatoes, page 275, or the Stewed Scarlet Runner Beans, page 276). Add the anchovies and break them up with a wooden spoon as they sizzle. Once they have completely dissolved, add the onions and stir to coat. Cook over medium heat until they are browned in parts, 3 to 5 minutes, then add the fennel wedges and garlic. Toss to coat, adding another drizzle of oil as needed.

After cooking for a couple minutes, add the gochujang, dragging the thick paste over all veggie surfaces until more or less incorporated.

Preheat the oven to 325°F with the rack placed in the lower third to accommodate the Dutch oven with its lid.

CONTINUED →

CREAMY BEANS

1½ cups dry navy beans

2 heels Parmesan cheese (see Note)

Kosher salt and freshly ground black pepper

SHORT RIBS

5 pounds pasture-raised beef short ribs (2 good-size or 3 small ribs per person)

Kosher salt

Extra-virgin olive oil

4 or 5 anchovies

12 cipollini onions

2 medium fennel bulbs, root and frond ends trimmed, leaving enough of the root end so when they are sliced lengthwise into 3-inch wedges they remain intact

5 garlic cloves, smashed

1 generous tablespoon gochujang

ingredients continued →

1 bay leaf

5 to 7 fresh thyme sprigs

1 bottle dry red wine—Syrah, Pinot Noir, Grenache all work nicely

4 cups beef, chicken, or mushroom stock, preferably homemade (pages 79 or 80)

½ cup fresh shiso leaves, torn, or a combination of fresh parsley and chervil

½ cup bittercress, or coarsely chopped arugula or watercress

Finely grated zest from half a lemon for garnish

Flake salt and freshly ground black pepper

Add the bay leaf and the thyme sprigs, tied with kitchen twine into a bundle, to the pot. Pour in the wine. Free up any browned bits as it bubbles, scraping the bottom of the pot with a wooden spoon. Bring the mixture to an active simmer, then cook for 1 minute. Tuck the ribs into the vegetable mixture and add back any accumulated juices. Add the stock so it comes nearly to the top of the ribs but does not submerge them, and once the pot returns to a simmer, place the lid on and transfer it to the oven.

Cook 1 to 2 hours, until ribs are fall-apart tender. Leave enough time to allow the pot to cool and refrigerate overnight: the stew tastes better the second day as the flavors will have melded, and you can more readily scrape away the surface fat once it has solidified. (Do this when you bring the pot out the next day, prior to reheating.)

Reheat the pots of stew and beans on a low heat, stirring occasionally to heat evenly. Remove and discard the bundle of herbs from the stew and the Parmesan heels from the beans. Serve the braised ribs hot, spooned atop the creamy beans, and garnish with an abundant amount of fresh shiso, bittercress, lemon zest, flake salt, and ground pepper.

NOTE: I save the heels of hard cheeses such as Parmesan over time, stored in the freezer in a resealable bag, where they keep indefinitely. They give their final magic in preparations such as this.

POMEGRANATE-PERSIMMON PUFF PASTRY TART

MAKES 2 SERVINGS

There are days where you want to serve an impressive dessert but simply do not have the time or bandwidth to make it happen. Enter good-quality, store-bought, all-butter puff pastry and the season's fruit gems. In the oven, ripe persimmon effectively becomes its own jam, an earthy-sweet base layer for bright pomegranate and ground black pepper. After you roll out the pastry, the dessert takes less than 40 minutes start to finish and delivers big on *wow*. Unnecessary but delicious additions: a dollop of crème fraîche or a scoop of ice cream.

Preheat the oven to 400°F.

Lay out the puff pastry on a piece of parchment. Brush the egg wash across the surface of the puff pastry all the way to the edges. Use a thin sharp knife to score a border ½ inch in from the edge, all the way around.

Cut the persimmon open and scoop out its flesh, spreading it in an even layer across the base of the pastry, inside the confines of the scored border. Add a few generous grinds of black pepper.

Transfer the tart to a sheet pan and bake for 25 minutes or until the crust is deeply golden, rotating the pan two-thirds of the way through for even baking.

When the tart is deeply golden, remove it from the oven and set on a wire rack to cool for 5 minutes. Transfer the tart to a serving platter. Shower it with pomegranate arils, followed by the slivered almonds, and dust with the sugar. Serve with a dollop of crème fraîche or a scoop of ice cream, if desired.

½ sheet puff pastry, rolled to a rectangle roughly 9 by 6 inches (use the other half toward a mini version mushroom tart, page 194)

1 egg, beaten, for egg wash

1 very ripe Hachiya persimmon

Freshly ground black pepper

Arils from half a pomegranate

1 tablespoon slivered almonds, toasted

1 teaspoon confectioners' sugar

A dollop of crème fraîche or a scoop of ice cream (optional)

CHERRY-RYE-GANACHE SANDWICH COOKIES

MAKES 18 SANDWICH COOKIES

It is the holiday season, our last hurrahs of the year. These not-too-sweet but exceedingly indulgent sandwich pretties are pure seduction. Dried tart cherries and flake salt present contrast to the chocolate, lightening the richness. You can make the cookies on one day, then make the ganache and sandwich them the next. Allow them to set fully before diving in so their flavors have a chance to meld. After tasting, you may end up coveting the lot for yourself.

Make the cookies: Sift the cocoa, flours, baking soda, and kosher salt into a medium bowl. Stir to combine and set aside.

In a large bowl, cream the butter using an electric mixer. Gradually incorporate the sugars and cream until fluffy, about 3 minutes. Add the scraped vanilla seeds and the eggs, one at a time, blending in between additions to incorporate. Add the flour-cocoa mixture and blend until just combined, stopping occasionally to scrape down the sides with a rubber spatula as you mix all together. The mixture will be dense, like earthy clay. Using the spatula, fold in the chocolate and cherries.

Preheat the oven to 375°F.

Scoop tablespoon portions of the dough onto two parchment-lined sheet pans, leaving at least 2 inches between them to accommodate for spreading as they bake. Flatten each slightly and top half of the portions with a little flake salt. Bake for 9 to 12 minutes until the cookies are puffed and slightly cracked. Transfer them to cool completely on a wire rack.

Make the ganache: In a small saucepan, bring the cream just to a boil and then remove from the heat. Add the chopped chocolate and let sit for a minute. Stir the mixture with a silicone spatula until fully incorporated—the cream and chocolate should meld and become richly dark and satiny. Allow the mixture to cool until thickened and spreadable, 8 to 10 minutes. When it's cool, dollop a small spoonful onto one cookie and sandwich with the second. Repeat with all remaining cookies.

Allow them to set fully before serving. The cookies will keep sealed in a container at room temperature for up to 1 week. If you refrigerate them, allow the cookies to come to room temperature before serving.

COOKIES

1¼ cups Dutch process cocoa

1 cup all-purpose flour

1 cup rye flour

1 teaspoon baking soda

¼ teaspoon kosher salt

2½ sticks salted butter, at room temperature

1 cup packed dark brown sugar

½ cup cane sugar

1 vanilla bean, seeds stripped from pod

2 eggs

10 ounces bittersweet dark chocolate, chopped

1½ cups dried sour cherries

Flake salt, such as Maldon, for sprinkling

GANACHE

½ cup heavy cream

¾ cup bittersweet chocolate wafers, chopped into small pieces, or chips

ORANGE–CARDAMOM ICE CREAM + SABLÉ COINS

MAKES 1 QUART ICE CREAM AND 16 COOKIES

Don't let this Plain Jane–looking dessert fool you. The salt-flecked Breton cookie derives its name from the fine texture of generously applied butter rubbed into flour and eggs, emulating the texture of sand, and after a few hours' rest to meld, they are ready to be formed. They are rich, delicate, and simple, perfect for a holiday cookie swap. Because they are simple, use the best quality butter you can find, as well as high quality salt and flour. These cookies are also infinitely adaptable. Add spice, citrus zest, sanding sugar, or nuts. Or keep them perfectly simple and pair with ice cream as I've done here. The orange and cardamom flavors make a delightful foil to the crumbly, buttery cookie. The ice cream is a variation of Julia Moskin's no-egg recipe I produced for the *New York Times* years ago. Once the ice cream is made, it will keep indefinitely, sealed tightly in its container in the freezer. Thanks to their abundant butter, the sablés keep for a few weeks, sealed in a container at room temperature, but they likely won't last that long.

ICE CREAM

1 cup half-and-half

1 cup heavy cream, not ultra-pasteurized

3 cardamom pods, bruised with the flat of a chef's knife

Wide strips of peel from half an orange, any white pith cut away

½ cup cane sugar

¼ teaspoon kosher salt

SPELT SABLÉS

2 egg yolks

⅓ cup cane sugar

½ cup all-purpose flour

⅓ cup spelt flour

2 teaspoons baking powder

8 tablespoons salted butter, at room temperature

½ teaspoon flake salt

Sunflower or coconut oil for greasing

Prepare the ice cream: In a medium saucepan, combine the half-and-half and cream. Bring the mixture to a simmer, stirring occasionally. Remove from the heat and mix in the cardamom pods and orange peels. Let steep for 5 minutes.

Add the sugar and kosher salt and mix until the sugar dissolves, 3 to 4 minutes. Taste and add more sugar and kosher salt as needed to balance the flavors. The mixture should taste slightly too sweet when warm; the sweetness will be muted when the ice cream is frozen. Refrigerate at least 4 hours, or overnight.

The next day churn according to the manufacturer's instructions, first spooning any cream solids directly into the machine, then straining the spice pods and peels from the cream before adding it to the machine. Transfer the ice cream to a container, seal, and freeze. This step can be done up to 2 weeks in advance.

Make the spelt cookies: In a medium bowl, use a fork to whisk together the yolks and sugar until fluffy and quite pale, about 2 minutes.

Sift together the flours and baking powder, then work the dry ingredients into the wet in intervals, using a spatula. The mixture will become crumbly and dry. Add the butter and smear it in with the spatula, scraping down the sides of the bowl as needed, until fully incorporated into the dough. Add the flake salt and fold it in.

Cover the dough with plastic wrap and refrigerate. Rest the dough for at least 4 hours, up to overnight.

Preheat the oven to 300°F. Grease a metal mini-muffin tin with sunflower oil (see Notes). Portion the dough into 16 equal balls. Place them into the greased hollows and press each once with your thumb, to flatten it a bit.

Bake the sablés for 30 minutes or until golden and fragrant. Invert the pan over a clean, dry work surface and give it a brief thwack to turn out the cookies. You may need to repeat this one or twice more until all have released. Transfer them to a wire rack to cool completely.

Serve a scoop or two of ice cream per person and a dish filled with sablé coins at the table to pass around.

NOTES: If you have a silicone rather than metal tin, there is no need to grease the molds. Also bake the sablé cookies 4 to 6 minutes longer, until deeply golden, and wait 10 minutes before releasing the cookies from the tin so they hold their shape.

You can make sablé dough, portion it, and freeze, up to 2 months in advance. Pull as needed to bake as many as you'd like to use at a given time. Bake from frozen, adding 5 to 7 minutes to the baking time.

CANDIED MEYER LEMON ICE CREAM + PISTACHIO TUILES

MAKES 1½ QUARTS ICE CREAM AND SEVEN 5-INCH TUILES

For some years now, I've swapped care packages with my friend Mindy, a forager and farmer to chefs, out on the West Coast. In recent memory, she has twice sent boxes of Meyer lemons harvested from her grandmother's tree. Upon receiving these boxes of cheer, I go to work preserving the season. I have made various batches of Preserved Meyer Lemons (page 97), infused spirits, and candied bright windowpane slices. Bonus is the richly lemony syrup left over, added to all kinds of things, including the Rye + Spruce Tip Last Word cocktail (page 103). I love capturing the candied brightness in ice cream and the fragrance of fresh zest in these crunchy tuiles. You could be perfectly happy making just the ice cream or the tuiles, but the two are excellent together. A perfect brightening indulgence for frosty days. Make the candied lemon slices at least 3 days in advance.

ICE CREAM

2 cups half-and-half

2 cups heavy cream, not ultra-pasteurized

½ vanilla bean, split lengthwise, seeds scraped out with the tip of a sharp knife

1 cup cane sugar

½ teaspoon kosher salt

2 Candied Meyer Lemons (about half a batch; page 102)

TUILES

½ cup lightly salted pistachios

2 tablespoons sesame seeds

¼ cup all-purpose flour

4 tablespoons cane sugar

Pinch kosher salt

2 tablespoons freshly squeezed orange juice

Zest from 1 orange

Zest from 2 Meyer lemons (use regular lemons if you cannot find Meyers)

3 tablespoons salted butter

1 tablespoon sesame oil

Make the ice cream: In a medium saucepan, combine the half-and-half and cream. Bring the mixture to a simmer, stirring occasionally to prevent scorching. Remove from the heat and stir in the vanilla bean and seeds. Let steep for 5 minutes.

Add the sugar and salt and mix until the sugar dissolves, about 4 minutes. Taste, and add more sugar and salt as needed to balance the flavors. The mixture should taste slightly too sweet when warm. The sweetness will be subtler when the ice cream is frozen. Refrigerate for at least 4 hours, or overnight.

Chop the candied lemons into a fine dice prior to churning the ice cream. Strain the cream mixture as you transfer it to the ice cream maker and churn according to the manufacturer's instructions. In the last 5 minutes of churning, add the chopped candied lemons. Transfer the ice cream to an airtight container and freeze until solid. This step can be done up to 1 week in advance.

Make the tuiles: Chop the pistachios until they resemble a coarse meal. Combine the sesame seeds, chopped pistachios, and flour in a small bowl and stir with a fork to combine.

Combine the sugar, salt, orange juice, citrus zests, butter, and sesame oil in a small saucepan. Heat the saucepan over medium heat until the sugar-butter mixture is dissolved and melted together. Stir until uniform.

Remove from the heat and stir the liquid into the flour mixture until fully incorporated.

Rest the batter at room temperature for 1 hour, or up to overnight, to allow the butter to re-solidify so you can more easily portion it.

Preheat the oven to 375°F. Line two sheet pans with parchment and scoop 2 level tablespoons of the batter per tuile, two per sheet, spaced evenly apart.

Flatten the mounds into 3-inch flat disks with wetted fingers to prevent the mixture from sticking. Bake until they spread thin and turn golden, 10 to 12 minutes, rotating the pans after 8 minutes. Cool the tuiles fully on the sheet pans. Use a spatula to lift them and set aside. Repeat with the remaining batter, baking them evenly spaced on the sheet pans.

Spoon two scoops of the candied lemon ice cream and one tuile per person. Tuiles should be eaten within 1 or 2 days, as any atmospheric humidity will soften them.

SUSTENANCE, EATING IN BETWEEN THE FEASTS, AKA BONUS TRACKS

This addendum is nourishing, humble food that comes to the rescue. They are simple dishes, mostly cooked passively, that siphon leftover bits from the grand affairs. This is relief food when days are long and hunger cannot wait.

PIQUANT FRENCH LENTILS

MAKES 2 TO 4 SERVINGS

There is a pot of lentils on my stove every other day. I love them because they don't require presoaking like dried beans usually do. In usual rotation are beluga, also known as black lentils, and these French lentils. These legumes can be as meaty or creamy as you like—just add more (or less) liquid to suit the meal or your taste. I eat the cooked lentils by the spoonful straight out of the pan if I'm pressed for time, but I love to sit down to a bowl with elements neatly piled to entice, feeling like a whole being eating such nourishment.

1 cup French lentils

2 to 3 tablespoons Tomato Confit, made with shallots (page 60), plus 1 to 2 tablespoons of their oil

½ cup brine from Moroccan Pickled Carrots (page 86)

Kosher salt

1 medium sweet potato, peeled and sliced in half lengthwise, then into ½-inch-thick half-moons

Extra-virgin olive oil, for drizzling

FOR TOPPING

Harissa (page 59)

Greek yogurt or vegan sour cream

Fermented Green Garlic (page 89)

Radish greens or other micro greens

Chives, snipped finely with scissors

Flake salt and freshly ground black pepper

In a medium saucepan, combine the lentils with enough water to barely cover them, the tomato-shallot confit, and the confit oil and bring to a boil. Cover and lower to a simmer. Cook the lentils for 20 minutes or until the liquid is absorbed.

Add ¼ cup of the pickle brine to the mixture and continue to simmer until the lentils are tender, 10 to 15 more minutes. If additional liquid is needed, taste and add either the remaining brine, or a splash of water if the acidity feels balanced. Season with ½ teaspoon kosher salt, or more to taste.

Preheat the oven to 400°F. Toss the sweet potatoes in olive oil to coat, season with kosher salt, and roast in a single layer for 15 minutes on a sheet pan. After 15 minutes, turn the potato slices over and roast for 7 to 10 minutes more, until soft and slightly browned. Remove the sweet potatoes from the oven and set on a wire rack.

Serve the lentils in bowls, topped with a pile of roasted sweet potatoes, harissa, dollops of yogurt, Fermented Green Garlic, and a cluster of greens. Scatter with chives, flake salt, and a few generous grinds of ground pepper to taste.

This dish can be eaten warm or at room temperature.

BROWN RICE, PICKLED SPICES, POTATOES

MAKES 4 SERVINGS

There is almost always a pot of grains on my stove, helping to save the day in between all the cooking for guests and commissioned projects. This kind of meal is nearly completely hands-off, vegan or vegetarian, and can be prepared in innumerable ways. As it makes no demands while cooking, it is also a lifesaver. I save and add the potato poaching oil from the Spanish Tortilla (page 115) or the rich stock from the aromatic poached veggies (page 222). For a slightly richer dish (and not vegetarian) I use the leftover fat from the lamb skewers (page 177) or some of the skimmed beef tallow from the Braised Short Ribs + Creamy Beans (page 263). At the end, I add pickled seeds and brine from any of my jars of pickles. I hate waste, so everything gets used in one way or another to flavor-packed, nourishing results. The somewhat sweet field garlic oil makes a zippy addition to any food. Use it to finish dishes once they are brought to the table, spooned as generously as you like.

Cook the rice: Bring the stock, fat, potatoes, peels, and rice to a boil in a medium saucepan. Cover, lower the heat to simmer, and cook for 30 minutes or until you can hear steam but no bubbling inside the pot (the liquid having been fully absorbed). Remove from the heat, fold the greens into the rice mixture, place the lid back on, and allow to sit for 7 to 10 minutes until the leaves are bright green and wilted. Add enough brine so that the mixture is made more savory.

Divide the rice among bowls or transfer to a serving dish. Top with a generous amount of pickled seeds, ground pepper, a shower of parsley, and spoonfuls of the Field Garlic Oil. Any leftovers can be stored in the refrigerator for up to 3 days.

BROWN RICE

2 cups mushroom stock (page 80) or vegetable stock

2 tablespoons leftover fat or extra-virgin olive oil

3 medium Yukon gold potatoes, peeled and cubed

3 to 5 ½-inch strips lemon peel, the length of the lemon, bitter white pith removed

1 cup short grain brown rice

Half a bunch of the innermost tender leaves of bok choy, kale, mustard greens, or other tender dark leafy green, coarsely chopped

2 to 3 tablespoons brine from any of the pickle projects (pages 85 to 98), to taste

3 or 4 teaspoons pickled seeds from any of the pickle projects (pages 85 to 98)

Freshly ground black pepper

¾ cup chopped parsley

Field Garlic Oil (page 58) for topping

STEWED SCARLET RUNNER BEANS

MAKES 4 SERVINGS

Beans are here for us. They don't ask for much and they give reliable sustenance with gusto. As you read earlier in these pages, I fell hard for scarlet runner beans—a popular variety of Ayocote bean—after growing them one year and have become a devotee ever since. Scarlet runner beans are thought to be among the first domesticated food plants, cultivated in the highlands of Mexico and Guatemala around 2,000 BC. Young beans are exquisitely crunchy and juicy, and I happily eat them straight from the vine. When the pods mature, the plump shelled beans resemble pink-and-black leopard print. They are a feast in any form. If time isn't on my side but hunger must be reckoned with, a pot of these with my go-to repertoire of preserved and fermented foods does exactly what I need, and in style. The zingy Juniper + Cumin Meyer Lemon Kraut and sweet caramelized onions are good friends to any bean. Here, they harmonize in a fully plant-based meal.

BEANS

2 cups dry scarlet runner beans

4 tablespoons extra-virgin olive oil

6-inch stem fresh rosemary

Kosher salt

8 medium watermelon radishes, thinly shaved on a mandoline

4 handfuls mixed greens, such as garlic mustard, ground elder, parsley, pea shoots, or other soft herbs and microgreens

Squeeze of lemon (optional)

Extra-virgin olive oil (optional)

½ to ¾ cup Juniper + Cumin Meyer Lemon Kraut (page 90)

¼ to ½ cup caramelized onions (page 116)

Freshly ground black pepper

Cook the beans: Soak the beans in enough water to cover by 3 inches for 8 hours or overnight. Drain the beans in a colander, then transfer to a large saucepan and fill with enough water to submerge beans by ½ inch. Add the olive oil and rosemary and bring to a boil. Cover the pan with its lid and lower the heat to simmer, and cook until tender, 50 to 60 minutes. Once the beans are tender, season with ½ to 1 teaspoon (or more) salt.

Combine the radish slices and tender greens in a bowl and toss together, adding a squeeze of lemon and/or a drizzle of oil if desired.

Ladle the beans and some of their liquor into wide shallow bowls. Arrange the radish-greens mixture on one side, followed by a pile of the kraut. Add a cluster of caramelized onions and season all with freshly ground black pepper. This dish can be eaten warm or room temperature, depending on the mood or the season.

RECIPES BY DIETARY LIFESTYLE

In addition to highlighting responsibly sourced fish, seafood, meat, and dairy, plant-based eating takes an ongoing center stage at home. In an effort to share the range of dishes available for food-conscious or otherwise mindful diets, I've constructed a list of the dishes by type for easy reference.

VEGAN

Field Garlic Oil (page 58)

Harissa (page 59)

Tomato Confit (page 60)

Ramp Salt (page 63)

Pistachio Dukkah (page 64)

Seeded Rye Lavash (made with date syrup; page 67)

Sourdough Bread (page 68)

Mushroom Stock (page 80)

Immunity Elixir (page 81)

Corn Stock (page 82)

Quick Pickled Red Onions (page 85)

Pickled Ramps (page 85)

Moroccan Pickled Carrots (page 86)

Fermented Green Garlic (page 89)

Juniper + Cumin Meyer Lemon Kraut (page 90)

Wild Mushroom Escabeche (page 93)

Preserved Meyer Lemons (page 97)

Tarragon-Shallot Summer Squash Pickles (page 98)

Autumn Olive Jam (page 99)

Wild Blueberry Compote (page 100)

Rosé + Spice Poached Quince (page 101)

Rye + Spruce Tip Last Word (page 103)

Honeysuckle Cordial (page 104)

Spring Fling Salad in Green (page 124)

Vegan Morning Bowl (page 156)

Pickled blueberries (page 168)

Vegan Umami Udon (page 172)

Pineapple, Tequila Granita, Brittle (page 178)

A Rosy Salad for Darker Days (minus the cheese; page 251)

Piquant French Lentils (page 272)

Brown Rice, Pickled Spices, Potatoes (page 275)

Stewed Scarlet Runner Beans (page 276)

VEGETARIAN

All from vegan, plus . . .

Sourdough Crackers (page 75)

Spiced Nuts (page 77)

Eggs, Beans, Garden Greens (page 111)

Spanish Tortilla, Sauce, Pickles, Salad (page 115)

Buttermilk Panna Cotta (page 136)

Sour Cherry Pie (page 139)

Ginger-Pecan Strawberry Streusel Cake (page 141)

Eat'cha Garden (page 148)

Pillowy French Toast + Wild Blueberry Compote (page 151)

Buttery Scrambled Eggs + Chanterelles (page 152)

Summer Skillet: Fried Eggs + Scarlet Runner Beans (page 155)

Brown Butter + Lemon Cecamariti (page 157)

Stone Fruit, Pecan + Pistachio Crisps (page 180)

Kahlúa Chocolate Mousse (page 181)

Double Rye Buckwheat Plum Cake (page 182)

Black Raspberry–Bourbon Mascarpone Tartlets (page 185)

Wild Mushroom–Potato–Onion Tart (page 194)

Quinoa + Quince Porridge (page 197)

Two Toasts (page 203)

Sunchoke Soup + Crispy Mushrooms (page 204)

Roasted Whole Cauliflower with Harissa + Yogurt (page 207)

Ultimate Nibbles Platter (page 208)

Quince Tarte Tatin (page 226)

GLUTEN-FREE

COOK-UP-A-PLAN RECIPE LISTS

FEEDS A CROWD

It is very handy to know how to feed a group of people and do so in style. Feeds-a-crowd dishes make for great communal feasting and scale up easily.

Wild Salmon Gravlax (page 94)

Pâté, Elderberry Gelée, Pickled Ramps (page 119)

Wild Salmon + Fried Sage Gremolata (page 134)

Sour Cherry Pie (page 139)

Ginger-Pecan Strawberry Streusel Cake (page 141)

Brown Butter + Lemon Cecamariti (page 157)

Maple-Gochujang Ribs, Pickle Platter, Cornbread (page 168)

Kahlúa Chocolate Mousse (page 181)

Quinoa + Quince Porridge (page 197)

Sunchoke Soup + Crispy Mushrooms (page 204)

Roasted Whole Cauliflower with Harissa + Yogurt (page 207)

Ultimate Nibbles Platter (page 208)

Braised Lamb Shanks + Melted Onions (page 214)

Pasta Puttanesca (page 217)

Quince Tarte Tatin (page 226)

Autumn Olive Linzer Tart (page 229)

Wild Salmon Rillettes + Seeded Rye Lavash (page 241)

A Rosy Salad for Darker Days (page 251)

Spicy Tomato Clams + Thick Sourdough Toast (page 252)

Roast Chicken, Hen of the Woods, Leeks, Pan Sauce (page 255)

Sage-Buttermilk-Rye Pot Pies (page 257)

Braised Short Ribs + Creamy Beans (page 263)

Cherry-Rye-Ganache Sandwich Cookies (page 267)

Orange-Cardamom Ice Cream + Sablé Coins (page 268)

Brown Rice, Pickled Spices, Potatoes (page 275)

ONE PAN RECIPES

Sometimes, it is nice to throw it all together and call a meal done—relatively low maintenance one-pan dishes mean you'll be washing fewer actual dishes at the night's end. Worthy of its own celebration.

Tomato Confit (page 60)

"Deli Sandwich" Dutch Baby (page 112)

Spring Skillet: Duck Eggs + Crispy Brown Rice (page 118)

Mussels for Betty (page 127)

Braised Lamb Shanks + Melted Onions (page 214)

Pasta Puttanesca (page 217)

Chicken Thighs, Quince, Cipollini, Preserved Lemon (page 221)

Spicy Tomato Clams + Thick Sourdough Toast (page 252)

Roast Chicken, Hen of the Woods, Leeks, Pan Sauce (page 255)

Brown Rice, Pickled Spices, Potatoes (page 275)

NO COOK + NEARLY NO COOK

Achieve the wow factor in food that requires simply being beautifully sliced, blended, or marinated, and not always time spent cooking. No-cook recipes are essential accents to any cooked dishes. I rely on these bright preparations throughout the seasons.

Field Garlic Oil (page 58)

Garlic Mustard Pesto (page 62)

Pistachio Dukkah (page 64)

All the pickles (pages 85 to 98)

Juniper + Cumin Meyer Lemon Kraut (page 90)

Wild Salmon Gravlax (page 94)

Preserved Meyer Lemons (page 97)

Spring Fling Salad in Green (page 124)

Eat'Cha Garden (page 148)

Oaxaca-Meets-the-Mediterranean, Tomatoes, Corn (page 162)

Scallop-Shiso Ceviche (page 165)

Pineapple, Tequila Granita, Brittle (page 178)

Puntarelle + Tardivo with Punchy Dress (page 200)

Cured King Salmon, Persimmon, Pickles (page 248)

A Rosy Salad for Darker Days (page 251)

MAKE-AHEAD

Finally, I swear by foods that can be made ahead, otherwise I'd really be at my wit's end. These preparations create a bit of breathing room as you plan whatever celebration, so you can be fresh and ready for revelry with the special people you've made such efforts for.

Eggs, Beans, Garden Greens (page 111)

Spanish Tortilla, Sauce, Pickles, Salad (page 115)

Pâté, Elderberry Gelée, Pickled Ramps (page 119)

Asparagus + Artichokes (page 123)

Sour Cherry Pie (page 139)

Ginger-Pecan Strawberry Streusel Cake (page 141)

Roasted Salmon + Spicy Cucumber-Orange Salsa (page 167)

Maple-Gochujang Ribs, Pickle Platter, Cornbread (page 168)

Pineapple, Tequila Granita, Brittle (page 178)

Wild Mushroom–Potato–Onion Tart (page 194)

Sunchoke Soup + Crispy Mushrooms (page 204)

Roasted Whole Cauliflower with Harissa + Yogurt (page 207)

Bouillabaisse + Rouille-Slathered Toasts (page 211)

Braised Lamb Shanks + Melted Onions (page 214)

Chicken Thighs, Quince, Cipollini, Preserved Lemon (page 221)

Quince Tarte Tatin (page 226)

Autumn Olive Linzer Tart (page 229)

Pawpaw Crème Brûlée (page 232)

Wild Salmon Rillettes + Seeded Rye Lavash (page 241)

Braised Short Ribs + Creamy Beans (page 263)

Cherry-Rye-Ganache Sandwich Cookies (page 267)

Orange-Cardamom Ice Cream + Sablé Coins (page 268)

Brown Rice, Pickled Spices, Potatoes (page 275)

MENU IDEAS

SPRING-SUMMER MENUS

BIRTHDAY BREAKFAST

"Deli Sandwich" Dutch Baby (page 112)
Spring Fling Salad in Green (page 124)
Sour Cherry Pie (page 139)
Rye + Spruce Tip Last Word (page 103)

MOTHER'S DAY

Asparagus + Artichokes (page 123)
Seared Scallops + Veggie Gravel (page 133)
Kahlúa Chocolate Mousse (page 181)
Honeysuckle Cordial (page 104)

FATHER'S DAY

Spring Skillet: Duck Eggs + Crispy Brown Rice
(page 118)
Crispy Pork + Fennel Meatballs in Umami Broth
(page 128)
Maple-Gochujang Ribs, Pickle Platter, Cornbread
(page 168)
Pineapple, Tequila Granita, Brittle (page 178)
Rye + Spruce Tip Last Word (page 103)

EPIC SMALL BITES

Pâté, Elderberry Gelée, Pickled Ramps (page 119)
Asparagus + Artichokes (page 123)
Grand Aioli Summer Feast (page 158)
Buttermilk Panna Cotta (page 136)

SATURDAY BRUNCH

Spanish Tortilla, Sauce, Pickles, Salad (page 115)
Mussels for Betty (page 127)
Buttermilk Panna Cotta (page 136)

BRIGHT + LIVELY

Spring Fling Salad in Green (page 124)
Crispy Pork + Fennel Meatballs in Umami Broth
(page 128)
Seared Scallops + Veggie Gravel (page 133)
Stone Fruit, Pecan + Pistachio Crisps (page 180)

EASTER FEAST

Spring Fling Salad in Green (page 124)
Seared Scallops + Veggie Gravel (page 133) and/or
Wild Salmon + Fried Sage Gremolata (page 134)
Buttermilk Panna Cotta (page 136)

BRUNCH PARTY

Eat'cha Garden (page 148)
Brown Butter + Lemon Cecamariti (page 157)
Pillowy French Toast + Wild Blueberry Compote
(page 151)
Pineapple, Tequila Granita, Brittle (page 178)

VEGAN FEAST

Vegan Morning Bowl (page 156)
Vegan Umami Udon (page 172)
Pineapple, Tequila Granita, Brittle (page 178)
Honeysuckle Cordial (page 104)

CLEAN EATS

Eggs, Beans, Garden Greens (page 111)
Eat'cha Garden (page 148)
Oaxaca-Meets-the-Mediterranean, Tomatoes, Corn
(page 162)
Spring Fling Salad in Green (page 124)
Vegan Umami Udon (page 172)

PICNIC AFTERNOON

Buttery Scrambled Eggs + Chanterelles (page 152)
Oaxaca-Meets-the-Mediterranean, Tomatoes, Corn (page 162)
Sour Cherry Pie (page 139)

BBQ LUNCH

Maple-Gochujang Ribs, Pickle Platter, Cornbread (page 168)
Double Rye Buckwheat Plum Cake (page 182)
Sour Cherry Pie (page 139)

BIRTHDAY WITH FRIENDS

Scallop-Shiso Ceviche (page 165)
Oaxaca-Meets-the-Mediterranean, Tomatoes, Corn (page 162)
Lamb Skewers with Alliums Three Ways (page 177)
Roasted Salmon + Spicy Cucumber-Orange Salsa (page 167)
Kahlúa Chocolate Mousse (page 181)

AL FRESCO LUNCH

Grand Aioli Summer Feast (page 158)
Oaxaca-Meets-The-Mediterranean, Tomatoes, Corn (page 162)
Double Rye Buckwheat Plum Cake (page 182)

ANNIVERSARY DINNER

Spring Fling Salad in Green (page 124)
Scallops, Corn Confit, Milkweed (page 173)
Black Raspberry–Bourbon Mascarpone Tartlets (page 185)
Honeysuckle Cordial (page 104)

GLUTEN-FREE DINNER

Grand Aioli Summer Feast (page 158)
Roasted Salmon + Spicy Cucumber-Orange Salsa (page 167)
Seared Scallops + Veggie Gravel (page 133)
Buttermilk Panna Cotta (page 136)
Stone Fruit, Pecan + Pistachio Crisps (page 180)

FALL-WINTER MENUS

HARVEST BRUNCH

Fall Skillet: Pumpkin + Brussels Leaves (page 198)
Roasted Whole Cauliflower with Harissa + Yogurt (page 207)
Sunchoke Soup + Crispy Mushrooms (page 204)
Quince Tarte Tatin (page 226)

VEGAN COMFORT FOOD

Roasted Whole Cauliflower with Harissa + (Vegan) Yogurt (page 207)
Beet, Mandarinquat, Celery Salad (page 247)
Stewed Scarlet Runner Beans (page 276)
Piquant French Lentils (page 272)
Quinoa + Quince Porridge (page 197)

HOLIDAY FEAST

Puntarelle + Tardivo with Punchy Dress (page 200)
Braised Short Ribs + Creamy Beans (page 263)
Quince Tarte Tatin (page 226)
Autumn Olive Linzer Tart (page 229)
Rye + Spruce Tip Last Word (page 103)

VEGETARIAN DATE NIGHT

Two Toasts (page 203)
A Rosy Salad for Darker Days (page 251)
Wild Mushroom–Potato–Onion Tart (page 194)
Pawpaw Crème Brûlée (page 232)

ANNIVERSARY MEAL

Pasta Puttanesca (page 217)

Cured King Salmon, Persimmon, Pickles (page 248)

Halibut + Poached Vegetables with Aioli Slather
(page 222)

Persimmon-Date Ice Cream + Spiced Nuts (page 225)

Rye + Spruce Tip Last Word (page 103)

CHRISTMAS BRUNCH

Apple + Pomegranate Flognarde (page 245)

Cured King Salmon, Persimmon, Pickles (page 248)

A Rosy Salad for Darker Days (page 251)

My Mother's Gruyère Soufflé (page 246)

Autumn Olive Linzer Tart (page 229)

Cherry-Rye-Ganache Sandwich Cookies (page 267)

CHANNUKAH LUNCH

Ultimate Nibbles Platter (page 208)

Wild Salmon Rillettes + Seeded Rye Lavash (page 241)

Beet, Mandarinquat, Celery Salad (page 247)

Chicken Thighs, Quince, Cipollini, Preserved Lemon
(page 221)

Orange-Cardamom Ice Cream + Sablé Coins (page 268)

WOW THE IN-LAWS

A Rosy Salad for Darker Days (page 251)

Wild Mushroom–Potato–Onion Tart (page 194)

Bouillabaisse + Rouille-Slathered Toasts (page 211)

Sage-Buttermilk-Rye Pot Pies (page 257)

Candied Meyer Lemon Ice Cream + Pistachio Tuiles
(page 270)

Pawpaw Crème Brûlée (page 232)

QUICK AND IMPRESSIVE

Winter Skillet: Fried Duck Eggs, Wilted Greens,
Furikake (page 242)

Beet, Mandarinquat, Celery Salad (page 247)

Pasta Puttanesca (page 217)

Pomegranate-Persimmon Puff Pastry Tart (page 265)

RESOURCES, GUIDES, SUPPLIES

MAKERS I LOVE

There are people whose beautiful pieces make appearance throughout these pages. The unique sensibilities and flair of their handiwork add greater interest and beauty to my food and also enhance the world I live in. Needless to say, I cherish these objects.

abc carpet & home—abchome.com

Clam Lab ceramics—clamlab.com

DBO Home—dbohome.com

Degrenne glassware—degrenne.com

Etsy—Etsy.com

Food52—food52.com

Goodwill Stores—goodwill.com

Malinda Reich Studio Ceramics—malindareich.com

Marité Acosta pottery—mariteacosta.com

Nicole Brunner ceramics—wildbowerstudio.com

Schoolhouse electric—schoolhouse.com

FORAGING RESOURCES

There is a wealth of people who study nature and teach any who are interested about the landscapes in which we live. Here are some who have offered their wisdom on my path and their books. Support your local bookstore and order these valuable resource guides from them. Or visit your local library: many locations are well stocked with these helpful resources.

AUTHORS + BOOKS

David Arora, *Mushrooms Demystified* (Ten Speed Press, 1986) and *All the Rain Promises and More* (Ten Speed Press, 1991)

Dina Falconi, *Foraging & Feasting: A Field Guide and Wild Food Cookbook* (Botanical Arts Press, 2014)

Euell Gibbons, *Stalking the Wild Asparagus* (David McKay, 1962)

Leda Meredith, *Northeast Foraging* (Timber Press, 2014) and *The Skillful Forager* (Roost Books, 2019)

Samuel Thayer, *The Forager's Harvest* (Foragers Harvest Press, 2006)

Marie Viljoen, *Forage, Harvest, Feast* (Chelsea Green Publishing, 2018)

National Audubon Society Field Guide to Mushrooms (Knopf, 1981) and *National Audubon Society Field Guide to North American Trees* (Knopf, 1980)

Timber Press Regional Foraging Series

ONLINE RESOURCES + SUPPLIES

66 Square Feet Plus—66squarefeet.blogspot.com

Alexis Nikole Nelson—@Blackforager

Botanical Arts Press—botanicalartspress.com

Eat the Weeds—eattheweeds.com

The Forager Chef—foragerchef.com

Good Life Revival—thegoodliferevival.com

Kitchen Curandera—kitchencurandera.com

Lady Bird Johnson Wildflower Center—wildflower.org/plants-main

Native Invasive Species Information Center—invasivespeciesinfo.gov

Opinel hinged foraging knives—opinel-usa.com

Outside Institute—theoutsideinstitute.org

Plant Finder—missouribotanicalgarden.org

Victorinox foldable blades—victorinox.com/us

Xtratuf rubber boots—xtratuf.com

GARDENING RESOURCES

Whenever confronted with a new conundrum or question, these resources provide solid breadth and depth of information, and high quality, niche products that enhance my gardens, year after year.

ONLINE RESOURCES

Gardening Know How—gardeningknowhow.com

Gardenista—gardenista.com

Homestead and Chill—homesteadandchill.com/category/garden/all-things-garden

The Old Farmer's Almanac—almanac.com

Rural Sprout—ruralsprout.com

The Spruce—thespruce.com/gardening-4127780

NURSERIES AND GARDENING SUPPLIES

Baker Creek Heirloom seeds—rareseeds.com

Best Nest—bestnest.com

Catskill Native Nursery—catskillnativenursery.com

Gardener's Supply—gardeners.com

Hudson Valley Seed Company—hudsonvalleyseed.com

Johnny's Selected Seeds—johnnyseeds.com

Prairie Nursery—prairienursery.com

Row 7 Seeds—row7seeds.com

A Rustic Garden—arusticgarden.com

FERMENTATION, PRESERVATION, AND BAKING

Preserving vessels for every project, the right tool for the job is true in every field.

Ball and Kerr mason jars—freshpreserving.com

Kilner—kilnerjar.co.uk

Kraut Source—krautsource.com

Le Parfait—leparfait.com

Roots and Harvest—rootsandharvest.com

Sarah Kersten Studio—sarahkersten.com/collections/fermentation-jars-1

Slap and Fold Process—youtube.com/watch?v=Qzx7dxuvaCo

Specialty Bottle—specialtybottle.com

SPECIALTY FOODS

Though by no means comprehensive, here is a list of purveyors whose goods I keep stocked on my shelves. They help make my food dynamic.

CHEESE, MEAT, FISH, SEAFOOD

Adams Fairacre Farms—adamsfarms.com

Catsmo trout roe—catsmo.com

Cheese Louise—cheeselouiseny.com

D'Artagnan—dartagnan.com

Drifters Fish—driftersfish.com

Four Fat Fowl—fourfatfowl.com

DRY GOODS + SPICES

Burlap + Barrel—burlapandbarrel.com

Dual Variety store—https://dualsnatural.com

Peace and Plenty Farm—peaceplentyfarm.com

Rancho Gordo—ranchogordo.com

Ziba foods—zibafoods.com

FLOURS

Arrowhead Mills—arrowheadmills.com

Bob's Red Mill—bobsredmill.com

Farmer Ground—farmergroundflour.com

King Arthur Baking Company—kingarthurbaking.com

OILS, SAUCES, VINEGARS

Buon Italia—buonitalia.com

The Date Lady—ilovedatelady.com

La Tourangelle—latourangelle.com

Maille—us.maille.com

ACKNOWLEDGMENTS

To my husband, my other human, Jim. For being willing to taste every single thing, be prompted for feedback, whether flavors, edits, or impromptu art direction—and offer it brilliantly—even when you had no moments to spare. Thank you for finding ingredients for me, for cooking when I could not, and for all of the dishes you washed. Thank you for uplifting me to make everything possible. Especially during a pandemic.

Thank you, Adriana, for seeking me out, coming to Catbird Cottage that first time to eat my food and believing so much in me. You saw what I could not at the beginning of our journey. I am grateful for your steadfast spirit, empowering me to dig deep. Thanks for holding my hand, for being that crucial sounding board over and over as I refined all the layers.

To our many and wonderful guests, you all are the inspiration—and the literal reason that so many of these dishes even exist. Thank you for your particularities and requests. You helped me think in new ways so I could dream up iconic, legendary meals for you, commemorating your special moments. We are so grateful you've made our cottage a destination; it is a great honor to play a role in making your cherished new memories.

Thank you, Annie. Your willingness to refine the many jotted notes I sent along—and bring my vision into this gorgeous, tangible work—has been such an exhilarating piece in the puzzle. There was so much anticipation, sending you oodles of images, wondering how you would make beautiful sense of it all.

Thank you so much, Dervla, for harnessing each idea and coaxing out the clarity in all these pages! You are a master at gelling the narrative arcs and my story feels more grounded because of your keen insights.

Thank you, Nancy and Lisa, for your incredible sleuthing, page to page. Your honing required I re-examine, defend, and clarify every passage, and your combined attention to detail meaningfully strengthened the impact I could make with this book.

To my sweet parents, thank you always for supporting me. Your hurrahs and care and "twist my arm" willingness to eat all the things have spurred me on year after year, and your perspectives shaped my vision of what I could make of my life.

Dear Guiseppe and Megan, thank you for troubleshooting—and lauding—the special recipes I sent your way, graciously taking on recipe testing while your lives were taking a breakneck new momentum. I hope eating them together offered you nourishment and a piece of joy in your hectic lives.

Thank you to the many wonderful testers, from Detroit to Denmark, who helped make this book possible: Heidi Robb, Matt Berlin, Laura Silverman, Adriana Stimola, Tory

Shelley, Temperance David, my dear parents Karen and Frank Hammer, and Jalyn Spencer. Special thanks to Becky Collins and Kimmy Meinelt, whose combined enthusiasm really kept me going as I ran the gauntlet. You two made me tear up more than once, affirming that my food was in fact uniquely delicious. An extra special shout-out to Xina Giatas, my very first tester who kept welcoming new cooking experiments, rising to the occasion and testing throughout the many months, and, to sibling power duo Martin and Maria Høier in Denmark, who with repeated enthusiasm tested *so many* of my creations, always interested in more and helping to save the day as I waded through the sea of making this book. You two gave me such help, and your reflections made this process unexpectedly profound. I could not have done it without all of you.

Thank you Dennis, Galen, Zoya, and David at The Green Cottage. On days when we ready every nook and cranny of the cottage for guests, your magical shop is a breath of fresh air. I am beyond grateful for your good taste in beautiful blooms, each and every week. The curated bouquets I bound away with bring me joy, and back home, arranging them for the special people who come for a stay extends that joy.

Malinda, thank you so much for your offer to ship so many beautiful pieces, it was so generous of you. Your wonderful ceramics go perfectly with my food, making a textural, lush affair of each and every image.

I could not make such beautiful images and delicious dishes without the tireless problem-solving and care of the great local farmers in my region. Christine at Maynard Farm, Sam and Erin at Long Season Farm, Oleh at Rusty Plough Farm, Bryn and Wes at Solid Ground Farm, Jeff and Megan at 518 Farms, and Jenna and Rick at Pura Vida Fisheries, thank you for growing some of the finest, tastiest produce ever, and curating a selection of quality, sustainable East Coast seafood.

Ilse and Aya, two of my favorite people, you sadly live oceans away. I cannot wait to cook for you again, your bright and loving spirits have buoyed my growth over the years. Thank you for always cheering me on.

To those who shaped how I saw food, from early days through NYC days: thank you, so very much, Mark Tulloss, Lauren Collura, Leda Meredith, Jon Rowley, Betty Fussell, Joel Hough, and Gregory Porter for helping me see how simple food can be the best eating of our lives.

INDEX

Published in the United States by Ten Speed Press, an imprint of Random House, a division of Penguin Random House LLC, New York.
www.tenspeed.com

Ten Speed Press and the Ten Speed Press colophon are registered trademarks of Penguin Random House LLC.

Library of Congress Control Number: 2021950220

Hardcover ISBN: 978-1-9848-5970-9
eBook ISBN: 978-1-9848-5971-6

Printed in China

Photographs on pages 20, 53, 66, 70, 73, 117, 192, and 258 by Jim Lafferty
Acquiring editor: Dervla Kelly | Production editor: Lisa Regul
Designer: Annie Marino | Art director: Kelly Booth | Production designer: Mari Gill
Typefaces: Adobe Fonts' Freight Text and P22's Underground
Production manager: Serena Sigona | Prepress color manager: Jane Chinn
Copyeditor: Nancy Bailey | Proofreader: Kathy Brock | Indexer: Ken DellaPenta
Publicist: Natalie Yera | Marketer: Andrea Portanova

10 9 8 7 6 5 4 3 2 1

First Edition